60 DAYS TO BECOMING A MISSIONARY DISCIPLE

Fr. John Bartunek, L.C., S.Th.D.

SOPHIA INSTITUTE PRESS

Manchester, New Hampshire

Sophia Institute Press
Box 5284, Manchester, NH 03108
1-800-888-9344

www.SophiaInstitute.com

Sophia Institute Press® is a registered trademark of Sophia Institute.

This is a combined and edited version of the books previously printed as *Seeking the Kingdom: 30 Meditations on How to Love God with All Your Heart, Soul, Mind, and Strength* and *Go! 30 Meditations on How Best to Love Your Neighbor as Yourself.*

Imprimi Potest, Luis Garza, L.C., J.D.C.

Cover design: David Ferris Designs
Cover art: Domenico Ghirlandaio, *The Calling of St. Peter and St. Andrew*, 1481 (TWAGJW) © Art Heritage/Alamy Stock Photo

Library of Congress Control Number: 2020938136
Print edition ISBN: 978-1-64413-260-9
Electronic formats ISBN: 978-1-64413-261-6

First printing

Contents

CONTENTS

Living the Great Commandments

THIS BOOK IS FOR ALL those who find themselves wanting to follow Jesus Christ more closely. That desire is the most precious gift God can give to a human heart, because friendship with Jesus Christ is the only path to lasting fulfillment. This path, moreover, is twofold, as Jesus revealed when he gave the two great commandments:

> "The first is: 'Hear, O Israel! The Lord our God is Lord alone! You shall love the Lord your God with all your heart, with all your soul, with all your mind, and with all your strength.' The second is this: 'You shall love your neighbor as yourself.' There is no other commandment greater than these." (Mark 12:29-31)

Followers of Christ are called not only to know and love God more and more, but also to be God's partner in bringing others to do the same, thereby lovingly helping them discover the "pearl of great price" (Matt. 13:46). Those two loves—love for God and love for neighbor—constitute the only path of true, lasting fulfillment. In these commandments lies the meaning of our very existence.

This book is an extended reflection on the wealth of wisdom that God has poured into these two commandments. In sixty short daily meditations, it unpacks and explores the many implications of what it means to seek Christ by loving "the Lord your God with all your heart, with all your soul, with all your mind, and with all your strength, and your neighbor as yourself."

The first thirty days will focus on the first great commandment. We will reflect on what it means to love God "with all your heart, with all your soul, with all your mind, and with all your strength" and how we must bring every dimension of our being and personality into play in our relationship with God. This spiritual integration will keep our desire for God strong in the face of roadblocks we may encounter on our journey.

The remaining thirty days will be devoted to the second great commandment: to love your neighbor as yourself. We will delve into our call to the apostolate, clear the air of some mistaken attitudes, explicate the different forms or dimensions in which we can and should fulfill our share in the apostolate, and end by setting a few expectations for our work in the kingdom.

THE FIRST GREAT COMMANDMENT: LOVING THE LORD OUR GOD

To love Christ is to have a unique relationship with him, because Jesus is a unique friend. He is not only a loyal and loving companion; he is also the Lord—Creator and Redeemer of the human race, uniquely worthy of worship and obedience. Friendship with Christ grows, therefore, by allowing Christ's companionship and lordship to touch and transform every sector of our existence: all our internal powers, which subsequently manifest themselves in all our external activities. This extension of Christ's influence to every corner of our life is the essence of spiritual integration; we gradually integrate, more and more deeply, every facet of our person and experience into our friendship with Jesus Christ. We learn to live more and more in Jesus, and he comes to live more and more in us. This is the amazing journey toward spiritual maturity.

This mysterious connection between Christ and the Christian constitutes one of the main themes of the New Testament. St. Paul especially refers to the phrase "in Christ" over and over again. Everything changes for the person who has come to share in Christ's life: "So whoever is in Christ is a new creation: the old things have passed away; behold, new things have come" (2 Cor. 5:17). And Jesus himself becomes the life of the one who welcomes him through faith:

I have been crucified with Christ; yet I live, no longer I, but Christ lives in me; insofar as I now live in the flesh, I live by faith in the Son of God who has loved me and given himself up for me. (Gal. 2:19-20)

Normal friendship entails an intimate sharing between two people. As Aristotle is attributed with saying, friendship is "a single soul dwelling in two bodies." But when one of those two souls is infinite and perfect, then intimate sharing is not enough. In this case, the lesser of the two must also allow himself to be transformed and elevated by the greater. This is the case with a Christian and Christ. We must walk with Jesus through life, but we also must humbly and lovingly conform ourselves to Christ (this is what it means to "follow" Jesus Christ) in order to allow this grace-filled friendship to reach maturity. Only thus can we enter fully into Christ's kingdom—the one kingdom where our longings for an eternally meaningful life can be fulfilled.

GUIDED BY THE HOLY SPIRIT

We are not alone in our efforts to conform to Christ. Jesus accompanies us, and actually enables us, every step of the way, especially through the presence and action of the Holy Spirit. St. John Paul II, whose words will accompany you along your journey through these sixty meditations, repeated that essential truth over and over again. For example, St. John Paul II said in *Veritatis Splendor*, 21:

Following Christ is not an outward imitation, since it touches man at the very depths of his being. Being a follower of Christ means becoming conformed to him who became a servant even to giving himself on the cross. Christ dwells by faith in the heart of the believer, and thus the disciple is conformed to the Lord. This is the effect of grace, of the active presence of the Holy Spirit in us.

REQUIRING OUR FREE COOPERATION

And yet, Jesus refuses to do all the work himself. He includes us in the project, sharing the work with us. We have to choose, freely and repeatedly, to be faithful to the friendship. Otherwise, it would not be a friendship at all—we would just be pre-programmed Christian robots. But that's not what we were created for. We were created in God's image, to give glory to him by freely living in communion with him, in whom alone we find our lasting happiness.

And so, in this Christian adventure, in this journey toward spiritual maturity, we have a part to play. We are co-protagonists in the process of integrating every facet of our existence into our friendship with Jesus. We are co-conquerors in the battle to bring every sector of our personality and experience and activity under the infinitely wise and sure rule of Christ the Lord.

How do we do our part? How do we cooperate with Jesus to Christianize every single corner of our lives? Jesus sums up the answer with a liberating simplicity: "But seek first the kingdom (of God) and his righteousness, and all these things will be given you besides" (Matt. 6:33).

Seeking God's kingdom first, seeking to allow Christ the Eternal King to rule and guide our lives in accordance with his wisdom, goodness, and love, seeking to abide by the Lord's life-giving standards in all that we think, say, and do—this is every Christian's primary task. It is the basic commitment that we make when we fall in love with God and give our hearts to him. Following through on that commitment is how we do our part in allowing God's grace free rein to order and energize our lives on earth, and to bring us to the fullness of eternal life in heaven.

LOVING WITH EVERYTHING WE'VE GOT

Seeking something involves knowing about it, wanting it, and going out to take possession of it. These three activities correspond to the three basic powers of the human soul: the *mind*, which knows and understands; the *emotions*, which feel attraction and repulsion; and the *will*, by which one makes decisions and takes action.

And so, in essence, seeking God's kingdom means seeking to let Jesus, the everlasting King, rule our minds with his infinite truth, our feelings with his endless beauty, and our decisions with his overflowing goodness. This is how our friendship with Christ matures. This is how we integrate our entire lives into his unique and life-giving friendship. This is how we allow God to transform and bring to full spiritual maturity our minds, our emotions, and our wills — our whole selves, every corner of our lives.

LOVE: AN ONGOING ADVENTURE

The process of integration takes a lifetime, because we are always changing and growing, and because God himself, the one we are seeking, is infinite. Seeking first the kingdom, then, is not something that we can check off our to-do list once and for all. But the more intentionally and intelligently we engage in it, the more quickly and fully God's grace will extend the Lord's rule in our lives and move us further along the path of spiritual maturity.

These initial reflections on what it means to "seek first the kingdom of God" point toward Christ's own instructions about how to do just that. When he was asked to identify the first and greatest commandment, the path to spiritual maturity, he answered by saying:

> "The first is: 'Hear, O Israel! The Lord our God is Lord alone! You shall love the Lord your God with all your heart, with all your soul, with all your mind, and with all your strength.' The second is this: 'You shall love your neighbor as yourself.' There is no other commandment greater than these." (Mark 12:29-31)

By using the verb *love*, Jesus centers the human vocation to holiness and happiness not simply on personal achievements, but rather on a relationship — on a personal relationship of intimate and mutual self-giving with God, which happens through friendship with Jesus.

Then, by specifying "heart, soul, mind, and strength," Jesus points out the importance of integrating our whole personality—every facet of our humanity—into our friendship with God. In this book we will explore each one of those four areas individually, even though in real life they always go together; each one influences and affects all the others.

Finally, by emphasizing that we are to love God with all our "heart, soul, mind, and strength," Jesus indicates the dynamism of this lifetime adventure; it has no limit—we can always deepen our intimacy with God, expand our spiritual integration, and discover new depths of meaning and fulfillment.

THE SECOND GREAT COMMANDMENT: LOVING OUR NEIGHBOR

The essence of our earthly mission is to love as God loves—we are created in his image and likeness, and his nature is love (see 1 John 4:8). Our fulfillment flows from entering fully and consciously into the stream of divine love. Loving means, essentially, affirming the goodness of someone else's existence and doing good to that person in such a way that his or her existence can truly flourish. Love involves desiring, giving, and working to help others be all they can be, all God calls them to be. And since every human being is "made to live in communion with God, in whom he finds happiness" (CCC, 45), the best way to love someone is to help that person discover, establish, and deepen that communion with God.

That is our most basic and indispensable mission in the world; that is how we best fulfill the second great commandment and find the meaning we most yearn for. In his Message for the Twenty-Eighth Youth Day, Pope Benedict XVI put it well:

> To make Christ known is the most precious gift that you can give to others. . . . When you work to help others and proclaim the gospel to them, then your own lives, so often fragmented because of your many activities, will find their unity in the Lord. You will also build up your own selves, and you will grow and mature in humanity.

Recognizing the Universal Call to Mission

Not all Catholics realize they are called to be missionaries. Many of us simply assume that this aspect of the Church only has to do with priests, nuns, and other consecrated persons who have been called to explicit missionary status. The rest of us laypeople, so the misunderstanding goes, are off the hook. As the *Catechism* explains, however, every Christian has a "share in the priestly, prophetical, and kingly office of Christ . . . By Baptism they share in the priesthood of Christ, in his prophetic and royal mission" (CCC, 873, 1268).

Every Catholic truly is a missionary, and the first step to discovering and fulfilling our mission is to let that fact seep into our consciousness. Each of us has received a call to be missionaries, evangelizers, and apostles—to be part of the solution God wants to bring to the troubled world through his Church.

Discovering Your Mission of Love

The universal call to mission, however, does not mean that every individual Christian should go to uncharted lands, seeking to convert those who have never before heard of Jesus. That is only one kind of mission, though critical. Nor does it mean that every Christian has to have a PhD in theology. Rather, each person's mission of love unfolds in a unique and unrepeatable way, since each of us is a unique and unrepeatable person. Yet within that unique unfolding, certain elements and patterns are shared by all Christians. Jesus has told us a lot about them in the Gospels, and the Church has become more acutely aware of them through her two thousand years of being involved in this mission.

Discovering them—or rediscovering and reflecting more deeply on them—is essential to being fully engaged in the Christian quest, and only full engagement in that quest will quench the existential thirst we have for meaning and happiness. We are created for more than simply making a living and trying to have a good time. And we all recognize that, deep down inside. Each of us is looking for the deeper meaning of our lives, and that meaning is connected with Christ's call to mission, with his call to making a lasting impact on the world by loving our neighbor as ourselves. The mission is there to be discovered.

As we reflect on our mission of love, we will both explore some key presuppositions that will help us accept and rejoice in our call to be missionaries and also reflect on three dimensions of our Christian mission—the "priestly, prophetical, and kingly" dimensions that the *Catechism* refers to. Many readers will be surprised to discover how every single thing we do can have a missionary impact that reverberates into eternity. It's easier than you think to be the missionary you are called to be.

USING THIS BOOK

And yet, while becoming a witness to Christ's love may be easier than you think, you will surely run up against obstacles and roadblocks every step of the way. This is inevitable for anyone who truly burns with a longing to know Jesus more and more clearly, to love him more and more dearly, and to follow him more and more nearly (to borrow three phrases from a medieval prayer by St. Richard of Chichester).

These obstacles can easily drain that precious desire to seek greater intimacy with God and fellowship with neighbor. They can disorient, discourage, and jade even the most well-intentioned Christians. And that can happen at any point in the spiritual journey: the beginning, the middle, or the end. Both those who are newly intrigued by Christ and those who have consistently loved him and their neighbor on a daily basis can face burnout and any number of dangerous obstacles.

Often, these obstacles arise when we don't allow the basic ideas that make up our Christian identity to sink into our hearts. Instead, we keep these ideas in our heads. We agree with them, but we don't really allow them to have a deep impact on the way we see ourselves and the way we live our lives. That's why I decided to present these basic ideas in the form of meditations. A meditation gives us a chance to take one or two critical ideas, reflect on them with calm focus, and allow them to penetrate our souls.

The sixty short meditations in this book provide explanations and reflections that can help you love God and your neighbor with everything you've got, intentionally and intelligently. Working through one chapter a day can give you two month-long retreats. Working through one chapter a week with a group of friends can provide a richly rewarding path of Christ-centered fellowship.

The abundant biblical quotations contained in these meditations are presented in red in order to make prayer and meditation on God's sacred Word easier, if you use the book in this way. The questions for reflection at the end of each chapter can serve either as aids for personal reflection and prayer or as helps to spark invigorating small-group interaction. Each chapter's concluding prayer, drawn from various sources that make up the vast, two-thousand-year-old treasury of Christian spirituality, can be prayed individually or as a group. The introductory quotations from Pope St. John Paul II, Pope St. Paul VI, and Pope St. John XXIII are meant to link the themes of each chapter to the Church's ongoing mission of renewed evangelization, which was so dear to these great popes who led the Christian family through the second half of the twentieth century and across the threshold of the third millennium.

However you choose to take advantage of this resource, if you are truly seeking God, you can't go wrong. After all, the Lord himself made the solemn promise: "Seek, and you will find" (Matt. 7:7, RSV).

PART I

GOD'S PART AND MY PART

When a large crowd gathered, with people from one town after another journeying to him, [Jesus] spoke in a parable. "A sower went out to sow his seed. And as he sowed, some seed fell on the path and was trampled, and the birds of the sky ate it up. Some seed fell on rocky ground, and when it grew, it withered for lack of moisture. Some seed fell among thorns, and the thorns grew with it and choked it. And some seed fell on good soil, and when it grew, it produced fruit a hundredfold."

LUKE 8:4–8, 11–15

How Much Is Up to Me?

We now need to profit from the grace received, by putting it
into practice in resolutions and guidelines for action.
— St. John Paul II, Novo Millennio, 3

J ESUS SEEMS TO CONTRADICT HIMSELF. On the one hand, he tells us that "apart from me you can do nothing" (John 15:5, RSV). He is the vine, he explains in the same passage, and we are only branches, completely dependent on the flow of sap and life that comes to us through the vine. The word used for nothing in the Greek, in fact, is the simple, total negative—nothing at all, absolute zero.

Yet on the other hand, Jesus looks us in the eye and implores us, "Strive to enter by the narrow door; for many, I tell you, will seek to enter and will not be able" (Luke 13:24, RSV). Here he begs us to put all our effort into following him, obeying him, seeking him. The Greek word for strive connotes struggle, fight, and the kind of intensity that amazes us when we watch, riveted, as Olympic athletes battle for the gold.

What is going on here? How can we reconcile our Lord's injunction that we are absolutely helpless and dependent in the spiritual life with his command to fight to the death, as it were, in order to achieve spiritual maturity and salvation?

ST. PAUL TO THE RESCUE?

What a relief it would be if St. Paul were to resolve the dilemma for us! But, this time anyway, he comes up short. He too, it seems, contradicts himself. In defending his apostolic credentials, he points out to the Christians in Corinth that "by the grace of God I am what I am, and his grace to me has not been ineffective. Indeed, I have toiled harder than all of them; not I, however, but the grace of God with me" (1 Cor. 15:10).

Paul attributes all that he is and all that he has accomplished as a follower of Jesus to "the grace of God." But in the same breath, he claims to have contributed to his Christian greatness by having "toiled harder" than anybody else. The Greek word used for *toil* connotes wearisome, backbreaking exertion. Etymologically, it harkens back to a term associated with the demanding, harsh, and unrelenting work of an agricultural laborer before the advent of mechanized farm equipment. That's the kind of contribution St. Paul feels that he has made to his Christian mission, even while he affirms that God's grace is the sole source of all the good fruits his mission has borne.

We can see no light at the end of this tunnel. We are stuck with the paradox: Our Christian life depends entirely on God's grace, yet it also depends on our human efforts in order to make that grace bear fruit. It is a partnership. The theologian-pope, Benedict XVI, affirmed this paradox without trying to explain it away when commenting on our Lord's parables about seeds:[1]

> Every Christian, then, knows well that he must do all that he can, but that the final result depends on God: this knowledge sustains him in daily toil, especially in difficult situations.

The Holy Father went on to quote the cavalier-turned-mystic, St. Ignatius of Loyola, to drive the point home: "Act as if everything depended on you, knowing that in reality everything depends on God."

THE RIGHT PROPORTION

Here we have one of the many binary star systems, spiritually speaking, in the galaxy of the Gospels.

A binary star system happens when two stars share a common center of mass. In such a situation, their orbits are perfectly harmonized and inextricably interdependent. As one moves, the other moves. As one turns, the other turns. They seem to pull against each other, and yet the tension between them is actually the source of their dynamism. Likewise, in our growth toward spiritual maturity, the mysterious partnership between God's action and our action creates a healthy kind of tension from which spiritual dynamism flows.

Each binary star system consists of a brighter star (the primary star) and a dimmer star (the companion star). In our pursuit of intimacy with God—of the spiritual maturity that alone will yield the lasting fulfillment we are created for—God's grace is the primary star, and our effort is the companion star. God's grace is primary, 99 percent. Our striving is secondary, 1 percent. And yet, both are necessary; without the 1 percent, the job will not be done.

To switch analogies, think of cooking. The ingredients for a plate of primavera pasta come from myriad suppliers: the farmers who grow and harvest the wheat and the vegetables, the olive oil and the tomatoes (not to mention the God-given natural forces that give and sustain the lives of those plants); the transportation companies that bring those products to food-processing plants; the food-processing plants themselves; more transportation companies to put the goods in the grocery store; the grocery store team that preserves and arranges and sells. . . . By the time those ingredients are lined up on the kitchen counter and ready to be prepped and cooked, hundreds if not thousands of people have already contributed to the meal. That's like the 99 percent. And yet, unless someone chops, simmers, boils, and stirs, the meal will never make it to the table. That's like the 1 percent.

True Partners

St. Augustine, the great bishop from North Africa who helped the Church survive the cataclysmic fall of the western Roman Empire early on in Christian history, expressed this truth cleverly when he wrote: "God created us without us: but he did not will to save us without us."[2] God created us to live in a relationship with him, not to be robots. So, even though we are entirely dependent on him for our existence and our spiritual growth, he chooses to limit his omnipotence, in a sense, in order to leave us room to become true partners in salvation history.

Questions for Personal Reflection or Group Discussion

1. What idea in this chapter struck you most and why?

2. In what ways have you personally experienced this paradox of Christianity, this binary star system of God's grace and your effort?

3. Explain why God chooses to make the fruitfulness of his grace in your life depend so much on your collaboration.

4. What will you do today to keep yourself in better harmony with God, the "primary star" of your life?

   - I will say a short prayer of thanksgiving before each meal.
   - I will write a "note to God" thanking him for a specific blessing.
   - (Write your own resolution) I will _____

   _____

   _____

   _____

Concluding Prayer

O God, strength of those who hope in you, graciously hear our pleas, and, since without you mortal frailty can do nothing, grant us always the help of your grace, that in following your commands we may please you by our resolve and our deeds.

— ROMAN MISSAL, COLLECT FOR THE
ELEVENTH SUNDAY IN ORDINARY TIME

DAY 2

God Is Faithful

Christianity is grace, it is the wonder of a God who is not satisfied
with creating the world and man, but puts himself on the same
level as the creature he has made, and after speaking on various
occasions and in different ways through his prophets, "in these
last days . . . has spoken to us by a Son" (Hebrews 1:1–2).
—St. John Paul II, Novo Millennio Ineunte, 3

GOD'S GRACE IS NEVER LACKING. His 99 percent is always available. He never fails us. He never forgets about us. He never goes on vacation leaving us to fend for ourselves for a while. No—"God is faithful," St. Paul reminds us (1 Cor. 1:9). Just as he took the initiative to create and redeem us, beginning in us the "good work" of holiness, so he "will bring it to completion at the day of Christ Jesus" (Phil. 1:6). The *Catechism of the Catholic Church* reminds us of this in its very first paragraph:

> For this reason, at every time and in every place, God draws close to man. He calls man to seek him, to know him, to love him with all his strength. (CCC, 1)

God's grace, his action, his part, is never lacking. It reaches out to us and surrounds us and sustains us at every time and in every place, like the very atmosphere we breathe.

This is the bottom line in our friendship with Christ. This is the starting line and the finishing line. Jesus, his trustworthiness, his faithfulness, his absolute dependability and unlimited loyalty—this is the "Alpha and the Omega, the first and the last, the beginning and the end" (Rev. 22:13, RSV).

A Message from the Cross

This was one of the reasons that God chose to save us through the betrayal, humiliation, torture, crucifixion, and death of his only-begotten Son. Saving us that way shows, once and for all, that nothing we do can cause God to give up on us. He stayed faithful to us, loving and forgiving us, throughout the horrible injustices and crimes that we committed against him during Christ's passion and death. And after all that, he still loves us and reaches out to us and offers us his grace. Because of that, we have absolute assurance of his undying faithfulness.

St. Paul understood this as well as anyone, and better than most. He put it like this in his letter to the Christians in Rome:

> What then shall we say to this? If God is for us, who can be against us? He who did not spare his own Son but handed him over for us all, how will he not also give us everything else along with him? (Rom. 8:31–32)

In his encyclical letter *Lumen Fidei* (15–16), Pope Francis gave this fundamental truth brilliant expression. He wrote (emphasis added):

> The history of Jesus is the complete manifestation of God's reliability. . . . The clearest proof of the reliability of Christ's love is to be found in his dying for our sake. If laying down one's life for one's friends is the greatest proof of love (cf. John 15:13), Jesus offered his own life for all, even for his enemies, to transform their hearts. This explains why the evangelists could see the hour of Christ's crucifixion as the culmination of the gaze of faith; *in that hour the depth and breadth of God's love shone forth.*

Learning to Trust

It's easy to say but hard to live; it's hard to trust that God will always be doing his part, the 99 percent, even when we waver or get sloppy in doing our 1 percent.

Our modern, post-Christian culture steadily feeds us the lie that if we just work a little bit harder, or a little bit smarter, we can create heaven on earth; we can perfect ourselves. We tend to believe the lie, because even in the safest of harbors, in the bosom of our family when we're growing up, we discover that human approval and affection can (and sometimes even *must*) be earned. And so this lie seeps into our relationship with God. We feel as if we need to make ourselves worthy of God's grace; he will only do his part, we mistakenly tell ourselves, if we do our part really, really well.

God knows how hard it is for us to trust him, and he is always looking for ways to help us out. As a result, the story of salvation that unfolds in the pages of the Bible comes back to the truth of God's utter reliability over and over again, like a refrain. God manifests his faithfulness to his people all the way from the very beginning, through the experiences of Abraham, Moses, all the kings and prophets of the Old Testament, and all the apostles and saints of the New Testament. Maybe the Blessed Virgin Mary expressed it best when she simply proclaimed: "His mercy is from age to age" (Luke 1:50, RSV).

IMAGES THAT INSPIRE CONFIDENCE

The prayer book of the Old Testament (and of the Church), the Psalms, draws on images from the natural world to dispel the hesitancy of our fallen nature and emblazon confidence in God on our hearts. Read Psalm 36:5-6, for example:

> LORD, your mercy reaches to heaven;
> your fidelity, to the clouds.
> Your justice is like the highest mountains;
> your judgments, like the mighty deep.

The psalmist compares the immeasurable qualities of God to some of the most evocative scenes of the created world. The vast expanse of the sky, the atmosphere that surrounds and upholds us every moment, whether or not we are aware of it, is a pale reflection of the Lord's "mercy and faithfulness." Is there a limit to the sky, to the heavens? Not one that we can see or experience. Just so, God's forgiveness, goodness, and love have no limits.

The solidity, the firmness, the unflagging and monumentally

dependable presence of the mountains show forth to the inspired psalmist the absolute firmness of God's justice—a Hebrew word connoting truth and faithfulness, utter reliability.

The vast and mysterious power and motion of the sea, so mesmerizing, inviting, and awe-inspiring, are for the psalmist a glimpse of the untiring wisdom of God—his judgments, his will, his attentive and intimate governance of all things.

This is our God. This is the Lord who is always doing his part. This is the bedrock of our faith and the steady assurance that allows us to stumble along joyfully at his side as we make a decent effort to do our part. It starts with him. It always starts with him.

Questions for Personal Reflection or Group Discussion

1. What idea in this chapter struck you most and why?

2. When have you experienced personally God's amazing faithfulness? (Remember, consider, and give thanks.)

3. What are some of the factors in your life that keep you from trusting God more fully?

4. Confidence in God can show itself in many different ways throughout the ups and downs of your daily life. It can soften the blows of disappointment or loss, since you know that God loves to work wonders out of weakness. It can fill you with courage to do the right thing, what you know is truly right, even when peer pressure is violently pulling you in the wrong direction, because you know that God's way is always the better way. It can free you to rejoice in the successes of other people, instead of resenting them, because you know that God's love for you doesn't depend on winning competitions. What will you do today to express your confidence in God?

   - I will humbly accept my human limitations by saying "no" to good opportunities or invitations that would require me to overcommit.

   - I will simply say a prayer for someone who is struggling and wants to unreasonably draw me into their tangled situation, instead of thinking that it's up to me to solve everyone's problems.

- I will visit the grave of a loved one and surrender that person into God's care once and for all, letting go—through prayer—of the resentment or fear that still accompanies my feelings of loss.

- (Write your own resolution) I will _____

  _____

  _____

  _____

Concluding Prayer

*We give you praise, Father most holy, for you are great and
you have fashioned all your works in wisdom and in love.
You formed man in your own image and entrusted the
whole world to his care, so that in serving you alone, the
Creator, he might have dominion over all creatures.
And when through disobedience he had lost your friendship,
you did not abandon him to the domain of death.
For you came in mercy to the aid of all, so
that those who seek might find you.*

—Roman Missal, from Eucharistic Prayer IV

The Spiritual Combat

*St. Paul's words (especially in the Letters to the Romans and
Galatians) enable us to know and feel vividly the strength of the
tension and struggle going on in man between openness to the action
of the Holy Spirit and resistance and opposition to him . . .*
—St. John Paul II, Dominum et Vivificantem, 55

T HE DEVIL, OUR ANCIENT ENEMY, really exists. Jesus talked about
him a lot. The *Catechism* emphasizes the reality of this fallen
angel, who is interested in interfering with the adventure of love we
are called to live:

> Evil is not an abstraction, but refers to a person, Satan, the
> Evil One, the angel who opposes God. The devil is the one
> who 'throws himself across' God's plan and his work of salva-
> tion accomplished in Christ. (CCC, 2851)

And the devil knows the truth that we examined in the last chapter,
that God is faithful, that divine grace will never fail us. The devil
knows that he cannot obstruct the flow of God's grace at its source.
He can, however, clog up the channels by which we normally receive
that grace. He can confuse and distract the minds and hearts to
which God's grace is directed, turning us into bad receivers, bad
cooperators, irresponsible partners. This is his strategy.

ENEMIES OF OUR SPIRITUAL GROWTH

And our ancient enemy has powerful allies: the fallen world (all the
corrupting and wounding influences that come from the proliferation

of sin in human society and culture) and our fallen human nature (our own internal divisions and insecurities that make us vulnerable to temptation). Because of these, we have built-in tendencies that continually nudge us away from God's grace and disturb the spiritual docility needed for that grace to be fruitful in our lives. St. John refers to these negative influences when he warns the early Christians:

> Do not love the world or the things of the world. If anyone loves the world, the love of the Father is not in him. For all that is in the world, sensual lust, enticement for the eyes, and a pretentious life, is not from the Father but is from the world. (1 John 2:15-16)

The fallen world in which we live—though good in its essence because it was created by God—can be a snare for us fallen human beings. This is why the Church has never ceased to remind us that the spiritual life is, at least in part, also a spiritual combat:

> Therefore man is split within himself. As a result, all of human life, whether individual or collective, shows itself to be a dramatic struggle between good and evil, between light and darkness. . . . The whole of man's history has been the story of dour combat with the powers of evil, stretching, so our Lord tells us, from the very dawn of history until the last day. Finding himself in the midst of the battlefield man has to struggle to do what is right, and it is at great cost to himself, aided by God's grace, that he succeeds in achieving his own inner integrity.[3]

AN INTERIOR BATTLE

This spiritual combat doesn't happen with guns and swords and tanks and missiles. It takes place much more subtly, often invisibly, in the intimate arena of human freedom. It has to do with our daily choices, whether large or small. It has to do with how we use the gift of free will that we have received.

God, as well as our better self, wants us to use that freedom to choose, step after step, the path of union and friendship with

Christ, the path of abundant life, the path of obedience to his wise and loving plan for the human family: "I came so that they might have life and have it more abundantly. I am the good shepherd" (John 10:10-11).

Our enemy and our fallen nature, on the other hand, want us to use our free will in order to choose a different path, a path strewn with false promises (that we can somehow be fulfilled without God, for instance) and false ideas about God and ourselves (we are unloveable, God is untrustworthy, holiness is beyond our reach, it's not worth trying anymore, etc.).

This path often appears to offer easier and quicker access to happiness, but in fact it leads to interior disintegration and emptiness, because the devil is "a murderer . . . a liar and the father of lies" (John 8:44, RSV) and because sin always has evil consequences: "For the wages of sin is death" (Rom. 6:23, RSV).

Spiritual combat is the ongoing battle between these contrary forces: Which will we choose to follow? St. Peter sums it up vividly in his first letter. First, he points out our need to be watchful:

Be sober and vigilant. Your opponent the devil is prowling around like a roaring lion looking for [someone] to devour. Resist him, steadfast in faith . . .

And then he reminds us that our vigilance should never be harsh and desperate, but calm and joyful, even when it's hard, because God is with us:

The God of all grace who called you to his eternal glory through Christ [Jesus] will himself restore, confirm, strengthen, and establish you after you have suffered a little. (1 Pet. 5:8-10)

Sometimes our choices are stark and obvious, as when the Israelites abandoned God in the wilderness by worshipping the golden calf, or when David laid his life on the line by going out to face Goliath.

Yet, although some individual choices may be stark, the process by which we make those choices is complex. We arrive at big-decision moments with a predisposition for self-giving or self-centeredness, for docility or resistance to God's action in our lives. The gradual formation of that predisposition is the real, day-to-day spiritual battleground. The predisposition is built up from many little, seemingly insignificant choices that gradually fill in our spiritual profile: choices about how we spend our time; whom we befriend; what we say and how we say it; and how we react to unforeseen opportunities, difficulties, or temptations.

Through the exercise of our free will in the little choices we make, we are either furthering Christ's kingdom and growing in spiritual maturity, or we are inhibiting that kingdom and stunting our spiritual growth. As Jesus put it:

> The person who is trustworthy in very small matters is also trustworthy in great ones; and the person who is dishonest in very small matters is also dishonest in great ones. (Luke 16:10)

SMALL BATTLES PREPARE US FOR BIGGER BATTLES

Jesus illustrated the relationship between the many small choices that prepare us for bigger decisions by using a construction image. He likened the spiritual life to the construction of a house. We build gradually, through choices in or out of harmony with his wisdom. Then comes a storm, a stark choice, a big decision, a decisive temptation. Our response to the storm is conditioned by all the small choices that went into building up our spiritual edifice:

> Everyone who listens to these words of mine and acts on them will be like a wise man who built his house on rock. The rain fell, the floods came, and the winds blew and buffeted the house. But it did not collapse; it had been set solidly on rock. And everyone who listens to these words of mine but does not act on them will be like a fool who built his house on sand. The rain fell, the floods came, and the winds blew and buffeted the house. And it collapsed and was completely ruined. (Matt. 7:24-27)

SPIRITUAL RESPONSIBILITY

Before he became bishop and then pope, St. John Paul II was known for his wise advice in the confessional. But he was also known for the delicate respect he showed to those who came to confession. After helping them sort through their confusion and their trouble, and after identifying some possible next steps, he would always say, "But now it is up to you; you must choose."

This is the battlefield of the spiritual combat: the intimate and mysterious arena of human freedom. Every day we enter that arena anew. There, through our decisions, we make ourselves more into one of two kinds of people—either the kind of person who stays faithful to what is true, good, and beautiful, or the kind of person who prefers an easier path, namely, the wide gate and the broad road that lead to destruction (see Matt. 7:13).

Questions for Personal Reflection or Group Discussion

1. What idea in this chapter struck you most and why?

2. How aware are you of your interior freedom, your God-given capacity to choose how you will act and react?

3. How does the reality of spiritual combat make you feel: excited, frightened, confused, humble? How do you think God wants this truth to make you feel?

4. Victor Frankl was a Jewish psychologist sent to a concentration camp in Nazi Germany. His experience of surviving the camp led him to develop a new school of psychology based on what he termed "logotherapy."One of his key principles was: "Everything can be taken from a man but one thing: the last of the human freedoms—to choose one's attitude in any given set of circumstances, to choose one's own way." What will you do today to exercise more consciously this great gift of interior freedom?

   • I will say a prayer instead of retaliating when I feel attacked or misunderstood.

- I will say no to my usual tendency to procrastinate regarding important things.
- I will give myself some silence today, a few minutes to simply let my interior settle down and listen to what God may be saying to my heart.
- (Write your own resolution) I will _____

  _____

  _____

  _____

Concluding Prayer

*Grant, O Lord, that we may begin with holy fasting
this campaign of Christian service, so that, as
we take up battle against spiritual evils, we may
be armed with weapons of self-restraint.*

—ROMAN MISSAL, COLLECT FROM
THE MASS FOR ASH WEDNESDAY

DAY 4

Good Soil

Baptism is the sign that God has joined us on our journey,
that he makes our existence more beautiful, and that he
transforms our history into a history of holiness.
— St. John Paul II, World Youth Day Vigil, 1997

OUR LORD FREQUENTLY DESCRIBED HIS kingdom, the growth of his lordship in each heart and in the world, by comparing it to plants. The mustard seed (see Matt. 13:31), the farmer's field (see Matt. 13:24), the sower who sowed seed on various types of soil (see Luke 8:1-15) — all these images illustrate the essential partnership at the heart of our Christian journey.

The seed has an intrinsic power to grow and bear fruit. That power comes directly from God, not from anything the farmer can do. But the power to grow is only released under proper conditions: good soil, water, sunlight. Creating and maintaining the proper conditions for growth is the farmer's job. And it's a hard job. Lots of work is involved. But even if he did all that work extremely well, it would have no result without the God-given life inside the seed.

Which is more essential to a healthy crop, the seed or the soil? Neither. Both are equally essential. So it is with our growth in holiness. God's grace is the seed of new spiritual life planted in our souls through faith and baptism, the potential to become a saint, a unique reflection of God's infinite beauty, the glorious truth about God and ourselves in God's eyes. The soil is our part, our cooperation with and response to God, the healthy or unhealthy exercise of our freedom in the midst of the spiritual combat.

Our efforts — our choices and decisions — can provide and

maintain healthy soil for the seed of God's grace to take root and flourish. Our lack of effort or misguided efforts can harden that soil or otherwise corrupt it, so that the seed of the kingdom is stolen, choked, or has its growth truncated.

SEASONS OF GROWTH

Myriad practical lessons flow from this concept of spiritual growth. First of all, patience. Have you ever seen a farmer standing in his fields, yelling at his crops to grow faster? That would be absurd. Yet isn't that exactly what we do when we become frustrated with our slow spiritual progress, or the slow spiritual progress of others?

Then there is the lesson of rhythm. Spiritual growth goes through seasons. Plants need to grow to maturity before they bear fruit. Likewise, we need time in our Christian journey to get to the point where we can really bear abundant spiritual fruit. We need Nazareth seasons—seasons of quiet, ordinary, and undramatic activity and experience, when we are being prepared for the mission.

Even when plants are mature, they have periods when they are seemingly dry and dormant, under attack, so to speak, by harsh conditions: the wintry months. So too, in the spiritual life, we experience wintry seasons, when all we find in our souls is dryness, darkness, the brittle starkness of bare branches coated with frost. Jesus had these seasons, too—when he sweat blood in the Garden of Gethsemane, or when he suffered rejection and crucifixion on Calvary.

Other periods are full of blossoms and buds, vigor and hope: spiritual springs, like Jesus during the early part of his public life, being followed and admired by huge crowds as he preached and healed and performed miracles. Those springs are followed by seasons of waiting and guarding and weeding and watering: spiritual summers, like the latter period of our Lord's public life, when he spent time with his twelve apostles, keeping a lower profile because he was becoming so controversial. Harvest season comes, too—the Resurrection, the Ascension into heaven, the Holy Spirit-filled Pentecost.

Love Is Patient

Our mechanized, technology-driven world prepares us poorly for the seasons of spiritual growth. We are conditioned to expect immediate results, to be able to go to the spiritual grocery store and buy exactly what we need at any time, regardless of the season. We are conditioned by a consumer-centered, on-demand culture; we rebel at the spiritual realm, where humility and faith and wisdom can't be downloaded with the touch of a finger but must be asked for simply, sought after avidly, and cultivated perseveringly over various seasons of gestation.

It's hard to change our expectations, to travel life's pilgrimage at God's pace instead of trying to force him and ourselves to go at the world's 24/7-news-cycle pace. We all need to reflect frequently and deeply on this mysterious partnership between God's part and our part, between the seed and the soil. The Lord comes steadily and surely into our lives, transforming us gradually, the way that nature transforms a seed into a plant. We simply have to keep giving him the chance to do so.

St. James, who died a martyr's death at the hands of his own people in first-century Jerusalem, learned this lesson well. He wrote to the Christians of his time:

> Be patient, therefore, brothers, until the coming of the Lord. See how the farmer waits for the precious fruit of the earth, being patient with it until it receives the early and the late rains. You too must be patient. Make your hearts firm, because the coming of the Lord is at hand. (James 5:7–8)

Heeding the Call

Yet the most comforting lesson flowing from our Lord's parables about seeds and soil is the assurance that we are never alone in this work of following Christ and building his kingdom. The seed and the soil go together, always. God is not only our goal; he is also our companion, our light, our support, and our guide: "I am the way and the truth and the life. . . . I will not leave you orphans" (John 14:6; 14:18).

Certainly, God loves us too much to force our hand, but he also loves us too much to ever give up on us. He will always do his part, his 99 percent. But he will always respect our freedom, giving us space to do our part, our 1 percent. He will give us rest and comfort; he will make our lives fruitful; he will lead us into complete joy—but only if we heed his call, a heartfelt call that he never stops issuing: "Come to me . . . follow me . . . abide in me" (Matt.11:28; 4:19; John 15:4, RSV). This is the great adventure, the joyful striving, the glorious toil of being a follower of Christ.

Questions for Personal Reflection or Group Discussion

1. What idea in this chapter struck you most and why?

2. Sometime today, read prayerfully the parable of the sower (Matt. 13:1–23), asking the Holy Spirit to show you what you need to see.

3. Reflect on your spiritual progress since you began to open your heart to God. What positive changes have you seen in yourself? Where would you most like to experience more growth? How would you describe the season you are currently in?

4. What will you do today to keep the soil of your heart ready to receive the seed of God's Word, in whatever form it comes?

   - I will take time away from the hustle and bustle just to be with God and let his love sink into my heart—maybe going for a quiet walk in a beautiful setting, or sitting silently in a chapel.

   - I will take a chunk of my drive time and simply sit in silence, reflecting on my life and asking God to speak to my heart, without listening to anything or talking on the phone.

   - I will finally do that kind but inconvenient deed that has been nagging my conscience for a while now, but that I have been trying to ignore.

   - (Write your own resolution) I will _____
   _____
   _____
   _____

Concluding Prayer

Let nothing trouble you,
Let nothing frighten you,
Everything passes; God never changes.
Patience obtains all;
Whoever has God wants for nothing;
God alone is enough.

—A PRAYER BY ST. TERESA OF AVILA[4]

Full Freedom

The commitment to imitating Christ is the triumph of God's love that
takes hold of a man and demands of him every possible effort in the service
of this love, while at the same time he stays fully aware of human weakness.
— *St. John Paul II, Homily, October 29, 1995*

D IFFERENT PERSONALITIES TEND TO REACT to this truth about our partnership with God in different ways. If carried to the extreme, these reactions can lead to a lack of interior balance, inhibiting the "glorious freedom of the children of God" (Rom. 8:21) that we are called to begin experiencing even as we travel along our pilgrimage in this fallen world. Each of us needs to develop an awareness of how these tendencies show up in our own case, so as to gradually develop a healthy sense of balance while our interior freedom matures.

THE ACHIEVER'S TRAP

High achievers and perfectionists will tend to overemphasize the 1 percent that is our part. They can interpret the parable of the sower and the seed, and other parables of the kingdom, as threats. They tend to think that if they are not doing their absolute best at every moment, God won't be pleased and won't be able to send his grace. They feel that God is watching closely over them, but more analytically than lovingly. They can fall into subconsciously perceiving God as if he were a judge in a gymnastics competition, paying special attention and taking a perverse delight in all the flaws, all the shortcomings, of their Christian performance. They forget what God himself has told us about his unconditional love, a love that doesn't have to be earned: "I have loved you with an everlasting love; I have continued my faithfulness to you" (Jer. 31:3, RSV).

If this tendency is given free rein, the spiritual life can gradually become twisted and oppressive. The sweet and jubilant fascination that accompanied the soul's first personal encounters with the Lord gets worn down by fear, tension, and pressure, which are for the most part self-imposed. The deep, rich satisfaction that came from discovering the ultimate meaning of life (living in communion with God) and redirecting one's actions and desires toward that meaning, fades and almost disappears. The Christian quest for holiness comes to be felt as a stifling shackle and an exhaustive, unfair burden.

Unpleasant Repercussions

This path of overemphasizing our own efforts can have various eventual outcomes; the self-imposed pressure cooker can explode in a variety of directions. It can leave the soul brittle, harsh, and dry. This creates Christians who are pious but not holy, who are cold and judgmental and holier-than-thou. On the other hand, it can lead a person to rebel against God, to come to the conclusion that Christianity is nothing more than a spiritual and emotional prison constructed out of controlling lists of sadistic, inhuman obligations. The constant disappointment of not living up to unrealistic, self-imposed standards of performance can also lead to seemingly perennial discouragement, and even depression, paralyzing the soul or sparking addictions.

The Antidote

The tendency to overemphasize our own efforts needs to be balanced out by frequent contemplation of God's goodness, of his undying commitment to always be there with his 99 percent, and of his delight in our slightest efforts to put forth our 1 percent.

The achiever or perfectionist needs to think frequently and intentionally about all God has done through the ages, and all he continues to do, to further his loving plan of salvation. These individuals need to think frequently and intentionally of all God has done and continues to do to further their own individual stories of salvation. Like St. Paul, they need to renew their confidence in God, the senior partner of our Christian quest:

> I am confident of this, that the one who began a good work in you will continue to complete it until the day of Christ Jesus. . . . For God is the one who, for his good purpose, works in you both to desire and to work. (Phil. 1:6; 2:13)

THE LULL OF MEDIOCRITY

For more social and spontaneous types, the tendency tilts to the other extreme: underemphasizing our role in spiritual growth. Casual and easy-going folks can fall into being lazy Christians, satisfied with comfortable mediocrity, because "God will take care of it."

Comfortable Christians habitually let their good, God-inspired resolutions languish and die. They may avoid the big dramatic sins, but they also avoid the taxing demands of mature love. They hear the Lord's call, and they feel the attraction of spiritual maturity (and sincerely desire it), but, like the rich young man in the Gospel who "went away sad" (Mark 10:22) after rejecting the Lord's invitation to leave behind his comfort zone, they have difficulty mustering up enough spiritual energy to keep on giving of themselves to God and neighbor until it hurts. They may not even allow themselves to consciously realize that they are resisting the nudge of grace.

SIGNS OF STAGNATION

Sometimes this tendency is hard to diagnose, because comfortable Christians are often jovial and quite engaged in good, holy activities that they enjoy. But they are not growing in their spiritual lives, because they are continually refusing, directly or indirectly, God's invitations to go deeper. They usually have good excuses, but their repeated refusals gradually create a kind of gray spiritual undertone in their lives, a hazy sense of inadequacy and dissatisfaction, a vague sadness lurking in the corners of their consciousness. This can even deepen into hidden but spiritually destructive self-loathing if the tendency fails to be identified and faced.

This underemphasizing of our part is hard to live with. So, comfortable Christians frequently develop attachments to superficial pastimes that serve as distractions and temporary escape routes. God is continually calling out to them, because he never gives up on any of us. But they are afraid of answering the call and stepping out of their comfort zone, so they find ways to drown out that still, small voice.

CULTIVATING COURAGE

Comfortable Christians need to develop courage and perseverance. They need to allow the Holy Spirit to remind them of what's at stake in the spiritual battle. St. Paul is a sure guide in these reflections:

> Working together, then, we appeal to you not to receive the grace of God in vain. . . . Work out your salvation with fear and trembling. . . . Let us not grow tired of doing good, for in due time we shall reap our harvest, if we do not give up. (2 Cor. 6:1; Phil. 2:12; Gal. 6:9)

Here again, contemplating God's goodness can provide powerful fuel for growth: The more convinced we are of God's wisdom and love toward us, the better chance we will have of trusting him when he invites us to step into uncomfortable territory. And even if we just keep taking very little steps, he will work wonders: "Draw near to God, and he will draw near to you" (James 4:8).

Questions for Personal Reflection or Group Discussion

1. What idea in this chapter struck you most and why?

2. Which of the two tendencies discussed in this chapter is stronger in you? How can you tell?

3. How deeply do you consider and reflect on God's goodness and love toward you? In other words, who is God for you, and how deeply have you experienced his personal, unconditional love? Are there perhaps some interior blocks that make it hard for you to accept and feel God's personal love for you?

4. Whether you tend to fall into the Achiever's Trap or the Lull of Mediocrity, growing in intimacy with God requires counteracting those tendencies by forming habits of thought and behavior that correspond more harmoniously with the full truth of who you are in Christ. Forming new habits takes time (most experts say about forty days) and consistent, intentional effort. What new habit will you begin to form today to help you grow in the full freedom of the children of God?

- Today, and every day for the next month, I will consciously choose to step out of my comfort zone at least one time, when my conscience nudges me to—whether by doing an inconvenient (to me) favor for someone, speaking the truth when it's risky, or reaching out to someone who ought to be reaching out to me.

- Today I will begin a Journal of Glory, where every day I will write down at least one good thing that God did for me during the day in order to cultivate a deeper awareness of his goodness—whether allowing me to marvel at a beautiful sunset, to experience a small success, or simply to enjoy a pleasing coincidence.

- (Write your own resolution) I will _____

_____

_____

Concluding Prayer

Take, Lord, and receive all my liberty,
my memory, my understanding
and my entire will,
All I have and call my own.
You have given all to me.
To you, Lord, I return it.
Everything is yours; do with it what you will.
Give me only your love and your grace.
That is enough for me.

—A PRAYER FROM ST. IGNATIUS OF LOYOLA

PART II

LOVING GOD WITH ALL MY HEART

One of the scribes, when he came forward and heard them disputing and saw how well he had answered them, asked him, "Which is the first of all the commandments?" Jesus replied, "The first is this: 'Hear, O Israel! The Lord our God is Lord alone! You shall love the Lord your God with all your heart, with all your soul, with all your mind, and with all your strength.' The second is this: 'You shall love your neighbor as yourself.' There is no other commandment greater than these."

MARK 12:28–31

DAY 6

Loving with My All

I praise the Lord with you, because he is so great and beautiful
a Love as to deserve the priceless gift of the whole person in
the unfathomable depths of the heart, and in the concrete
unfolding of daily duty through the various stages of life.
—St. John Paul II, Homily, February 2, 2002

THE MERE FACT THAT YOU are reading this book—and have gotten this far—should fill you with deep, intense joy. It shows that you already desire the most important thing: to know, love, and follow Jesus Christ more fully every day. That desire is supernatural. You couldn't have stirred it up on your own. Its presence in your soul shows without any doubt that God is with you and acting in your life. The engine of holiness is already humming in the depths of your heart, just as it was for the Blessed Virgin Mary. As the Preface of the Mass for Advent puts it: " . . . The Virgin Mother longed for him with love beyond all telling." Your longing to love God more fully, even if it seems to be a small or dim longing way down in the basement of your being, is in itself a movement of a very deep love for him, a love that gives him immense pleasure.

The deep longing for fulfillment, the yearning to come closer to Christ, is itself the work of Christ. He plants good, holy desires in the human heart so that he can later fulfill them. Through this longing, God is drawing you closer to his divine heart, where you will find more than you could ever have imagined, where your most intense desires will be satisfied to overflowing. As St. Thomas Aquinas put it when commenting on the fullness of love that the faithful experience in heaven: "Eternal life is the perfect fulfilment of desire; in as much as each of the blessed will have more than he desired or hoped for."[5]

Knowing that God is leading us to this glorious, indescribable destination should be an ongoing source of encouragement for all of us, as it was for St. Paul: "What eye has not seen, and ear has not heard, and what has not entered the human heart, what God has prepared for those who love him . . . " (1 Cor. 2:9). We have that to look forward to.

A PRECISE TOTALITY OF LOVE

Jesus summarized our part in the fulfillment of this longing when he gave us the two great commandments. But fulfilling those commandments requires understanding them. What exactly was Jesus trying to tell us when he commanded us: "You shall love the Lord, your God, with all your heart, with all your soul, with all your mind, and with all your strength"? This, according to our Lord, is the first and greatest commandment, which overflows into the second most important commandment, "You shall love your neighbor as yourself" (Mark 12:30–31, RSV).

We have two possible interpretations for the verse about loving God. First, Jesus may have simply been using many terms to say one thing: Love God totally! His use of the terms *heart, soul, mind,* and *strength* may have been simply a rhetorical device, a poetic way of expressing totality, emphasized by his fourfold repetition of the word *all*.

Yet, on the other hand, Jesus may have been consciously referring to the different powers of the soul when he listed those four modes of loving God. He may have meant exactly what he said, giving us clear instructions about what mature love for God looks like: it fills and overflows from the four main dimensions of human nature—the heart, the emotions, the intelligence, and the will.

These two interpretations are not mutually exclusive. They actually complement each other. To love God totally means to love him with every fiber of one's being. And that means integrating every sector of one's life and every capacity of our human nature into a true friendship with Jesus Christ.

BEYOND SELF-HELP LISTS

The self-help industry tends to divide up the art of living. It promotes "five ways to become happy," and "seven tricks to get ahead," and "ten secrets to success." This is not necessarily a bad thing. Lists like these often contain excellent advice. And in the face of real life's real complexity, they provide a certain degree of clarity, order, and understanding. The Ten Commandments themselves follow a similar structure.

Yet, in the Christian tradition, the Ten Commandments have always been seen as guidelines that point out the bare minimum requirements for staying on the path to happiness. The essence of happiness goes beyond the bare minimum; it goes deeper. Full spiritual maturity can never consist in mechanically fulfilling a list of dos and don'ts. Jesus knows this. And so, without completely erasing the lists, he brings us to the deeper level, to a more unified vision.

Authentic love is the essence of happiness: loving God totally, with all the powers of our human nature, and expressing that love through concrete decisions in daily life, through treating others (God's children, created in God's image and likeness) with the same concern and proactivity that marks every person's spontaneous attitude toward oneself.

FOUR ARENAS OF LOVE

Jesus chooses to describe this total love for God by referring to four separate arenas, so to speak, in which that love can be developed and grown and shown. This was no mistake. Three of the four terms Jesus uses were also used in the Old Testament; they formed part of God's original revelation to Israel (see Deut. 6:5). Jesus reiterates them. And so, surely they mean something. To penetrate this meaning will open up new possibilities in any Christian's life, because it will show concrete ways to channel every Christian's deep desire to love God more fully.

The following chapters will examine in depth each of these four arenas of love, showing how each of the four activates different powers built into human nature. Only by growing harmoniously in all four areas can we truly allow God's grace to transform every corner of our lives, gradually discovering the abundant life that Jesus identified as the goal of his life's mission: "I came so that they might have life, and have it more abundantly" (John 10:10).

Although we will examine each sector separately, it's important to keep in mind that they are all connected. What happens in the emotions, for example, reverberates in the mind and the heart, and the direction of our heart affects our will and our emotions, and so on. The human person is a unified whole, even though our human nature does indeed have various powers and faculties.

Savoring the Promise

But before branching into the distinctions between heart, soul, mind, and strength, we should pause and take some time to savor the promise hidden inside this first commandment—the promise that God's grace is working hard to bring us not merely to an earthly happiness that comes from following five secret tips, but rather to the full, glorious, and everlasting satisfaction of spiritual maturity. Here's how Pope Benedict XVI portrayed that maturity in the context of describing the implications of our faith in Jesus. Notice how his expression seems to brim over with joy, energy, and optimism, which is how all of us should approach the great adventure of growing in God's love:

> Faith in the Lord is not something that affects only our minds, the realm of intellectual knowledge; rather, it is a change involving the whole of our existence: our feelings, heart, mind, will, body, emotions and human relationships. With faith, everything changes in us and for us, and it reveals clearly our future destiny, the truth of our vocation in history, the meaning of our lives, the joy of being pilgrims en route to our heavenly homeland.[6]

Questions for Personal Reflection or Group Discussion

1. What idea in this chapter struck you most and why?

2. When did you first start experiencing a desire to know, love, and follow Jesus Christ more fully? Remember and savor that moment of grace.

3. What things in your life tend to encourage that holy desire, and what tends to drain it?

4. Think about the activities and commitments coming up in the next twenty-four hours. Which ones will be most threatening to the interior equilibrium that flows from loving God with your all? Think now about how you can react to those things more wisely.

   - With someone I tend to get into arguments with, I will listen and ask questions to understand what he or she means before responding.

   - With work I don't enjoy but have to do, I will make the Sign of the Cross and begin with a prayer to Jesus to ask for strength.

   - With a strong temptation that I often end up giving in to, I will avoid putting myself in the situation where the temptation usually arises.

   - (Write your own resolution) I will _____
   _____
   _____
   _____

Concluding Prayer

Soul of Christ, be my sanctification.
Body of Christ, be my salvation.
Blood of Christ, fill all my veins.
Water from Christ's side, wash out my stains.
Passion of Christ, my comfort be.
O Good Jesus, listen to me!
In thy wounds I fain would hide,
Ne'er to be parted from thy side.
Guard me should the foe assail me.
Guide me when my life shall fail me.
Bid me come to thee above,
With the saints to sing thy love,
World without end. Amen.

—ANIMA CHRISTI, A MEDIEVAL LATIN PRAYER,
TRANSLATED BY BLESSED JOHN HENRY CARDINAL NEWMAN[7]

DAY 7

Focusing on the Heart

Today, on this Lord's Day, I wish to invite all those who are listening to my words, not to forget our immortal destiny: life after death – the eternal happiness of heaven, or the awful possibility of eternal punishment, eternal separation from God, in what the Christian tradition has called hell. There can be no truly Christian living without an openness to this transcendent dimension of our lives. "Both in life and death we are the Lord's" (Romans 14:8).
– St. John Paul II, Homily, September 13, 1987

THE FIRST ARENA OF LOVE that Jesus points out is the "heart." In all three New Testament versions of this greatest commandment, *heart* is always first on the list.

Sacred Scripture uses this term more than a thousand times, but never to refer simply to the biological organ. The term always has a fuller, more complete, and more spiritual cachet. With so many appearances, the word can't help but take on a variety of connotations, yet the core meaning always remains the same. The *heart* refers to the deepest center of the person, the irreplaceable and irreducible "I" of the unique human individual. All the other powers of human nature flow from and depend on the heart. A person can say, "My feelings, my decisions, my hopes, my desires, my thoughts . . . " But while all of those possessions belong to someone, the *heart* is the biblical term that refers to the core identity of that someone; it encompasses the substantive center of the possessor of everything else. The *Catechism* explores the mysterious origin of prayer:

The heart is our hidden center, beyond the grasp of our reason and of others; only the Spirit of God can fathom the human heart and know it fully. The heart is the place of decision, deeper than our psychic drives. It is the place of truth, where we choose life or death. It is the place of encounter, because as image of God we live in relation: it is the place of covenant. (CCC, 2563)

This is the heart. Jesus commands his followers to love him, in the first place, with all their heart. What does this mean?

THE TREASURE HUNT

Jesus gives us a revealing clue in another one of his discourses, when he says, "For where your treasure is, there also will your heart be" (Matt. 6:21). A treasure is what we value most, what we desire most, what we set our sights on attaining or maintaining. To love God with all our heart, therefore, means to make God—communion with him, friendship with him—into the overarching goal of our lives, into our most precious possession, into our deepest yearning. It means making our relationship with God the true north of our earthly journey, so that every decision, every desire, every hope and dream, every interpersonal interaction is evaluated, lived, and developed in light of that fundamental, orienting relationship.

As a result, anything that may damage our relationship with God must be cut away or re-dimensioned, especially sin and sinful habits, whereas anything that harmonizes with or may enhance our relationship with God is welcomed and integrated more and more fully into our life. As you can see, engaging the whole heart in our love for God is not something that happens from one moment to the next; it is a process. To love God with all your heart means intentionally and gradually making your relationship with him into the greatest—indeed, the only—treasure of your life.

KEEP ON SEEKING

Loving God with all our heart means wanting, above everything else, to grow continually in our communion with him, in our friendship with him. This desire may start small, but as we grow, it also grows. And as our heart comes to love God more and more fully, every other desire is slowly but surely subordinated to and harmonized with that overarching desire, and so every experience, circumstance, and activity serves to bring us into a deeper knowledge of him. This is why Jesus was able to assure us, "Blessed are the clean of heart, for they will see God" (Matt. 5:8).

In the end, we get what we want. If we truly want God, if our heart is set on pursuing God, on seeking him, on living in a deeper and deeper communion with him, God will not deny us that treasure, which is called heaven—after all, that's what he created us for. This is why he can solemnly promise: "Seek and you will find" (Matt. 7:7). In the original Greek, the verb *seek* has the sense of an ongoing process: "Keep on seeking, and you will find." If we keep our hearts pointed toward God, we will reach full communion with God, wherein we find our happiness.

On the other hand, if we persistently prefer to seek our fulfillment in something else, in some idol—whether other relationships, achievements, or pleasures—and leave communion with God as a secondary concern, or as no concern at all, God will honor our choice. He will keep trying to convince us to set aside our idols in favor of his friendship, but he won't force us to do so. If we keep declining his invitations to the end, the purpose for which we were created—living in communion with God—will be everlastingly frustrated, and this is called hell.

Two Kinds of People

C.S. Lewis put it simply and eloquently in his masterpiece, *The Great Divorce*, referring to our Lord's amazing promise about seeking and finding: "Ask and it will be given to you; seek and you will find; knock and the door will be opened to you. For everyone who asks, receives; and the one who seeks, finds; and to the one who knocks, the door will be opened" (Matt. 7:7-8). Lewis comments on that dictum as follows:

There are only two kinds of people in the end: those who say to God, "Thy will be done," and those to whom God says, in the end, "Thy will be done." All that are in Hell, choose it. Without that self-choice there could be no Hell. No soul that seriously and constantly desires joy will ever miss it. Those who seek find. To those who knock it is opened.[8]

When Jesus commands us to love God with all our heart, he is teaching us the right answer to the very first question he asked in the Gospel of John, a question that each of us must answer anew every single day of our lives: "What are you looking for?" (John 1:38). Where am I hoping to find the happiness I cannot resist desiring? If I hope to find it in God, I am loving God with my heart. As I progressively learn to hope to find it in God alone, and to order all the other smaller loves of my heart around that greatest love, I am learning to love God with all my heart.

Questions for Personal Reflection or Group Discussion

1. What idea in this chapter struck you most and why?

2. When you look into the depths of your soul, how do you answer Christ's question: "What are you looking for?"

3. If an observer were to follow you around for a typical week of your life, what would they conclude you are looking for in life?

4. Here on earth we find ourselves filled with conflicting desires. Even though, on the one hand, we do sincerely desire God, we also experience less worthy desires that often pop up uninvited. But God understands what you're made of! He will help you increase your good, God-centered desires, and purify the others. You just have to work with him. Today, what will you do to nourish your hope in God as the source of your lasting happiness?

   • I will take ten minutes to write down the most beautiful and satisfying experiences I have ever had—and then reflect on how they are connected to God and his love for me.

- After each meal today, I will say a short but sincere prayer of thanks before getting up from the table.
- (Write your own resolution) I will _____

_____

_____

_____

Concluding Prayer

Be Thou my Vision, O Lord of my heart;
Naught be all else to me, save that Thou art.
Thou my best Thought, by day or by night,
Waking or sleeping, Thy presence my light.
Be Thou my Wisdom, and Thou my true Word;
I ever with Thee and Thou with me, Lord;
Thou my great Father, I Thy true son;
Thou in me dwelling, and I with Thee one.
Be Thou my battle Shield, Sword for the fight;
Be Thou my Dignity, Thou my Delight;
Thou my soul's Shelter, Thou my high Tower:
Raise Thou me heavenward, O Power of my power.
Riches I heed not, nor man's empty praise,
Thou mine Inheritance, now and always:
Thou and Thou only, first in my heart,
High King of Heaven, my Treasure Thou art.
High King of Heaven, my victory won,
May I reach Heaven's joys, O bright Heaven's Sun!
Heart of my own heart, whatever befall,
Still be my Vision, O Ruler of all.

—IRISH MONASTIC PRAYER FROM THE SIXTH CENTURY

My Deepest Desire

St. Paul reminds us of two fundamental truths: first, that our ultimate
vocation is to glorify the God who created and redeemed us; and secondly,
that our eternal and highest good is to "attain to the fullness of God
himself" (Ephesians 3:19)—to participate in the loving communion
of the Father and the Son and the Holy Spirit for all eternity. God's
glory and our good are perfectly attained in the kingdom of heaven.
—St. John Paul II, Homily, September 18, 1987

LOVING GOD WITH ALL ONE's heart simply means making God—an
increasing communion with him, an ever-deepening friendship
with him—the highest priority and guiding principle of one's life.
It is love understood as the fundamental desire, the fundamental
orientation of one's life.

When Jesus began his public ministry with a call to conversion, this
is what he was getting at. By announcing that "the kingdom of God is
at hand" (Mark 1:15), he was pointing out that in him, God-become-
man, full communion with God is now truly possible. God has made
himself one of us, so that we can enter into a real friendship with him.
Jesus is Emmanuel, God with us. Before Jesus, God was close to his
people, but it was a closeness always mediated by something: by creation, by his revelation and his commandments, by his prophets.

In Jesus, who is truly God and truly man, God's closeness has
taken a definitive turn, and we can love God with all our heart truly,
through a fully human relationship with the eternal God, through
knowing and following the Son. All it takes is leaving behind any

idols, any fundamental desire that can't be subordinated to or harmonized with the desire to live in communion with God: "Repent, and believe in the gospel!" (Mark 1:15).

RUNNING TO WIN

A healthy professional football team has one overarching goal, one fundamental desire: to win the championship. All the decisions made by the coaches and players are made with that in mind. All the activities they engage in, all the sacrifices they make, all the intermediate objectives and challenges, are seen and dealt with in light of that goal. That goal is the ultimate source of the entire team's dynamism, effort, and yearnings. The championship is the treasure they are hunting and hoping for; everything else takes on meaning through its relationship with that treasure.

St. Paul draws a parallel between this kind of all-encompassing, athletic treasure hunt and a Christian's hunt for greater and greater intimacy with Christ here on earth and the definitive, total communion with him forever in heaven:

> Do you not know that the runners in the stadium all run in the race, but only one wins the prize? Run so as to win. Every athlete exercises discipline in every way. They do it to win a perishable crown, but we an imperishable one. Thus I do not run aimlessly; I do not fight as if I were shadowboxing. No, I drive my body and train it, for fear that, after having preached to others, I myself should be disqualified. (1 Cor. 9:24-27)

When I love God with all my heart, my relationship with him becomes the axis of my activity, the magnet that brings order and dynamism into all the otherwise scattered shards of my life, the organizing principle around which every other element is arranged.

LOVE'S PURIFYING FIRE

This is how love for God purifies us. As we allow ourselves to be drawn more fully into friendship with him, we let go of unhealthy attachments that are holding us back from spiritual maturity. We leave behind selfish habits, behaviors, and attitudes that feel comfortable, or maybe even necessary, but that in fact impede us from loving and living with full freedom. We leave them behind, because our growing intimacy with God leaves no room for them.

This is the "discipline" that St. Paul calls Christians to exercise. The Letter to the Hebrews echoes St. Paul's comparison of spiritual growth to running a race, while emphasizing more this purifying effect of a growing, heartfelt love for God:

> Let us rid ourselves of every burden and sin that clings to us and persevere in running the race that lies before us while keeping our eyes fixed on Jesus, the leader and perfecter of faith. (Heb. 12:1-2)

Sometimes this purification requires renouncing material objects, but it can never be only that. Material poverty in itself is no virtue. Poverty of spirit, the purity of our fundamental desire, is what matters. As St. Thomas Aquinas explained it, "It is abundantly clear that the human heart is more intensely attracted to one object, in proportion as it is withdrawn from a multiplicity of desires."[9] In other words, I can better focus my attention on one task if I am not distracted by trying to do five other tasks at the same time.

TANTO CUANTO

St. Ignatius of Loyola explored this aspect of loving God with all our heart in his famous meditation about *tanto cuanto*. That Spanish phrase can be translated "inasmuch as." St. Ignatius points out that everything in creation, from mountains to moods, from galaxies to good food, from rehearsals to relationships, is given to us by God out of love and for love. All these things are essentially good, and they exist to be a stepping stone toward greater intimacy with God, to be opportunities for experiencing God's love for us and for showing and growing our love for him. Inasmuch as we enjoy and use all things for that purpose, they are good for us. But if we turn any of God's gifts into idols, seeking our fulfillment in them instead of in loving God through them, they become bad.

To take a rather mundane example, watching football on the weekends is not intrinsically evil. It can be a healthy form of recreation. But when it impedes me from fulfilling my basic responsibilities—like attending to family needs or worshipping God on the Lord's Day—it has overstepped its bounds and become an obstacle, a little idol.

Jesus himself illustrated this principle with his parables of the treasure in the field and the pearl of great price. The treasure and the pearl symbolize the kingdom of God, our friendship with Christ, our living in communion with him. All other realities are given to us to help us achieve and deepen that communion.

> The Kingdom of heaven is like a treasure buried in a field, which a person finds and hides again and out of joy goes and sells all that he has and buys that field. Again, the kingdom of heaven is like a merchant searching for fine pearls. When he finds a pearl of great price, he goes and sells all that he has and buys it. (Matt. 13:44-46)

Loving God with all our heart means living in accordance with the truth of our treasure. Nothing matters more than our relationship with God. We believe that, and so we desire nothing more than an ever-deepening intimacy with him. And we spend our lives learning to live accordingly.

Questions for Personal Reflection or Group Discussion

1. What idea in this chapter struck you most and why?

2. What evidence is there in your daily life to show that you are "running to win"? What evidence is there in your daily life to show that you are not really "running to win"?

3. Are there any attachments in your life (possessions, dreams, relationships, habits) that are holding you back from loving God with all your heart?

4. Many of us have a tendency to clutter our lives with lots of

things that we don't really need, things that weigh us down in our pursuit of spiritual maturity instead of propelling us forward. What will you "rid yourself of" today that will free your heart to love God a little bit more fully?

- I will spend less time surfing the Web, chatting through social media, or indulging in entertainment.

- I will go through my closet and take out every outfit I haven't worn at least once in the last year and donate those clothes to someone who can use them.

- I will look over my credit-card bills from the last two months and see what kinds of whimsical purchases I can cut down on.

- (Write your own resolution) I will _____

_____

_____

_____

Concluding Prayer

Hear my voice, Lord, when I call;
have mercy on me and answer me.
"Come," says my heart, "seek his face";
your face, Lord, do I seek!
Do not hide your face from me;
do not repel your servant in anger.
You are my salvation; do not cast me off;
do not forsake me, God my savior!
Even if my father and mother forsake me,
the Lord will take me in.

—Psalm 27:7–10

Nourishing My Heart

*There is no doubt that spiritual formation ought to occupy a
privileged place in a person's life. Everyone is called to grow
continually in intimate union with Jesus Christ, in conformity to
the Father's will, in devotion to others in charity and justice.*
— St. John Paul II, Christifideles Laici, 60

LOVING GOD WITH ALL YOUR heart means desiring him above all
things and making your intimate, personal relationship with him
into the highest priority of your life, the center around which every
other facet of your existence finds its proper and glorious place. But
how do you do that? How do you make that happen?

The heart expresses itself through the other three modes that
Jesus identifies in the greatest commandment: loving God with all
our soul, mind, and strength. Attending to each of those arenas,
therefore, produces an indirect effect on the heart as well, educat-
ing and purifying it, and nourishing its Christian core. Nevertheless,
you can also attend to the heart directly.

THOUGHTS OF THE HEART

We spend a lot of time thinking about the things we desire. When
we treasure something, it occupies our mind. And, conversely, the
more we think about something, the more we tend to desire it.

This is part of human nature; it flows from the connection
between the two spiritual faculties that human nature possesses — intelligence and will, the power to know and the power to

choose. For us human beings, these faculties utilize instruments to operate: our senses, our imagination, our memory, our emotions, and our passions. Unlike angels, whose access to truth and goodness is purely spiritual and immediate, human persons discover truth and goodness gradually, through the mediation of spatial-temporal experience. This is why we can figure out a solution to a complex problem by making diagrams and pictures, doodling, trying various alternatives in our imagination, and discussing it with others.

And so, what we choose to look at, think about, and daydream about will affect the desires that grow and mature in our heart. The intensity of our love for a certain object can increase or decrease according to how much attention we pay to that object and how much space it takes up in our external and internal senses (memory and imagination).

TRICKS OF THE DEVIL

The devil understands this reality and uses it in the dynamics of temptation. St. James explains how temptation begins with something that stirs up a self-centered desire, and then, if we choose to pay attention to that desire, it grows. If we feed it with more attention, we will eventually act on it, committing sin. If we continue to act on it, the sin can become a habit and even choke off the life of grace:

> Each person is tempted when he is lured and enticed by his own desire. Then desire conceives and brings forth sin, and when sin reaches maturity it gives birth to death. (James 1:14–15)

The devil, agitating our fallen nature and the fallen world in which we live, will try to monopolize our attention with images, ideas, thoughts, and invitations that can lure us into self-absorption and eventually into destructive self-indulgence. The enemy of our souls wants to occupy our minds with a multiplicity of inputs that can divide our hearts, draining our desire for God and filling up our desires for any number of petty idols.

SPIRITUAL HEART SUPPLEMENTS

Forming our heart in Christ follows the contrary path. To feed our desire for God and our desire to make our relationship with him the core and fountain of everything we do requires thinking frequently about him and his magnificent plan for our lives. Just as a little boy will feed his desire for a new bike by looking at a picture of that bike every day, so too we need to gaze at the Lord and savor his dream for us as often as we can. We need to feed the central desire of our Christian heart with thoughts that are in harmony with that desire. And we need to intentionally stir up those thoughts all the time. The psalms frequently make choosing to think about God and his plans (his name, promise, judgments, testimonies) a central theme for prayer:

> In my heart I treasure your promise, that I may not sin against you. . . . At all times my soul is stirred with longing for your judgments. . . . Direct my heart toward your testimonies and away from gain. Avert my eyes from what is worthless; by your way give me life. When I recite your judgments of old . . . I am comforted, LORD. Even at night I remember your name in observance of your law, LORD. (Ps. 119:11, 20, 36-37, 52, 55)

Most of the traditional pious practices associated with Christianity have this as their goal. Displaying images of Jesus, Mary, and the saints on our walls, desks, rearview mirrors, and screen savers; wearing a cross or a crucifix around our necks; wearing blessed medals; dropping by a church and making the Sign of the Cross with holy water; asking for a priest's blessing; praying before meals—practices like these set reminders for us to think about God. They can nourish the core desire of our hearts.

EATING RIGHT

But the meat and potatoes of forming the Christian heart remain prayer and the sacraments (we will dive into these realities more fully in later chapters). Without a real, growing life of prayer—in all of its forms, but most essentially in a daily, personal God-time—our core desire for God will always remain undernourished, and our spiritual growth will be stunted. Infrequent or superficial contact with the sacraments, especially the Eucharist and confession, robs our souls of essential spiritual nutrients. Jesus made this clear so many times:

On Prayer: "Then Jesus told them a parable about the necessity for them to pray always without becoming weary . . . " (Luke 18:1); "If you remain in me and my words remain in you, ask for whatever you want and it will be done for you." (John 15:7)

On the Eucharist: "Jesus said to them, 'Amen, amen, I say to you, unless you eat the flesh of the Son of Man and drink his blood, you do not have life within you. Whoever eats my flesh and drinks my blood has eternal life, and I will raise him on the last day. For my flesh is true food, and my blood is true drink. Whoever eats my flesh and drinks my blood remains in me and I in him. Just as the living Father sent me and I have life because of the Father, so also the one who feeds on me will have life because of me.'" (John 6:53-57)

On confession (Jesus to his apostles): "Whose sins you forgive are forgiven them, and whose sins you retain are retained." (John 20:23)

God himself gives us a new heart when we become Christians, but he leaves it up to us to make that heart grow.

Questions for Personal Reflection or Group Discussion

1. What idea in this chapter struck you most and why?
2. Are you a better pray-er than you were a year ago, five years ago, ten years ago? Why or why not?
3. In a normal day, how often do you think about God and his plan for your life and for the world?

4. An old Native American story tells of a young brave talking with an elderly warrior. The old warrior explains that there are two wolves fighting a fierce battle against each other inside every human heart. One wolf fights to destroy all that is good through indulging in greed, lust, and cowardice. The other one fights to protect all that is good through fighting greed, lust, and cowardice. The young brave asks his elder which wolf will win the fight, and the wise warrior replies: "Whichever one you feed." What will you do today to feed the core desire of your life, the desire to make your relationship with God the organizing principle of everything you do?

- I will replace superficial images on my walls, desk, screen saver, and mobile devices with images that really mean something.

- I will take some time in the evening to reflect, prayerfully, on my behavior during the day, identifying how I can better reflect God's goodness tomorrow.

- I will avoid reading or watching things that cause unhealthy turbulence or distraction in my soul.

- (Write your own resolution) I will _____

_____

_____

_____

Concluding Prayer

*O God, let me know you and love you so that I may find
my joy in you; and if I cannot do so fully in this life, let me
at least make some progress every day, until at last that
knowledge, love and joy come to me in all their plenitude.
While I am here on earth let me learn to know you better, so
that in heaven I may know you fully; let my love for you
grow deeper here, so that there I may love you fully.
On earth then I shall have great joy in hope, and in
heaven complete joy in the fulfillment of my hope.*

—FROM THE PROSLOGION OF ST. ANSELM OF CANTERBURY

Freeing My Heart

*Undoubtedly, the journey is arduous; it demands availability,
courage, self-denial, in order to make one's life, as Christ did
his, a "gift" of love to the Father and to others. Only in this way
are we made capable, by the power of the Spirit, of proclaiming
the "Gospel of the Cross" and carrying out that "new evangelization"
that has in Christ crucified and risen its center and hinge.*
—St. John Paul II, Homily, February 24, 1991

I N HIS PARABLE OF THE sower and the seed, Jesus pointed out that having good soil is not sufficient to assure fruitful growth. Some seed fell on excellent soil, but it shared that soil with thorn bushes. The thorn bushes grew with the good seed and choked it. Jesus draws the lesson from his analogy: "As for the seed that fell among thorns, they are the ones who have heard, but as they go along, they are choked by the anxieties and riches and pleasures of life, and they fail to produce mature fruit" (Luke 8:14).

The anxieties and riches and pleasures of life aren't evil in themselves. The problem comes when we allow them to divide our hearts, when we begin seeking them, instead of seeking God, or paying more attention to them than to God. Jesus is trying to warn us about what will happen to our spiritual life when we allow contradictory desires to coexist in our heart, when we feed multiple desires, instead of feeding the one core desire and allowing that desire to bring all subordinate desires into harmony. He wants us to stay focused: "But seek first the kingdom (of God) and his righteousness, and all these things will be given you besides" (Matt. 6:33).

We need to nourish the Christ-centered desire at the core of our Christian heart, but we also need to protect that desire from thorns and parasites and other distractions that can starve it out.

THE ONE THING NEEDED

One of the Lord's most memorable teaching moments arose in this context. He and his apostles had been invited to dine at the home of Martha of Bethany. Martha was busy keeping everyone happy. She was perturbed that her sister, Mary, wasn't helping her. You probably remember what happened:

> As they continued their journey he entered a village where a woman whose name was Martha welcomed him. She had a sister named Mary [who sat] beside the Lord at his feet listening to him speak. Martha, burdened with much serving, came to him and said, "Lord, do you not care that my sister has left me by myself to do the serving? Tell her to help me." The Lord said to her in reply, "Martha, Martha, you are anxious and worried about many things. There is need of only one thing. Mary has chosen the better part and it will not be taken from her." (Luke 10:38-42)

Notice that Jesus didn't reprimand Martha for being busy, or for doing a lot of things, but for being "anxious and worried about many things." Martha was upset. Where did that come from? Clearly, she was not desiring only and principally the "one thing" needed—communion with God. In the hustle and bustle of entertaining, she had allowed her heart to be divided. She had become overly preoccupied with making a good impression by having everything come out just right. A tinge of vanity had temporarily upended the true priorities of her heart, leading her to overemphasize secondary things. She resented Mary for not sharing her desire to make the evening go perfectly according to plan. She lashed out at her sister in a typical family squabble.

Whenever we allow self-centered desires to compete with, instead of purified and ordered by, the one desire that we really need, we fall into the same trap.

Pulling Big Weeds

The lesson is clear. We not only need to nourish our desire for God, we also need to keep the soil of our heart free from suffocating, contradictory desires. This takes two forms of spiritual discipline. First, we need to uproot the thorns that are already growing in our souls. These include obvious sinful habits, like losing our temper, procrastinating, gossiping, using pornography, lying, cheating, abusing alcohol or drugs, and all the other destructive behaviors that flow from the seven capital sins of gluttony, lust, anger, sloth, arrogance, envy, and greed.

These are behaviors that the fallen world tolerates, and even encourages. Popular culture glorifies them in music, film, and advertising. But they are poison for the heart. They destroy and enslave us and those we love. They are sins because they are evil, because they go directly against everything that will make us flourish as human beings created in God's image.

Battles between Flesh and Spirit

St. Paul refers to these sins as the desires of our "flesh." Flesh in this context doesn't mean our bodies, our materiality, which is fundamentally good because it is created by God. Rather, it means our fallen nature, our wounded human nature that pulls us away from the path of life in God's Spirit.

> I say, then: live by the Spirit and you will certainly not gratify the desire of the flesh. For the flesh has desires against the Spirit, and the Spirit against the flesh. . . . Now the works of the flesh are obvious: immorality, impurity, licentiousness, idolatry, sorcery, hatreds, rivalry, jealousy, outbursts of fury, acts of selfishness, dissensions, factions, occasions of envy, drinking bouts, orgies, and the like. I warn you, as I warned you before, that those who do such things will not inherit the kingdom of God. (Gal. 5:16-21)

Because tendencies toward these behaviors are rooted deep within us (often connected to emotional wounds that we are barely aware of) and continuously stimulated by influences all around us, uprooting the thorns of sinful habits can be a long and difficult process. Traditionally, this phase of spiritual growth is called the purgative, or purification, stage.

PULLING LITTLE WEEDS

As the soil of our hearts is cleared of the big thorn bushes, we can focus more on watering and fertilizing the good desire for God, which is the topic of the rest of this book. But even then, we have to keep a lookout for the return of new weeds—this is the second spiritual discipline that keeps our heart's soil clean and rich. It involves sub-disciplines such as making room for silence in our daily lives, including some voluntary austerity in our lifestyle, keeping a healthy balance between work and rest, being more and more intentional as regards the kind of input we allow into our minds and imaginations—choosing, for example, types of entertainment and recreation that both delight and also edify. If we are careless in these little things, the weeds will surely come back, and the thorns will choke the precious core desire of the Christ-centered heart.

Questions for Personal Reflection or Group Discussion

1. What idea in this chapter struck you most and why?

2. What big weeds has God uprooted from your life in the past? Thank him for that grace. Are there any big weeds still choking your relationship with God? Ask him for the light and strength to root them out.

3. What types of situations typically make you "worried and anxious"? Why? Speak with God about any desires or fears that may be dividing your heart.

4. One of the greatest dangers for our spiritual growth is falling into routine. When we lose sight of the real purpose of our lives, of God's dream for us, we can just get stuck in a rut, doing

the same things over again, and maybe even doing them well but without the zest of consciously remembering how they fit into God's bigger picture. What will you do differently today to activate your desire to "seek first the kingdom of God"?

- I will serve someone who usually serves me.

- I will re-read something from my past (a diary or journal entry, a letter, an old essay) that will stir up afresh the best dreams of my heart.

- (Write your own resolution) I will _____

_____

_____

_____

Concluding Prayer

Too late have I loved you, O Beauty so ancient, O Beauty so new.
Too late have I loved you!
You were within me but I was outside myself,
and there I sought you!
In my weakness I ran after
the beauty of the things you have made.
You were with me, and I was not with you.
The things you have made kept me from you—the things
which would have no being unless they existed in you!
You have called, you have cried,
and you have pierced my deafness.
You have radiated forth, you have shined out brightly,
and you have dispelled my blindness.
You have sent forth your fragrance, and I have breathed it in,
and I long for you.
I have tasted you, and I hunger and thirst for you.
You have touched me, and I ardently desire your peace.

—St. Augustine of Hippo[10]

PART III

LOVING GOD WITH ALL MY SOUL

My child, when you come to serve the Lord, prepare yourself for trials. Be sincere of heart and steadfast, and do not be impetuous in time of adversity. Cling to him, do not leave him, that you may prosper in your last days. Accept whatever happens to you; in periods of humiliation be patient. For in fire gold is tested, and the chosen, in the crucible of humiliation. Trust in God, and he will help you; make your ways straight and hope in him.

SIRACH 2:1–6

Weak but Wonderful

But here is the great surprise: God has given the human person, the weak creature, a wonderful dignity: he has made him a little less than the angels or, as the original Hebrew can be translated, a little less than a god.
— St. John Paul II, Psalms and Canticles

T HORNS CAN CHOKE THE GROWTH of the good seed of God's grace, but shallow, rocky soil can wither it altogether. Jesus warned us of this, too. He used the analogy of bad soil that impedes a seed from putting down deep roots. Under the scorching sun, the plant simply withers and dies, because its shallow roots fail to find the moisture it needs for life under harsh conditions. The image describes the sentimental Christian, whose faith only goes as deep as his or her feelings:

"The seed sown on rocky ground is the one who hears the word and receives it at once with joy. But he has no root and lasts only for a time. When some tribulation or persecution comes because of the word, he immediately falls away." (Matt. 13:20-21)

Feelings, emotions, sentiments, and moods, along with psychic and biological drives, passions, and needs, make up an essential dimension of human experience. When Jesus commands his followers to love him with all their *soul,* he is referring to this wonderful, confusing, rewarding, and troubling dimension. If we fail to integrate this human richness into our loving relationship with God, sooner or later it will trip us up, and our desire for God and a deeper communion with him will wither away.

In the Old Testament, for example, King David failed to integrate healthily a natural and passionate attraction he felt toward a woman who was married to another man. This failure led him into the destructive moral chaos of adultery and murder. In the New Testament, we see how St. Peter's natural and understandable emotional fears, improperly acknowledged and channeled, led him to commit the most shameful deed of his life when he denied that he even knew Jesus (see Matt. 26:69–75).

The two-thousand-year tradition of Christian thought and experience has produced a deep, nuanced, and accurate understanding of these various facets of the human person. Becoming more aware of them frees us to be more intentional and effective in our journey toward spiritual maturity.

X-RAY OF A SOUL

Soul can be a confusing word. People often ask whether their dog has a soul. The answer often comes back as a simple no, which is disappointing, because people really want their loyal, beloved pets to be with them in heaven. But how can a dog get to heaven if it doesn't have a soul? We will set aside for now the theological question of whether pets join us in heaven; suffice it to say that if you need the accompaniment of a beloved pet in order to be absolutely, completely, infinitely happy (that's what life is like in heaven), you will not lack that pet.

Philosophically, though, we can give a better answer to the question of whether dogs have souls. Yes, they do have souls, but their souls are different than the human soul. Specifically, the soul is the principle of life in a living being. Anything alive, then, has a soul. But the different forms of life will have souls with different characteristics. Plants have nutritive souls that allow them to grow and reproduce, but without the power of locomotion. Animals have what are called sensitive souls. These add new powers to the nutritive souls, especially the powers of locomotion and sensory perception. These powers allow the more complex animal species (dolphins, for example, are more complex than spiders) to experience certain degrees of emotion, sense memory, and sense knowledge.

Human beings have rational souls, with the even greater additional powers of intellect and will, abstract thinking and free choice. These are spiritual powers shared in a certain way with the angels and with God himself. This is one reason why the Bible speaks of God having created the human person in the image of God: "in our image, after our likeness" (Gen. 1:26). These spiritual powers that go with personhood, integrally united to the other nutritive and sensitive powers still present in the human soul, are the root of human dignity. They show us why it is morally okay to kill a bothersome mosquito, but not a bothersome toddler.

PROBLEMS WITH THE SOUL

Those basic philosophical distinctions have been challenged in modern and post-modern times. Biologists have discovered so many varieties of life that were completely unknown to previous eras, for example, that the distinctions between vegetative and locomotive, or between sentient and nutritive, are much more fluid. Viruses, bacteria, extremophile—where do they all fit into the continuum between simple plant and complex animal? It's not always easy to tell.

Post-modern secularists also question the distinction between spiritual and non-spiritual souls. Many of them argue that what used to be considered spiritual is really just epiphenomenal, just an excretion of predetermined material and biological processes. According to this point of view, the human soul is no more spiritual, and therefore possesses no more dignity, than any other animal soul. The difference between a human being and a dolphin, therefore, is only a difference of degree, not a difference of kind.

These challenges to the Christian vision of the human person can be and have been met and overcome by Christian philosophers, scientists, and apologists. And their arguments simply reinforce the basic tenets of our faith, the basic truths revealed by God, that the human soul is unique among the many creatures of the visible universe, and uniquely valued and addressed by God.

THE BELOVED SOUL

Before we love at all, we are loved, infinitely and intimately, utterly and unconditionally, passionately and personally, by God. This must be the starting place for our reflection on what it means to love God with all our soul. Every component of our humanity is included in this love God has for us. The greatest proof of this astounding truth came with the Incarnation, when God himself took on human nature, becoming fully and truly man in Jesus Christ. Never again can we doubt that every aspect of the human condition, even though tangled and distorted by sin, is fundamentally good, and that God wants to redeem it all.

We have to consciously give ourselves permission, so to speak, to accept this truth. Otherwise, the difficult and often painful process of allowing God's grace to bring order and healing to the dizzying complexity of our souls may spark discouragement or resentment.

The *Catechism* announces our fundamental dignity and belovedness loud and clear:

> Of all visible creatures only man is "able to know and love his creator." He is "the only creature on earth that God has willed for its own sake," and he alone is called to share, by knowledge and love, in God's own life. It was for this end that he was created, and this is the fundamental reason for his dignity. (CCC, 356)

In his inaugural homily, Pope Benedict XVI expressed the same truth with even more gusto:

> We are not some casual and meaningless product of evolution. Each of us is the result of a thought of God. Each of us is willed, each of us is loved, each of us is necessary.[11]

Questions for Personal Reflection or Group Discussion

1. What idea in this chapter struck you most and why?

2. When you consider the truth that God loves you personally and infinitely, how deeply does it resonate? Is there something in you that sometimes resists accepting that truth?

3. How much do your emotional ups and downs affect the firmness of your faith? Do you only pray when you feel like it? Do you only forgive and show kindness when you are in a good mood? How often do bad moods and emotional low tides lead you to say and do things you later regret?

4. In spite of our weakness and brokenness, God loves us without limit. Jesus once told St. Faustina that even if she had on her soul all the sins of the world, in comparison with his mercy they would be nothing more than a drop of water thrown into a blazing furnace. What will you do today to express your faith in your true, God-given dignity and that of every human person?

   • I will take a break to stop and smell the roses (to enjoy one of the simple, healthy pleasures of life), and I will thank God for that blessing.

   • I will pray sincerely for a person that I have given up on.

   • I will engage in sincere conversation with someone that I normally wouldn't talk to.

   • (Write your own resolution) I will _____

   _____

   _____

   _____

Concluding Prayer

O LORD, our Lord,
how awesome is your name through all the earth!
I will sing of your majesty above the heavens
with the mouths of babes and infants.
You have established a bulwark against your foes,
to silence enemy and avenger.
When I see your heavens, the work of your fingers,
the moon and stars that you set in place—
What is man that you are mindful of him,
and a son of man that you care for him?
Yet you have made him little less than a god,
crowned him with glory and honor.
You have given him rule over the works of your hands,
put all things at his feet:
All sheep and oxen,
even the beasts of the field,
The birds of the air, the fish of the sea,
and whatever swims the paths of the seas.
O LORD, our Lord,
how awesome is your name through all the earth!

—PSALM 8

Understanding Emotions

You live with great hopes, with so many fine plans for the future.
But do not forget that the true fullness of life is to be found only in
Christ, who died and rose again for us. Christ alone is able to fill
in the deep space of the human heart. He alone gives the strength
and joy of living, in spite of any limit or external impediment.
— St. John Paul II, *Message for World Youth Day, 1989*

JESUS SPECIFIES TWO INNATE POWERS of the human soul when he issues the great commandment: He commands us to love God with
all our mind and all our strength. These correspond to the specifically
spiritual powers of the soul—the intellect and will, our capacity to
know and to choose. When he commands us to love God with all our
soul, then, it is safe to assume that he is referring to the other powers
of the soul. He is commanding us to align those with the core desire,
with the heart that seeks God above all things, or that at least wants
to seek God above all, because it knows and believes that "God alone
suffices," as St. Theresa of Avila once put it. His command to love
God with all our soul is an invitation to integrate our emotions and
passions, or psychic drives, into our friendship with him so that the
friendship can reach new heights. How do we do that? What does
that look like?

THE GIFT OF EMOTIONS

Emotions come from God. God created human nature, and emotions are part of human nature. When we come into contact with
external realities, we often perceive that those realities can help or

harm us. That perception produces a reaction in our soul, a feeling that moves us toward action. We were created to function that way. We have this internal dynamism that attracts us toward what seems good for us and repels us from what seems bad for us. This is our capacity for feelings or emotions (sometimes called passions). Their complexity and intensity contribute to making human experience as rich and wonderful as it is.

Categories of Emotion

Through the ages, philosophers have identified basic emotions. In modern times, psychologists have offered numerous other classifications. So far, no one has come up with a perfect synthesis of the wisdom of the philosophers and the science of the psychologists. In our effort to understand emotions, we will utilize insights from both sources.

An unavoidable obstacle in this effort has to do with language. The words that describe emotions—which are simple reactions to stimuli, simple feelings that have no moral weight in themselves—are often the same words that can also describe moral actions, vices, or virtues. Anger, for example, can refer to the simple emotional reaction of feeling anger, something which is natural and good in itself. But the word *anger* can also refer to a capital sin, the sin of anger, of choosing to act unjustly, violently, and self-centeredly in response to the feeling of anger. This language problem has no easy solution, so keep in mind that this discussion of feelings will use words such as *anger* (and *love*, and *hate*, and *desire*) strictly as emotional descriptors, not as moral terms linked to virtue and vice.

The Nine Most Basic Emotions

The nine basic emotions flow from the two contrary, foundational urges of our embodied human nature, which Christian philosophy labels love and hate. At their most fundamental level, these urges are connected to our senses and our bodies, and they are morally neutral; they are simple, emotional reactions to exterior stimuli; they are spontaneous feelings of love and hate without any moral decision to love or hate. Certain things in the world are good for us, and the urge of love, or attraction, kicks into gear when we come into contact with those things. Certain other things in the world are bad for us, and the urge of hate, or repulsion, kicks into gear when we come into contact with those things.

The experience of attraction stirs up four of the nine basic emotions. When we perceive something that would be good for us, we feel a desire for it. Desire—this is the first basic emotion. When that good, desirable thing seems as if it will be hard to acquire, but we think that if we make an effort, we will indeed acquire it, we feel the basic emotion of hope (the feeling, not the virtue). If the good, desirable thing seems impossible to acquire, we experience a feeling of despair, discouragement, or hopelessness (again, just the feeling, not the sin). When we actually acquire the good, desirable thing and are enjoying it, we feel pleasure, the fourth emotion connected to the urge of attraction.

The experience of repulsion stirs up the other five basic emotions. If we perceive something that will harm us, some evil thing, we feel the basic emotion of aversion, or revulsion. If that hateful thing actually comes upon us or happens to us, we feel sorrow or pain. If it comes upon us and we judge that by resisting we can actually get rid of it, we feel anger (the emotion, not the sin). If the hateful thing is out there somewhere and seems hard for us to avoid, we experience fear. If the hateful thing out there seems hard to avoid, but we judge that we can indeed avoid or eliminate it, we experience feelings of courage or audacity.

EMOTION IN ACTION

A few simple examples will help clarify. If I am hungry and I see a ripe apple in the fruit basket (and if I like apples), I will feel desire—the good, desirable apple is perceived as something that will help me. If the last time I took that kind of apple out of that particular basket, it had a big, fat worm in it, I may feel revulsion when I see that apple, which by association I perceive as something that may harm me. If I am penniless and hungry and see a basketful of apples at the store, I may feel *hope* if there is some way I can get enough money to buy one, and I may feel despair if I can't think of any way to get any money. If I get the money and I am on the way to the store, and someone much bigger than me knocks me down and steals the money, I will feel sorrow. If I get some more money and make my way back to the store, and while I am walking along I see the same thief staring at me from across the street, I may feel fear. If I make it to the store and offer my money to the clerk, and am told I need more than that to buy the apple, I may feel anger and courageously start to argue with the clerk, pointing out that, according to the price tag, I have the right amount.

This is a simple profile of human emotions, a good starting place for reflection on how God wants us to integrate emotions fully into our relationship with him.

Questions for Personal Reflection and Group Discussion

1. What idea in this chapter struck you most and why?

2. On a day-to-day basis, what role do your emotions tend to play in your activities and relationships? What is your habitual attitude toward feelings and emotions in general?

3. Try to remember specific instances in which you have felt each of the nine basic emotions. What triggered those feelings? How did you respond to them?

4. When your heart is in the right place, when you truly want, as your deepest desire, to grow in communion with God, you are better able to bring harmony into the often chaotic flurry of your emotions. For example, someone whose heart is set on winning a highly competitive scholarship may enter a severe crisis of circumstantial depression if he loses the competition. It may take months for this individual to recover an emotional balance and a healthy optimism about life. Someone else might compete for the same scholarship but see it merely as one excellent way to develop his or her talents so as to put them at the service of God and neighbor (the central desire of his or her heart) and thus will

recover much more quickly from the disappointment of not winning the competition. What will you do today to allow your desire for God to shape and order your emotional world?

- I will take some time this evening to talk with God in prayer about the high point and low point of the day, sharing my feelings with him and allowing his loving wisdom to temper them.
- I will read Matthew 26 and list all the emotions that Jesus might have felt during those dramatic events. I will observe how Jesus reacts to those emotions and try to learn from that.
- The next time I experience intense pleasure or joy, I will share it immediately with God by saying a prayer of thanksgiving.
- (Write your own resolution) I will _____

_____

_____

_____

Concluding Prayer

Lord, I desire that in all things your will be done, because it is your will, and I desire that all things be done in the manner that you will them. Grant that I may always esteem whatsoever is pleasing to you, despise what you abhor, avoid what you forbid, and do what you command. I beg you to enlighten my understanding, to inflame my will, to purify my body, and to sanctify my soul. My God, give me strength to atone for my sins, to overcome my temptations, to subdue my passions, and to acquire the virtues proper to my state of life. Fill my heart with tender affection for your goodness, hatred of my faults, love for my neighbor, and contempt of the world. May your grace help me to be obedient to my superiors, kind and courteous to my inferiors, faithful to my friends, and charitable to my enemies. Assist me to overcome sensuality by self-sacrifice, avarice by almsdeeds, anger by meekness, and carelessness by devotion. My God, make me prudent in my undertakings, courageous in danger, patient in trials, and humble in success.

—FROM POPE CLEMENT XI'S UNIVERSAL PRAYER

Emotions in a Fallen World

In the Christian plan human beings are called to union with God as
their last end, in whom they find their proper fulfillment, although they
are impeded in the achievement of their vocation by the resistance which
arises from their own concupiscence [selfish, unruly desires and tendencies].
—St. John Paul II, Address to Roman Rota, February 5, 1987

THE NINE BASIC EMOTIONS ARE just the raw material for this complex, powerful, and intriguing dimension of the human soul—the dimension of our feelings. The varied reality of day-to-day experience rarely stirs up any single one of them with perfect purity and clarity. Rather, they get mixed together in potent, and sometimes disturbing, combinations that include innumerable variations of intensity and hue. Life is simply too rich and multifaceted to fit neatly into predictable and easily manageable emotional boxes. Jesus alluded to this when he advised us to try to rise to the challenge of each day without fretting over vain attempts to control the bigger picture: "Do not worry about tomorrow; tomorrow will take care of itself. Sufficient for a day is its own evil" (Matt. 6:34).

THE VARIABILITY OF EMOTIONS

The intensity of feelings will depend on just how significantly we judge that the stimulating object will promote or inhibit what is good for us. The greater the good or the more threatening the evil, the more intense the emotion: someone on the verge of winning a million dollars, for example, will usually feel more intense anticipation than someone on the verge of winning five dollars. Likewise, the specific quality or character of the object will give the basic emotion different flavors or levels of appeal or repugnance. The attraction of a beloved person, for example, will feel wildly different than the attraction of a good night's sleep. Objects can even both attract and repel us at the same time, under different aspects. Such is the complexity of the human experience.

Variations in external objects are not the only factors affecting our emotional world. Sometimes emotions seem to surge up from within, not responding to external stimuli at all, but preconditioning how we respond to those stimuli. These passionate emotional impulses are sometimes simply referred to as the "passions of the soul." Moods, for example, can color our emotional reactions, tainting with dejection what should objectively be hope-filled, or intensifying anger beyond what the situation truly deserves.

Moods and other internal influences can flow from simple biological processes—from hormonal fluctuation or indigestion or exhaustion, for example. But they can also have their roots in subconscious emotional patterns linked to past experiences. In a fallen world, no one escapes trauma of some kind or another. No one grows up with perfect parents and a perfectly balanced personality. The internal and external harmony that God built into creation was shattered by original sin. The journey to human maturity necessarily involves facing and coping with our own confusing internal divisions (what theologians call concupiscence) and with pain caused by the sins of those around us. Even before we are fully aware of ourselves and the world, our coping mechanisms are already conditioning the way we experience and handle emotions, and this conditioning is not always healthy for the long run.

The Purpose of Emotions

All this wonderful complexity helps explain why navigating our feelings is often so difficult. Yet it doesn't change the basic purpose of feelings, a purpose invented by God and built into our human nature. Knowing this purpose frees us to engage our feelings in our Christian adventure, not simply to suppress them.

Emotions construct a bridge between the outside, material world and our inner, spiritual world. As human beings, we are both spiritual and material. Our spiritual vocation to know and love what is true and good is given to us and unfolds in this material world. Our access to a greater knowledge and love of God is through our experience of this world. Our senses put us in contact with the realities around us, our intelligence and our will are meant to interpret those realities, and our emotions are meant to give us the energy we need to act in this world, to pursue what is good and avoid what is evil. Here's how the *Catechism* explains it:

> Feelings or passions are emotions or movements of the sensitive appetite that incline us to act or not to act in regard to something felt or imagined to be good or evil . . . . The passions are natural components of the human psyche; they form the passageway and ensure the connection between the life of the senses and the life of the mind. (CCC, 1763–1764)

Angels, as purely spiritual beings, have direct access to spiritual realities. They are emotionless. They don't laugh, and they don't cry. Their soul is intelligent, but solely spiritual—not nutritive (like the souls of plants) and not sensitive (like the souls of animals). They are moved to action by the pure and immediate perception of the objects they may choose. But we are not angels. Our access to the spiritual realities that alone will fulfill our yearning for happiness (infinite truth and infinite goodness) is given through the mediation of this material world. Our emotional reactions are meant to give us the fuel we need to pursue what is good and true and to resist what is evil and false.

The Unruliness of Emotions

Yet, unfortunately, in our fallen human nature this feeling function has been damaged. Our natural emotional reactions to the world around us are not in perfect harmony with God's plan for our full spiritual maturity. This is why our emotional experience so often seems to contribute to the stresses that plague the human predicament.

Our feelings often seem to have a mind of their own, independent of what we know to be true by reason or by faith. At times, for example, I feel drawn to things that my conscience deems wrong and damaging but my emotions deem desirable (like sleeping in when I have important work to do, or spending money that I don't have just to keep up appearances). At other times, I feel repulsed by things that my reason or my faith tells me are good and important but my emotions label as undesirable (like taking time out of my busy schedule to simply sit with the Lord and pray, or making a difficult but necessary phone call).

At still other times, the intensity of my emotions seems to have no basis in reality, and my moods swing wildly up and down, making life turbulent and chaotic (as when I take out my internal frustrations on someone I love, someone who has nothing to do with the real cause of those frustrations).

Yet, in spite of being so complex by nature and so off-kilter because of original sin, emotions remain an essential element of the human experience, and as such, they are a crucial factor in growing to spiritual maturity. This is why Jesus singled them out, commanding us "to love the Lord your God with . . . all your soul" (Luke 10:27, RSV).

Questions for Personal Reflection or Group Discussion

1. What idea in this chapter struck you most and why?

2. What situations tend to trigger in you disproportionate emotional reactions?

3. In the past week, when have you experienced a clash between what you *felt* like doing and what you knew in your conscience that you *should* do? How did you react and why?

4. The first step in learning to better integrate our emotions into our love for God is to become more aware of the emotions that we feel. Some elements in our post-modern society don't want this to happen, because if we become more conscious of our

emotional worlds, we will be less vulnerable to emotional manipulation by insidious types of advertising. What will you do today to become more aware of how your emotions affect your decisions and behavior?

- After a conversation, I will take a few moments of silence to reflect on what I was feeling during the conversation, and the real reasons behind what I said and how I reacted.

- At the end of the day, I will think about how I used my free time and money during the day—what I occupied myself with and what I bought. Then I will reflect on *why* I made the decisions I did regarding free time and money, and how those decisions made me feel.

- (Write your own resolution) I will _____
_____
_____
_____

Concluding Prayer

May he support us all the day long,
till the shades lengthen and the evening comes,
and the busy world is hushed,
and the fever of life is over, and our work is done.
Then in his mercy may he give us a safe lodging,
and a holy rest and peace at the last.

—St. John Henry Cardinal Newman[12]

Forming My Emotions

*To follow in every instance a "real" emotional impulse by
invoking a love "liberated" from all conditionings, means nothing
more than to make the individual a slave to those human
instincts which St. Thomas calls "passions of the soul."*
—St. John Paul II, *Letter to Families, 14*

T HE PAINFUL AND COMPLEX DISCONNECT between where our emotions often do pull us and where they ought to pull us is an
undeniable aspect of life in a fallen world. We are made for God
and for authentic good, and that is our deepest yearning, but our
wounded human nature is easily distracted and deceived, and it
often leads us astray. St. Paul diagnosed this condition simply by
reflecting on his own experience of internal division between our
fallen nature and our redeemed nature:

> For I know that good does not dwell in me, that is, in my
> flesh. The willing is ready at hand, but doing the good is not.
> For I do not do the good I want, but I do the evil I do not
> want. . . . For I take delight in the law of God, in my inner
> self, but I see in my members another principle at war with
> the law of my mind. (Rom. 7:18-19, 22-23)

This is the human soul, an arena so often full of strife. This is the
soul with which Jesus commands us to love God.

THE EDUCATION OF EMOTIONS

The bottom line is simply that our capacity for these rich human experiences needs to be educated—and it can be educated! Under the Holy Spirit's guidance, we can bring our emotional potential into deeper and deeper harmony with what is true, good, and beautiful, so that our feeling function better fulfills its real purpose: energizing us in the pursuit of God's kingdom. This formation passes through three basic phases, which correspond to the three traditional stages of the spiritual life: the *purgative* way, the *illuminative* way, and the *unitive* way.

PURIFYING OUR EMOTIONS

In the first stage of spiritual growth, the *purgative* (or purifying) stage, our emotions need discipline. Like spoiled children who throw violent tantrums whenever their slightest whim is denied, undisciplined emotions tyrannically and violently seek to be indulged. But this is unhealthy. If we let our volatile emotional states and reactions dictate our behavior, we will stay spiritual infants forever.

A young wild horse has magnificent strength, great potential. But maximizing that potential requires training the horse to respond to the mind and will of its rider. The horse needs to learn how to carry a saddle, follow the reins, and recognize its rider's signals. In this way, the horse's raw strength can be harnessed for productive, fulfilling work.

Our emotions are kind of like that. They are a magnificent potential source of energy that can help our spiritual faculties flourish and lead us toward maturity and fulfillment. But they must learn docility to those higher faculties. And the first step in that process is holding them back from over-indulgence by disciplining them. We simply can't let them run our lives if we truly want to live life to the full.

INTEGRATING OUR EMOTIONS

Too often Christians stop the formation of emotions there, at the level of discipline and self-denial. But that is an incomplete view of the role of feelings. The purgative way is only the first stage. Discipline creates parameters for full freedom, but it is not the equivalent of full freedom. When that wild horse learns to sit still under tight rein, it is learning discipline. But unless it is also taught to walk and run without tossing its rider, the discipline will not have achieved its full purpose.

In the second stage of the spiritual life, therefore, God invites and helps us to move beyond seeing our emotions as the enemy of spiritual progress. Now that we are not enslaved to their every whim, we can learn to value them and understand them more deeply. We can face our own emotional wounds and coping mechanisms; we can give ourselves permission to feel our feelings deeply without fearing that they will sabotage us by always leading to sin. The horse is learning to run with and for its rider; our emotional world is expanding and making its powerful contribution to our pursuit of holiness, not just standing still with blinders on.

In this *illuminative* phase we learn the difference between life-giving emotional discipline and deadening emotional repression. God also gradually reveals to us the depth of our emotional needs, and he shows us how we can meet those needs in healthy ways, without reverting to the dangerous self-absorption of emotional immaturity. As our emotions thus truly become integrated into our relationship with God and our mission of building up his kingdom, our personality matures in harmony with our growing faith, and we become stable, content, joyful Christians.

PERFECT HARMONY

As our feelings enter more and more into the service of the truths of faith that are meant to govern our lives, as God teaches us to feel our feelings without letting them dictate our decisions, our emotional world gradually comes into almost perfect sync with our authentic good. This is what our feelings look like in the *unitive* way.

Emotionally mature Christians feel not only a *spiritual* attraction to prayer and the sacraments and works of mercy, but also an *emotional* resonance with those and similar God-centered activities. Their feelings have learned to perceive a truly good object in actions that used to be emotionally dry.

Likewise, as our emotions are fully integrated with our faith, we find ourselves spontaneously repulsed by spiritually dangerous objects that used to appear attractive. The prospect of a shady but lucrative financial deal can be an agonizingly seductive temptation for someone still in the purgative stage. But when our emotions have been formed by faith and conformed to Christ's own authentic desires for what is truly good and not just apparently good, an invitation to obvious material sin often elicits an emotional revulsion, regardless of the monetary benefits that it may proffer.

OUR DESTINATION

This was the experience of so many saints and martyrs—mature Christians who have cooperated generously with God's grace and found themselves desiring with their whole being whatever God desired for them, even if it was a cross. And the most comforting thing of all is that those saints and martyrs started out just like us, fallen and wounded and spiritually immature. The grand partnership of God's grace and their generous effort slowly but surely transformed them, just as it will do for us. Here's how St. Paul described it, showing us that discipline (being crucified with Christ) led him to a mature faith (illuminative way) and an indescribable union of mutual love with the Lord. This is where God is leading all of us—to love him with all our soul:

> I have been crucified with Christ; yet I live, no longer I, but Christ lives in me; insofar as I now live in the flesh, I live by faith in the Son of God who has loved me and given himself up for me. (Gal. 2:19-20)

At the beginning of our journey, and sometimes in the middle of it, St. Paul's words may not resonate with us—the discomfort caused by a feeling function in need of formation still predominates. But God is at work there, and every sacrifice and every small step we take at his side toward spiritual maturity will yield wildly disproportionate fruits: "Draw near to God, and he will draw near to you" (James 4:8).

Questions for Personal Reflection or Group Discussion

1. What idea in this chapter struck you most and why?

2. How fully are your emotions integrated into your life of faith? (Keep in mind that different sectors of your emotional experience can have different levels of integration.) How often, for example, does the prospect of obeying your conscience even when it's tough energize you instead of paralyzing you? Or how often do you go to prayer (personal prayer, Sunday Mass) only out of dry duty as opposed to out of duty bolstered by a real, emotionally felt desire?

3. Which of your emotional reactions need to be better disciplined? Which need to be more fully integrated into your relationship with God?

4. So many great pieces of music have been written out of faith in and devotion to God. And music is one of the main stimulants of emotion. This shows us, once again, that even though our emotional world is often hard to manage, it's something that God really wants to redeem. What will you do today to better harness the great potential of your emotions for the good of your life's mission?

   • I will sincerely express my affection to my spouse or another family member, rather than taking them for granted.

   • I will plan ahead this week, so as to be able to take time on Sunday, the Lord's Day, to really enjoy God's gifts and celebrate his goodness.

   • (Write your own resolution) I will _____

   _____

   _____

   _____

Concluding Prayer

O my God! I offer you all my actions of this day for the intentions and for the glory of the Sacred Heart of Jesus. I desire to sanctify every beat of my heart, my every thought, my simplest works, by uniting them to its infinite merits; and I wish to make reparation for my sins by casting them into the furnace of its merciful love. O my God! I ask of you for myself and for those whom I hold dear, the grace to fulfill perfectly your holy will, to accept for love of you the joys and sorrows of this passing life, so that we may one day be united together in heaven for all eternity.

—A MORNING OFFERING WRITTEN BY ST. THÉRÈSE OF LISIEUX

PART IV

LOVING GOD WITH ALL MY MIND

On the last and greatest day of the feast, Jesus stood up and exclaimed, "Let anyone who thirsts come to me and drink. Whoever believes in me, as scripture says: 'Rivers of living water will flow from within him.'" He said this in reference to the Spirit that those who came to believe in him were to receive. There was, of course, no Spirit yet, because Jesus had not yet been glorified. . . . Jesus spoke to them again, saying, "I am the light of the world. Whoever follows me will not walk in darkness, but will have the light of life."

JOHN 7:37–39; 8:12

Following the Light

*My special hope for you is this: that you will always have a great love
for truth—the truth about God, the truth about man and the truth
about the world. I pray that through truth you will serve humanity
and experience real freedom. In the words of Jesus Christ: "You
will know the truth and the truth will set you free" (John 8:32).*
—St. John Paul II, Address, September 11, 1987

E MOTIONS PROVIDE THE ENERGY WE need to take action in life. But
they need to be educated so they can move us toward actions
that truly contribute to what is best for us and for the world around
us. The wild horse needs to be taught to obey its wise rider.

That rider may want to go in the right direction—his or her
heart may be in the right place. But what if the rider simply
doesn't know the way to get there? What if the rider's intelligence
lacks the necessary knowledge and light and capacity to recognize
the proper landmarks and follow the true path? In that case, it will
be impossible to make progress. This is why our Lord singled out
this capacity of the human person when he gave us the great commandment: "You shall love the Lord your God . . . with all your
mind" (Mark 12:30).

A DARKENED MIND

Original sin ruptured the original harmony that God had built into the
human family's relationship with himself, with the created world, and
with each other. It also wounded human nature from within, including

our spiritual faculties (intelligence and will). Before the Fall, our first parents saw and grasped clearly God's plan for themselves and for the world. They saw things as God saw them.

Then, after the Fall, humanity became "subject to ignorance," as the *Catechism* puts it (CCC, 405). The world became a place full of shadows and threats. God became distant and mysterious, and religion degenerated, in most cases, into fear-inspired superstition. The human person became a puzzle to himself; the true meaning of human life, our origin, our purpose, and our path to achieve that purpose, became shrouded in darkness. Mankind became lost in a labyrinth of confusion that our own rebellion against God had constructed. St. Paul reveals the starkness of the situation, commenting on the persistent wickedness of a fallen race:

> For although they knew God they did not accord him glory as God or give him thanks. Instead, they became vain in their reasoning, and their senseless minds were darkened. While claiming to be wise, they became fools and exchanged the glory of the immortal God for the likeness of an image of mortal man or of birds or of four-legged animals or of snakes. Therefore, God handed them over to impurity through the lusts of their hearts for the mutual degradation of their bodies. They exchanged the truth of God for a lie and revered and worshiped the creature rather than the creator, who is blessed forever. Amen. (Rom. 1:21–25)

The Coming of the Light

An essential ingredient in God's plan for redeeming such a benighted human family, therefore, was light—the light of truth. The story of salvation includes a gradual, gentle, and glorious revelation of the truth about God, the world, and ourselves. This revelation began immediately after the fall of our first parents, continued and developed throughout the history of the Old Covenant, and reached its culmination in the incarnation, life, passion, death, and resurrection of Jesus Christ.

The New Covenant in Jesus, also known as the New Testament, explains and brings to fulfillment all that went before in the Old Testament. In Christ, we have been given new access to the truth that our minds were created to discover, explore, and grasp. We have been shown a sure path out of the deadening ignorance that forms part of the inheritance of sin: "I am the light of the world," Jesus proclaimed (and he certainly proclaimed it with a beaming and inviting smile, not with a fierce and ferocious frown); "whoever follows me will not walk in darkness, but will have the light of life" (John 8:12).

THE DEEPEST QUESTIONS

Who are we? Where do we come from? What is our purpose? What will make us truly happy? Why is there evil in the world? How can we live life to the full? What happens after death? How are we supposed to deal with the challenges and sufferings of life?

Mankind has posed these questions throughout its turbulent history. They are the basic questions of the human mind, because they respond to the fundamental human need and desire to know the truth—not just a few individual truths, like the laws of physics and the contents of our neighbor's cupboards, but the truth, the way things are. Until we know that, or at least some key elements of it, we cannot be completely free to flourish as God means us to; our minds remain unfulfilled, groping in the dark.

Since human nature is always the same, these questions are always the same. Every epoch, every culture, every religion has to face them. We are compelled by our own nature to answer these questions somehow, for the good of our minds, just as we are compelled by our own nature to find food and shelter for the good of our bodies.

THE FULLEST ANSWER

This is the real reason why the different religions seem so similar when they are looked at from certain perspectives: They all seek to give answers to the same basic questions that come with our fallen human nature. And some of the answers that the different religions and philosophies offer contain shards of the truth, because our minds are made to find truth, and we can indeed find some truth through sincere searching. St. Paul also made this point in his discussion about the wickedness of idolatry:

> Ever since the creation of the world, his invisible attributes of eternal power and divinity have been able to be understood and perceived in what he has made. As a result, they have no excuse. (Rom. 1:20)

And yet, if our own efforts were sufficient, Jesus would never have had to come to give us his revelation. Only in that revelation do we have access to the fullness of truth that we crave and are created for, the truth that will free us from darkness and allow us to live life abundantly, now and for all eternity:

> Jesus then said to those Jews who believed in him, "If you remain in my word, you will truly be my disciples, and you will know the truth, and the truth will set you free." (John 8:31-32)

As the *Catechism* instructs us, human reason unaided by the light of revelation will always remain, at some level, frustrated (see CCC, 37-38). Learning to love God with all our mind—coming to know, understand, and accept deeply all that he has revealed to us about himself, ourselves, and the world—is the path out of that frustration. We cannot truly seek God's kingdom without following it.

Questions for Personal Reflection or Group Discussion

1. What idea in this chapter struck you most and why?

2. Recall the time in your life when you first began to ask deeper questions. Are you still hungry for the truth that will set you free? Why or why not?

3. How well do you know the truths that God has revealed to you through Christ? Have you ever tried to explain the gospel to someone who hasn't heard it yet? If not, would you be able to do so?

4. St. Dominic, the medieval founder of the Dominican Order of

Preachers, required a radical poverty from his first members. They weren't allowed to own anything at all, either individually or corporately. They were to travel by foot, spreading the gospel. The only exception to their extreme austerity was books. He wanted all his men to be able to take their books with them wherever they went so they could constantly renew and deepen their knowledge of God's saving Word. What will you do today to deepen your knowledge of God's revelation?

- I will make a list of questions I have about the faith and then make an appointment to talk to a priest or expert about them.
- I will read the testimony of a non-Catholic who converted to Catholicism. (A resource for such testimonies is The Coming Home Network, www.chnetwork.org/converts.)
- (Write your own resolution) I will _____

_____

_____

_____

Concluding Prayer

Creator of all things, true source of light and wisdom, lofty origin of all being, graciously let a ray of your brilliance penetrate into the darkness of my understanding and take from me the double darkness in which I have been born, an obscurity of both sin and ignorance. Give me a sharp sense of understanding, a retentive memory, and the ability to grasp things correctly and fundamentally. Grant me the talent of being exact in my explanations, and the ability to express myself with thoroughness and charm. Point out the beginning, direct the progress, and help in completion; through Christ our Lord. Amen.

—St. Thomas Aquinas[13]

Where to Seek the Truth

The Church wishes to serve this single end: that each person may be able to
find Christ, in order that Christ may walk with each person the path of life,
with the power of the truth about man and the world that is contained in
the mystery of the Incarnation and the Redemption, and with the power of
the love that is radiated by that truth.
—St. John Paul II, Redemptor Hominis, 13

HEALTHY CHRISTIANS EXPERIENCE AN AVID yearning to learn more about God and how to live more and more in communion with him, just as healthy babies experience a driving hunger for the food that will enable them to grow. In different seasons of life, however, and for different reasons, the yearning itself can diminish, or we can silence it by focusing on less taxing or seemingly more practical aspects of following Christ. We need to keep an eye out for that. Loving God with all our minds means constantly seeking to get to know him better. When our knowledge of him becomes stale, our love too will become stale.

We live in a fallen world, and growing in spiritual maturity requires intentionally swimming against that fallen world's current. As soon as we stop, worldliness carries us backwards. This is why St. Paul encouraged the Christians in Rome, who had already received the gift of faith and the Holy Spirit, to continue seeking the renewal of their minds:

> Do not conform yourselves to this age but be transformed by
> the renewal of your mind, that you may discern what is the
> will of God, what is good and pleasing and perfect. (Rom. 12:2)

FINDING FOOD

In past ages, getting access to the message of Christ often required heroic efforts. Copies of the Bible were few, precious, and highly protected. And the vast majority of the population lacked enough education to be able to read the sacred Scriptures even if they had been more widely available. The faith was passed on largely through preaching and teaching, through the liturgical celebrations and the liturgical calendar, through the witness of consecrated men and women, and through local traditions. Even in difficult circumstances, however, God is still God, and the Holy Spirit has always found ways to instruct those who choose to make seeking a deeper knowledge of Christ and his kingdom a high priority—every era has its saints.

In post-modern times, the situation is different. Instead of a shortage of information, we have a glut of it. We are caught in a lava flow of information. We could spend all our waking hours reading, listening to, and watching the billions and billions of bytes that form the fluid and multimedia Internet library at our fingertips. Our problem isn't *finding* sources that can deepen our knowledge of God and his revelation; our problem is *choosing* which ones to use, and following through with the decision to use them.

WHOM TO LISTEN TO

The most important criterion to follow as we make those choices is Christ's own: "Whoever listens to you listens to me. Whoever rejects you rejects me" (Luke 10:16). Jesus has given to the world a teacher authorized to speak in his name, and he has promised to protect that teacher from error in all things regarding faith (what God has revealed about himself, his creation, and his plan of salvation) and morals (what God has revealed about how we must live in order to reach spiritual maturity). This teacher is his Church, the preserver and explainer of the gospel message as it comes to us, especially through sacred Scripture (the Bible) and sacred tradition (everything else the apostles received through the Holy Spirit and passed on to the Church).

The Church's authentic teaching office is called her Magisterium, and its dependability is guaranteed through the Holy Spirit's guidance of Christ's vicar on earth, the pope, and the bishops who teach in communion with him. As members of the Church, we all share in what theologians call the *sensus fidei*, or "supernatural sense of faith," by which revelation is maintained and understood down through the ages, but the Magisterium has a special role to play in that process.

> In order to preserve the Church in the purity of the faith handed on by the apostles, Christ who is the Truth willed to confer on her a share in his own infallibility. By a "supernatural sense of faith" the People of God, under the guidance of the Church's living Magisterium, "unfailingly adheres to this faith." (CCC, 889)

As we actively seek to expand and deepen our knowledge of God and his plan of salvation, the Magisterium provides clear reference points, firm anchors, and healthy parameters around which we can freely and confidently grow in our knowledge of the truth. These come primarily in the form of instructions from popes and bishops (such as encyclicals and the *Catechism*) and are explained by dependable Catholic sources (homilies, books, articles) that apply them to the different circumstances of life. Without those reference points, anchors, and parameters, we would return to the hesitant, fearful exploration that characterizes so many Christ-less paradigms. Without them, we could easily fall into seductive but destructive errors—for example, the heresies that have caused so many wounds throughout the centuries, the post-modern rationalizations of abortion and euthanasia, or even the false ideologies that have justified such horrific crimes as the Nazi holocaust and the Soviet gulags.

We need to stay humble and accept God's truth. We need to allow the Church to be for us, as it was for St. Paul, "the household of God, which is the church of the living God, the pillar and foundation of truth" (1 Tim. 3:15).

FEARLESS PURSUIT OF TRUTH

This doesn't mean that a good Christian is only permitted to read the Bible, the *Catechism*, and papal encyclicals—not at all. God draws each of us into a unique relationship with him. This uniqueness will be reflected in our individual journey of knowing God better. But whatever patterns emerge as we journey along the renewal of our mind, certain basic vitamins must never be depleted; we have to give ourselves daily doses of dependable truth, regular intellectual meals that only come with intentional and conscientious study of our authentically Catholic faith.

We have to gradually master the basic truths of revelation so we can recognize when they are contradicted or threatened by other ideas we run across. We have to continue developing our understanding of the implications of those basic truths so we cultivate the capacity to make mature and truthful judgments in tough situations. We have to seek greater familiarity with Christ's message so we can "always be ready to give an explanation to anyone who asks you for a reason for your hope, but . . . with gentleness and reverence" (1 Pet. 3:15-16).

And finally, we need to continually increase our knowledge about God, correcting any false ideas we may have about him and expanding our grasp of the truth about him so we can continually increase our love for and dedication to God. We cannot love what we do not know, and we cannot love more deeply what we know only superficially. Jesus came to earth to be our light, to roll back the suffocating darkness of ignorance and sin through his unique message of salvation. Loving him with all our minds means filling them, more and more every day, with that light (see 2 Pet. 1:19).

Questions for Personal Reflection or Group Discussion

1. What idea in this chapter struck you most and why?

2. How much time and effort do you currently put into getting to know your faith better and better?

3. When it comes to being informed about current issues and events from the point of view of the Magisterium, would you describe yourself as proactive or reactive? Why?

4. Very few of us are able to study our faith full-time. God understands this. But we do manage to find time every day to study something—we watch the news or our favorite TV series; we visit our favorite websites; we fill our minds with knowledge about things we are interested in. Daily learning more about our faith can happen in the same, natural, unexaggerated way. What will you do on a daily/weekly basis to learn something new about the "inscrutable riches of Christ" (Eph. 3:8)?

- I will attend an adult faith-formation event at my parish.
- I will attend a public lecture or guest-speaker event at a nearby Catholic college or university.
- I will search for a good Catholic website and sign up to receive daily or weekly e-mail updates.
- (Write your own resolution) I will _____

_____

_____

_____

Concluding Prayer

O Lord my God, I believe in you, Father, Son and Holy Spirit.
Insofar as I can, insofar as you have given me the power, I have
sought you. I became weary and I labored. O Lord my God, my
sole hope, help me to believe and never to cease seeking you.
Grant that I may always and ardently seek out your countenance.
Give me the strength to seek you, for you help me to find you
and you have more and more given me the hope of finding
you. Here I am before you with my firmness and my infirmity.
Preserve the first and heal the second. Here I am before
you with my strength and my ignorance. Where you have
opened the door to me, welcome me at the entrance; where
you have closed the door to me, open to my cry; enable me
to remember you, to understand you, and to love you.

—St. Augustine of Hippo

More Than Information

*This, then, is the marvelous yet demanding task awaiting all the lay faithful
and all Christians at every moment: to grow always in the knowledge
of the richness of baptism and faith as well as to live it more fully.*
—St. John Paul II, Christifideles Laici, 58

CHRISTIANIZING THE MIND, LEARNING TO love God with our whole mind,
involves more than simply filling our heads with information. The
mind is more than a hard drive. The human mind, our intellect, is a
directive power built into our nature. Our capacity to know shows us
the way things are and the way we should behave. To value and form
these capacities in harmony with our Christian vocation requires taking
some time to reflect on their various dimensions. As we show and grow
our love for Christ in this arena of our lives, we need to be aware of
at least three things, three interrelated functions of the human mind:
information gathering, thinking deeply, and training our memory.

GATHERING INFORMATION

Though information gathering—learning, coming to know more
both in breadth and depth—is not the only function of the mind, it
is a primary function. The healthy desire for more knowledge about
our faith, and about how to live out that faith, flows from this function. A steady increase of knowledge is necessary for spiritual
growth. Jesus is the Word of God, and a word communicates content, meaning. The more we know about God, about God's purpose
for the world, about God's plan of salvation, and about how God
sees us and wants to interact with and guide us, the better.

Receiving God's revelation and grasping it with our minds over-comes the natural ignorance of our human condition. It also gradu-ally purifies us of the malicious misinformation that we imbibe by living in a fallen world with a fallen nature. We are full of distorted ideas about ourselves, our world, and God. God's revelation is given to us to expose these lies and enlighten our darkened intellects.

Thirsting for deeper knowledge of our beloved Lord is a com-mon theme in the Scriptures. The Psalmist puts it succinctly: "Blessed are you, O Lord; teach me your statutes" (Ps. 119:12). The Book of Proverbs repeats it untiringly:

> Hear, O children, a father's instruction, be attentive, that you may gain understanding! Yes, excellent advice I give you; my teaching do not forsake. . . . The beginning of wisdom is: get wisdom; whatever else you get, get understanding. (Prov. 4:1-2, 7)

A healthy Christian is, among other things, a *learning* Christian.

GOING DEEPER

The second function of the intellect has to do not so much with gathering more and more information, but rather with deepening our understanding of the truths we already know and thinking deeply about them. A schoolboy can memorize the Gettysburg Address, but the words he memorizes will mean much less to him than they did to Abraham Lincoln when he wrote that address. Truth has breadth, but it also has depth.

The Latin root for the word *intelligence* includes two words: *intus* and *legere*. Together they connote "reading into" something—pene-trating the deeper meaning of things. Our minds are meant to do this, too. When we forget about this, we may grow in breadth of knowledge, but we will not necessarily grow in wisdom, in under-standing. We will be like a computer with lots of data, but not necessarily a deeper spiritual person, in tune with the true meaning of God's wonderful universe.

One of the Blessed Virgin Mary's traditional titles is "Seat of Wisdom." In the New Testament she models this dimension of the human mind, this quest not just for breadth but for depth. Multiple times, the Gospels show her mulling over, intentionally and prayerfully, God's revelation in Christ: "And Mary kept all these things, reflecting on them in her heart" (Luke 2:19).

Remembering

The third function of our intellect links our minds (a spiritual power) to our memories (a sensitive power). Loving God with our whole mind involves training our memory so that it easily retrieves whichever ideas, impressions, or experiences will help us most in each stage of our spiritual journey.

In order to interact with the world around us in a Christian way, we have to learn to recall the truths of revelation and allow them to guide and enlighten us in the various life situations we encounter. What good is it to be able to define Divine Mercy if we refuse to allow that mercy to give us hope and comfort after we commit a grievous sin?

Ancient Israel had a memory problem. God would perform amazing miracles for them, and a week later, when things got tough, they would forget about the miracles and stir up a tempest of whining and complaining. They would also forget about God's action in their lives in times of prosperity, slipping into a comfortable self-sufficiency that led them to neglect their relationship with him.

The temptation to forget about God's faithfulness and presence is a strong one. God vehemently warned Israel about it in the Old Testament: "Be careful not to forget the Lord, your God . . . " (Deut. 8:11). The entire chapter expands on this warning. We see the same warning in the Book of Revelation. In Revelation chapters 2 and 3, Jesus issues a series of reprimands and encouragements to the seven churches of Asia. In each one of them, he chastises or commends the members of the community in terms of what they have forgotten or kept in mind, what they have held onto or what they have lost. And his indications about how the churches should move forward usually include a reference to repenting and remembering, to persevering along the path that they took up at the beginning. Here is how he exhorts the church in Sardis, for example:

Remember then how you accepted and heard; keep it, and repent. If you are not watchful, I will come like a thief, and you will never know at what hour I will come upon you. (Rev. 3:3)

Keeping the truths of our faith constantly in sight so that we remain faithful to our calling in spite of the failures and successes, the sufferings and temptations that necessarily go along with life in a fallen world—this, too, is the job of a mind that seeks to love the Lord.

IMAGINING

Connected to this capacity for memory is the power of imagination, another bridge between the sensitive and spiritual powers of our soul. Our imagination allows us to picture in our mind's eye good things or bad things, noble things or base things. When we are feeling sad, for example, we can allow our minds to wander over to memories of even sadder situations or concoct images of how things could get worse. This would increase our sadness. On the other hand, we could also harness this power of our mind to help us rekindle hope, by picturing the crucifixion and the resurrection, for example, or by picturing the Sacred Heart of Jesus—the pledge of his undying love for us.

Our imagination can enhance all the other intellectual functions: gathering and learning information, penetrating the depths of the truths we learn, and recalling those truths in order to allow them to influence our daily living. But for this to happen, we have to educate and develop the imagination. Unfortunately, this training is severely handicapped by consumerism (which keeps our imaginations dependent and reactive so advertising images can be used to manipulate our emotions) and by media saturation (which keeps our imagination overloaded and therefore almost uncontrollably frenetic).

We need to recognize that the Christianization of our intellects involves developing harmoniously all these facets of our minds. A Christian mind is a mind that has learned God's revelation, assimilated it, and taken ownership of it. As a result, mature Christians will naturally see themselves, others, the world, events, and God through the clear window of truth. But reaching that maturity requires a daily decision to love the Lord with all our minds, actively seeking to grow in Christian knowledge and godly wisdom, the wisdom that addresses itself to us through the sacred Word:

> Happy the one who listens to me, attending daily at my gates, keeping watch at my doorposts; for whoever finds me finds life, and wins favor from the LORD; but those who pass me by do violence to themselves; all who hate me love death. (Prov. 8:34-36)

Questions for Personal Reflection or Group Discussion

1. What idea in this chapter struck you most and why?

2. Which do you tend to like more, gathering new knowledge or going deeper with the knowledge you already have? How can you achieve a better balance between these two complementary tendencies?

3. To form your memory and imagination, you have to be aware of them. How conscious are you, on a day-to-day basis, of what your memory and imagination are up to? How docile are they to your will?

4. St. John of the Cross, the sixteenth-century Spanish mystic and doctor of the Church, would very often spend large chunks of time simply gazing out his window at the beauties of God's creation. By contemplating God's works in this way, he absorbed God's wisdom and filled his mind with its light. What will you do today to grow in godly wisdom?

   - I will have a good conversation with a friend about how our faith sheds light on a major current event.
   - I will read my favorite Gospel passage, and then close my eyes and try to picture it—in every detail—in my imagination.
   - I will make a list of ten of the biggest blessings I have received throughout my life, remembering and savoring them.

- (Write your own resolution) I will _____

_____

_____

_____

Concluding Prayer

*O Mary, Mother of fair love, of fear, of knowledge, and of holy
hope, by whose loving care and intercession many, otherwise poor in
intellect, have wonderfully advanced in knowledge and in holiness,
you do I choose as the guide and patroness of my studies. I humbly
implore, through the deep tenderness of your maternal love, and
especially through that eternal Wisdom who deigned to take
from you our flesh and who gifted you beyond all the saints with
heavenly light, that you would obtain for me by your intercession
the grace of the Holy Spirit that I may be able to grasp with strong
intellect, retain in memory, proclaim by word and deed, and teach
others all things which bring honor to you and to your Son, and
which for me and for others are salutary for eternal life. Amen.*

—St. Thomas Aquinas[14]

Leveraging the Power of Literature and Art

Every piece of art, be it religious or secular, be it a painting, a sculpture, a poem or any form of handicraft made by loving skill, is a sign, a symbol, of the inscrutable secret of human existence, of man's origin and destiny, of the meaning of his life and work. It speaks to us of the meaning of birth and death, of the greatness of man.
—St. John Paul II, Address at Clonmacnoise, Ireland, 1979

INFORMING AND FORMING OUR INTELLECTUAL power is essential for learning to love God with our whole mind. Yet none of our human faculties exists in a vacuum—we can't really Christianize our mind without that having an indirect positive effect on our emotions and our will, as well as our heart. This is especially the case with regards to one specific intellectual pursuit, which at first glance doesn't even seem to be particularly relevant for our relationship with God: appreciating the fine arts, especially literature.

Not everyone loves literature, and certainly not every saint has been steeped in literary masterpieces. In fact, plenty of saints have reached the heights of holiness without even knowing how to read. And so, no one needs to feel obliged to utilize great literature as a means for spiritual growth. Yet it is a tested tool—a resource tried and proven, again and again, to enrich the human spirit. Understanding how the intelligent enjoyment of literature does that can give us another instrument to help us learn to love God with all our minds. Something similar can be said for all the fine arts, but since literature is the most accessible and all-embracing, we will focus our discussion here.

WHAT IS LITERATURE?

The literary arts include poetry, fiction, and drama, though some would add history to the list. Literature has come to be understood as a written art form, although the first great epics all originated as oral traditions, and the great dramas only really come to life when they are performed. From the earliest times, recited poetry and performed dramas also included musical elements. The literary arts, then, overlap with the other performing arts.

Because of this overlap, defining the different forms of literature can be problematic. But for the sake of discussing the role of literature in the spiritual life, we can identify certain defining characteristics.

All forms of literature give intelligible shape to what we experience in our human journey. They help us process our experience; they help us understand ourselves and our world; they help us move beyond what is superficial and live at the level of significance. They also give us joy. The beauty of good literature brings the disparate elements of our busy and demanding lives into a pleasing and inspiring harmony, reminding us of our true identity, our true potential, and our true destiny as creatures made in the image and likeness of God. This beauty also nourishes our heart by feeding good, true desires for the source of all beauty, goodness, and truth—God himself. Each form of literature achieves these noble goals in its own way.

THE MAGNIFYING POWER OF POETRY

Poetry, whether oral or written, tends to be more concise than prose. A poem will focus our attention on a detail of our human experience and delve into its meaning. Imagery and careful choice of words and rhythms give poetry its power to uncover the beauty and significance of every nuance of the human condition. Poetry encourages calm reflection on and appreciation of each precious piece of the mosaic of human experience.

The application of poetry to the spiritual life, then, is obvious.

Mental prayer, whether meditative or contemplative, involves deep reflection on God and his goodness. It creates space in the soul for the truth and beauty of God to shine on our minds and hearts. Poetry complements meditation. By revealing the deeper meaning hidden within the details of human experience, it sensitizes us to God's ubiquitous presence. It teaches us to read the first book of God's revelation – the created world.

THE MOTIVATING DYNAMISM OF DRAMA

In drama, the emphasis is on virtue: the power of the human spirit to seek and seize what is good. Good dramas – whether on stage or screen – show protagonists exercising their freedom, sometimes heroically, to avoid and conquer evil in pursuit of authentic happiness. Conflict, whether internal or external, is the core of drama. When sin and evil defeat the hero, we have a tragedy. When the hero overcomes sin and evil, we have a triumph. Both tragedies and triumphs have their place in our journeys.

Literary genius appears in drama through the author's capacity to include just the right amount and quality of events, conversations, and decisions, such that the audience feels deeply both the attraction of goodness and the threatening or seductive tug of evil. As the drama unfolds, the audience experiences vicariously the struggle of the protagonist. The better the drama, the deeper the identification between the audience and the protagonist, and it is according to the depth of that identification that the tragedy or the triumph will inspire audience members to repent of their own sins and to renew their hope-filled pursuit of what is true, good, and beautiful. Drama, then, can refresh, encourage, reinforce, or rekindle our good desires – an invaluable contribution indeed to our spiritual lives.

THE INTERIOR LANDSCAPE OF FICTION

The unique characteristic of fiction is the interior monologue. The great novels are almost poetic in their descriptions of the world and of human experience. They also involve the dramatic struggle between good and evil. But their specific contribution is opening a window into the human psyche. Tolstoy can spend a dozen pages describing a single moment of psychological experience: the mixed motives, the subconscious influences, the conflicting feelings, the waning or waxing hopes, and the nudging of conscience that are present in a person's interior at any given moment in life's journey. Through an author's description of what is happening inside the human person, readers get to know the characters much more profoundly than in a drama. And when the characters are developed truly, in consonance with our authentic identity as fallen and redeemed spiritual persons, this knowledge enriches us in two important ways.

First, it helps us reflect on and get to know ourselves better. The great literary authors are like expert psychologists: Their works are a mirror in which we are enabled to see parts of our own interiors that we normally cannot fathom. Second, it helps us understand other people and their experiences. We walk in their shoes for a while, and this vicarious experience can, if we let it, empower our efforts to be merciful, forgiving, understanding, compassionate, and supportive toward our neighbors.

Just a Means — Not the Goal

The other fine arts, like music, painting, and sculpture, can have a similar positive effect on our spiritual development, if we have the time and opportunity to learn their language. Of course, the realm of the arts poses spiritual dangers, too: False values can be paraded in attractive disguises; connoisseurship can devolve into snobbery; and entertainment can overrule edification. But all in all, an intelligent and prudent engagement with humanity's artistic achievements will be a boost for thinking about "whatever is true, whatever is honorable, whatever is just, whatever is pure, whatever is lovely, whatever is gracious" (Phil. 4:8, RSV).

Questions for Personal Reflection or Group Discussion

1. What idea in this chapter struck you most and why?

2. What stories (in whatever form—book, film, drama) have most inspired and influenced you over the years, and why?

3. Through the ages, the Church has been a consistent and avid patron of the arts. Why is that?

4. What will you do today to open yourself more to benefit from the human family's artistic treasures?

   - I will listen to a favorite piece of classical music.

   - I will start reading one of the classics that I have always wanted to read.

   - I will take some time to observe and admire the religious art present in my parish church.

   - (Write your own resolution) I will _____

   _____

   _____

   _____

Concluding Prayer

Lord, you are the hope of your people.
You give artists the gift of reflecting your splendor in their work;
Through the things they make, make the
world bright with hope and joy.

—FROM THE LITURGY OF THE HOURS

Spiritual Gluttony

The situation today points to an ever-increasing urgency for a
doctrinal formation of the lay faithful, not simply in a better
understanding which is natural to faith's dynamism but also in
enabling them to "give a reason for their hoping" (1 Peter 3:15)
in view of the world and its grave and complex problems.
—St. John Paul II, Christifideles Laici, 60

THE DESIRE TO LEARN MORE about our faith is a good one, a godly one, a desire planted and tended by the Holy Spirit. It leads us to engage our intellect, memory, and imagination in the quest to love God with our whole mind.

For some Christians, the need to know more, to learn more, to "think of what is above, not of what is on earth" (Col. 3:2), often feels like a burden. These Christians have to wage a constant battle against the sin of spiritual sloth—laziness when it comes to things of the spiritual life.

But for other Christians, the drive to expand and deepen our knowledge of God and his revelation provides not only supernatural benefits, but also natural pleasure. In some cases, it can stir up temptations to spiritual gluttony—a less obvious, and therefore more dangerous, arena of sin.

KEEPING TABS ON FRUSTRATION

God is infinite, so we will never come to know him so fully that nothing remains to discover. And yet sometimes we rebel against that reality. We become frustrated because we can't find more time to study and learn, to master everything there is to master about our faith, or about certain aspects of our faith. We yearn to learn more and more, but we run into so many obstacles: time limits, energy limits, resource limits. Even the basic responsibilities of our state in life seem to be obstacles in our going deeper with God, and so we begin to neglect them. All our free time, all our conversations, all our friendships—all our everything becomes more and more stuffed with devotions, and spiritual talks, and Bible studies, and faith-sharing groups, and conferences, and retreats, and seminars. And even then, we are frustrated because we can't fit more in.

This frustration seems holy, because it is directed toward wanting to know God better. But something deeper is going on. This is clear, because instead of leading us to greater internal peace and external generosity, the flurry of spiritual over-consumption seems to make us tense, anxious, brittle, and even judgmental. What's really happening?

Frustrations of this kind are dangerous traps along our spiritual journey, traps often set by the ancient enemy, the devil himself. Christians thirsting for more knowledge of the faith are too in love with God to be exceptionally vulnerable to temptations of *material* excess. So the devil has to change tactics in order to impede their spiritual progress. Enter spiritual and intellectual gluttony. If our spiritual and intellectual eyes get bigger than our stomachs, and we act on that, we will experience some spiritual indigestion, and that will become a nice ally in the devil's efforts to slow our progress along the path of Christian maturity.

Spiritualizing the Capital Sins

Both sloth and gluttony are capital sins—sins that give rise to other sins. We are used to seeing them in the material sphere, but we are not so used to seeing what they look like when they are spiritualized; yet sooner or later these sins do indeed show up on the doorstep of faithful, maturing Christians, dressed up in their spiritual disguises.

We experience pleasure in learning about the God we love. This is a good thing—all pleasures, in their proper settings, are good things.

God created both our capacity for pleasure and the objects that stimulate those pleasures. The devil can't change that. But he can twist it around a bit, and he can get us to be more and more attached to the pleasure to the point that we begin preferring the pleasure itself—in practice if not in theory—to the God who created it.

We understand this clearly in the material realm. The physical pleasures associated with gluttony, lust, and sloth are obvious. We are less aware of the spiritualized forms of these capital sins. If our eagerness to learn about God and our faith stirs up anxiety, tension, conflict, and frustration instead of contentment and joyful enthusiasm, some intellectual gluttony may be creeping in. When this happens, we need to nip it in the bud. We need to accept once again, intentionally, the truth that we already know: We will never be able to learn everything about God and the spiritual life; our journey to Christian maturity will continually present new vistas and discoveries, and we don't have to try to exhaust them.

THE RIGHT AMOUNT

The practical trick for keeping our God-given desire for greater knowledge healthy is to think in terms of the next step. We don't need to look at the 3.3 million volumes in the libraries at the great Catholic universities. Rather, we should look at the two or three books (or whatever other resources) that we really feel drawn to right now and dip into them, working through them and seeking to increase both the breadth and the depth of our knowledge. As we work through these books, other titles will come onto the radar screen. Put them on a wish list. When we are ready for another book, we can look through the list and see which ones draw us most intensely. This is often how the Holy Spirit guides us. He will draw us to certain titles or classes or other resources, and we will find ourselves just kind of following along. He knows what will help us most in each moment and each season of our journey, and he often guides us in subtle, gentle ways.

Another practical approach, for those who like planning and organizing, is to set some personal study goals for each liturgical season, or for each calendar year. Plan ahead what you would like to study, thinking through it intentionally, and then get all the materials, place them on your active bookshelf, and work through them gradually, enjoyably, peacefully. You might have a goal, for instance, of reading three books on prayer this winter, or reading all the works of St. Francis de Sales this year. As more items and ideas pop up, put them on your wish list and pile them onto your inactive bookshelf. This approach can be used as an individual, or by plugging into study circles with other fellow Christian travelers.

GRATEFUL TRUST

We should be grateful for the good, holy desire that we feel deep inside—the desire to know better and better all that God has revealed to us about himself, this world, and the way to live our lives to the full. We need to continue acting on this desire, but doing so with the child-like humility and joy that Jesus values so much. We will always have more to discover as we venture toward the Father's house, and that should fill our hearts with delight, not frustration.

Questions for Personal Reflection or Group Discussion

1. What idea in this chapter struck you most and why?

2. Are you more tempted to spiritual sloth or spiritual gluttony?

3. How intentional are you in your efforts to continually renew your mind in Christ? How intentional should you be, and what would that look like in your daily life?

4. While she was on her deathbed, St. Elizabeth of Hungary talked with her visitors about all the best spiritual sermons and homilies she had heard during her life. This shows that she had been eager to learn more about her beloved God, but that she had also taken enough time to digest what she heard. What will you do today to improve this area of your Christian living?

   • I will think about what tends to frustrate me, and try to discover why I get frustrated about those things.

- I will make a list of the types of things I tend to be slothful about, and the types of things I tend to be gluttonous about. I will choose one thing from each list to improve on this week.
- I will make a realistic personal reading list for the next couple of months.
- (Write your own resolution) I will _____

_____

_____

_____

Concluding Prayer

All holy Father, eternal God, in your goodness you prepared a royal throne for your Wisdom in the womb of the Blessed Virgin Mary; bathe your Church in the radiance of your life-giving Word, that, pressing forward on its pilgrim way in the light of your truth, it may come to the joy of a perfect knowledge of your love. Grant this through our Lord Jesus Christ, your Son, who lives and reigns with you and the Holy Spirit, one God, forever and ever. Amen.

—Collect from the Mass of Our Lady, Seat of Wisdom

PART V

LOVING GOD WITH ALL MY STRENGTH

As they were proceeding on their journey someone said to him, "I will follow you wherever you go." Jesus answered him, "Foxes have dens and birds of the sky have nests, but the Son of Man has nowhere to rest his head." And to another he said, "Follow me." But he replied, "[Lord,] let me go first and bury my father." But he answered him, "Let the dead bury their dead. But you, go and proclaim the kingdom of God." And another said, "I will follow you, Lord, but first let me say farewell to my family at home." [To him] Jesus said, "No one who sets a hand to the plow and looks to what was left behind is fit for the kingdom of God."

LUKE 9:57–62

The Strength to Decide

*Called to salvation through faith in Jesus Christ, "the true
light that enlightens everyone" (John 1:9), people become "light
in the Lord" and "children of light" (Ephesians 5:8), and are
made holy by "obedience to the truth" (1 Peter 1:22).*
—St. John Paul II, Veritatis Splendor, 1

BY LOVING GOD WITH ALL our mind, we open ourselves to receive
light and guidance about the right path to take through life. Our
intellect is bathed in and nourished by the truth of God's revelation,
and the ignorance and confusion we inherited from original sin is
gradually corrected and purified. But *knowing* something is not the
same as *doing* something.

The intellect is not the only spiritual power in human nature.
We also have the power of free choice, of decision: The human
intellect and the human will must work together, under the light
of faith and the strengthening of grace, in order to move us forward on the path of spiritual maturity. We must know the truth
more and more deeply, but we also must freely choose to act in
accordance with the truth we know, and we must make that
choice repeatedly, day after day, situation after situation. The wild
horse of our soul must have a rider that both knows where to go
and is fully determined to get there. To grow in our love for God,
then, includes loving him not only with all our mind and all our
soul, but also with all our *strength*.

THE SAD YOUNG MAN

The Gospels relate a memorable encounter that vividly illustrates how a weak will can impede spiritual progress. A rich and godly young man had heard about Jesus, the wonder-working rabbi from Nazareth. He had heard enough to come to believe in him, to believe that Jesus had the answers that his soul yearned for. And so, he went out to seek the Lord.

When he found him, he was so excited and eager that he "ran up, knelt down before him, and asked him, 'Good teacher, what must I do to inherit eternal life?'" (Mark 10:17). This was the right question! He wanted to know the deeper truth, and he believed Jesus could reveal it to him. His mind was open to the light.

Jesus recognized this and engaged in a conversation with him. He first told him to follow the commandments, since those were the path to fulfillment built right into human nature. But the young man replied that he was faithful to the commandments, and he wanted to know what else was missing, because he felt that his heart was still empty in some way. Again, we see that his mind was open to the light of truth; his conscience was making solid judgments and pushing him toward deeper immersion in God's revelation.

At that point, Jesus, "looking at him, loved him and said to him, 'You are lacking in one thing. Go, sell what you have, and give to [the] poor and you will have treasure in heaven; then come, follow me'" (Mark 10:21). Jesus gave him the answer. Jesus revealed to this sincere and well-instructed young man what was holding him back: an inordinate attachment to his wealth, and to the comfort and the apparent self-sufficiency that wealth brings. Jesus showed him the true path to deeper communion with God. The young man now knew the truth about how he could take the next step toward spiritual maturity.

In the man's response to this illumination, the Scriptures reveal the most common obstacle to spiritual growth: a weak will, a will enervated by inordinate attachments. St. Mark describes how the young man reacted to the answer he had been so avidly seeking: "At that statement his face fell, and he went away sad, for he had many possessions" (Mark 10:22). This man's capacity to choose the true good, his freedom—the precious gift we receive in order to enable us to love consciously and dynamically what is good, as persons, and not simply to follow unconscious instincts, like the rest of the animals—was hampered. He was not free to follow the higher good, the good he knew and desired, because his will was enchained, at least in part, to a lesser good.

THE TRUE AND THE GOOD

Jesus always linked knowledge of the truth with action in accordance with that knowledge. In his conversations with the Jewish leaders of his time, as well as his conversations with his own disciples, he repeatedly emphasized this connection. It is not enough to know and believe God's truth in the abstract; we must also choose to act and live in harmony with our faith—otherwise our union with God is impaired, and our wills remain divided and separated from God's will. And in fact, even knowledge of God's revelation remains immature without a growing obedience to that revelation:

> Jesus answered them and said, "My teaching is not my own but is from the one who sent me. Whoever chooses to do his will shall know whether my teaching is from God or whether I speak on my own." (John 7:16-17)

The spiritual life, as Jesus has revealed it, consists not merely of some secret or magical knowledge, as many non-Christian religions and heresies have asserted through the centuries. Rather, the spiritual life, the life of grace and growth in holiness, is an interpersonal relationship. More than just learning about God, it involves getting to know God. And getting to know someone means walking with them and living at their side, not only sharing common knowledge, but sharing *life* with them, being united in thought as well as in will, in both our spiritual faculties.

Jesus himself made this starkly, even frighteningly, clear at the end of his Sermon on the Mount. After pouring out his instruction, his light, his revelation regarding God and regarding the path to true happiness, he wraps things up with a stern warning against being satisfied with a mere knowledge *about* those things without advancing, through obedience, to a knowledge *of* them:

> "Not everyone who says to me, 'Lord, Lord,' will enter the kingdom of heaven, but only the one who does the will of my Father in heaven. Many will say to me on that day, 'Lord, Lord, did we not prophesy in your name? Did we not drive out demons in your name? Did we not do mighty deeds in your name?' Then I will declare to them solemnly, 'I never knew you. Depart from me, you evildoers.'" (Matt. 7:21-23)

The bridge between knowing and doing is built only by the spiritual power of our will. Engaging this power in our relationship with God is how we come to love him with all our strength. At this point, you may be wondering how you can do this better. That's what the following chapters will cover.

Questions for Personal Reflection or Group Discussion

1. What idea in this chapter struck you most and why?

2. Can you think of any inordinate attachments in your life, now or in the past, that have shackled or limited your freedom?

3. Jesus said, "Amen, amen, I say to you, everyone who commits sin is a slave of sin" (John 8:34). What do you think he meant? How is this relevant to your own spiritual journey right now?

4. St. Teresa of Avila, the sixteenth-century Spanish foundress and doctor of the Church, used to say that an eagle could be kept from flying either by chaining it to the ground, or simply tying it there with a little string. It's important for us to be humble and honest in our self-examination about what might be holding us back in our spiritual journey, so that God's grace can really get to work. Take some time to ask Jesus in prayer to show you, as he showed the rich young man in Mark 10, what is

lacking in your efforts to follow him more closely. At the end of the day, take some more time to reflect on what he showed you, and then renew your commitment to "do whatever he tells you" (John 2:5).

- I will take some time to sit alone with God and ask him what the rich young man asked him: "Lord, what must I do to keep growing in my relationship with you?" Prayerfully reflecting on this question, I will write down all the things that come to mind.

- I will consciously look for an opportunity today to do a good deed, a deed that fulfills, even in a small way, the commandment "Love your neighbor as yourself" (Mark 12:31).

- I will look at my list of daily duties each day this week and start with the least enjoyable item, the one I would rather put off until later. I will offer this as a sacrifice to God, uniting it to Christ's redeeming cross through a little prayer.

- (Write your own resolution) I will _____

_____

_____

_____

Concluding Prayer

O Mary, Mother of Mercy,
watch over all people, that the Cross of Christ
may not be emptied of its power,
that man may not stray from the path of the good
or become blind to sin, but may put his hope ever more
fully in God who is "rich in mercy" (Ephesians 2:4).
May he carry out the good works prepared
by God beforehand (see Ephesians 2:10) and so live
completely "for the praise of his glory" (Ephesians 1:12).

—St. John Paul II[15]

Building Well

*Revelation teaches that the power to decide what is good and what
is evil does not belong to man, but to God alone. Man is certainly
free, inasmuch as he can understand and accept God's commands.
And he possesses an extremely far-reaching freedom, since he can
eat "of every tree of the garden." But his freedom is not unlimited:
it must halt before the "tree of the knowledge of good and evil"
(Genesis 2:16–17), for it is called to accept the moral law given
by God. In fact, human freedom finds its authentic and complete
fulfillment precisely in the acceptance of that law. God, who alone
is good, knows perfectly what is good for man, and by virtue of
his very love proposes this good to man in the commandments.*
—St. John Paul II, Veritatis Splendor, 35

MANY POST-MODERN IDEOLOGIES AND THEORIES of human behavior
tend to either over- or underemphasize the power of human freedom. These have seeped into popular culture at every level, and in some
cases they have even affected how we understand the gospel itself.

A DANGEROUS DISCONNECT

Behaviorist and immanentist schools of thought tend to blame all
of our behaviors and choices on influences beyond our control.
According to them, subconscious or unconscious complexes and
urges or circumstantial and social pressures exercise so much influence on a person's decisions that moral responsibility disappears.
Some secularist and relativistic schools of thought, on the other
hand, see the human mind as all-powerful. For them, not only can

we freely determine what we choose to do, we can also freely and independently determine the very nature of good and evil.

Both of those errors shatter the link between freedom and truth, between truth and goodness. If the human person is completely determined by urges and circumstances, then our dignity disappears, as does our capacity for spiritual creativity, friendship, loyalty, love, and any other moral virtue that would give authentic meaning to life. If, on the other hand, the human person is actually divine, unlimited in our capacity to create meaning and truth simply by willing to do so, then every individual becomes, in essence, a universe unto himself, and the possibility of true communion between persons (human and divine) disappears. In either case, the theoretical divorce between truth and goodness is a lie that, if accepted, makes interior peace, fulfillment, and authentic happiness impossible.

Jesus Believes in Us

Jesus freed us from these lies. In the first place, he acknowledged and accepted the complex influences that contribute to conditioning our freedom in this fallen world. This is why he commanded us not to judge the interior intentions and culpability of other people—we simply cannot know enough to make a full and accurate judgment about a person, even when a particular action is objectively wrong. Only God sees clearly the many circumstantial and subconscious influences that may be at work inside a person's soul. It is enough for us to seek light regarding our own soul, without trying to manage the souls of others:

> "Stop judging, that you may not be judged. For as you judge, so will you be judged, and the measure with which you measure will be measured out to you. Why do you notice the splinter in your brother's eye, but do not perceive the wooden beam in your own eye? How can you say to your brother, 'Let me remove that splinter from your eye,' while the wooden beam is in your eye? You hypocrite, remove the wooden beam from your eye first; then you will see clearly to remove the splinter from your brother's eye." (Matt. 7:1–5)

Our Lord, however, never exaggerated the role of external influences. He always believed in us. He always appealed to our spiritual ability to make good choices, to exercise our freedom in harmony with the truth, and in that way to achieve the maturity, wisdom, and holiness that we are created for.

Yet he didn't fall into the other trap either. He never exaggerated the power of our freedom, exonerating us from the duty to humbly obey the truth. We are called not to be gods, but to love God, and that includes following God's plan for the human family in general, and for our individual life in particular. This conscious, free obedience to the truth promotes the fulfillment of our highest spiritual potential, and it alone leads to the meaning, fruitfulness, and happiness that will last. His respect for our capacity to do what is right and true, his hope in us, shines through in the finale of the Sermon on the Mount, a passage we have already seen:

> "Everyone who listens to these words of mine and acts on them will be like a wise man who built his house on rock. The rain fell, the floods came, and the winds blew and buffeted the house. But it did not collapse; it had been set solidly on rock. And everyone who listens to these words of mine but does not act on them will be like a fool who built his house on sand. The rain fell, the floods came, and the winds blew and buffeted the house. And it collapsed and was completely ruined." (Matt. 7:24–27)

THE TRUE AND THE GOOD

The same tone fills the pages of the entire New Testament. In Christ, with him and through the gift of his grace, each of us has become "a new creation: the old things have passed away; behold, new things have come" (2 Cor. 5:17). As a result, if we remain in the Lord and stay united to the vine, our collaboration with God's grace can truly work wonders in us and through us: "I am the vine, you are the branches. Whoever remains in me and I in him will bear much fruit, because without me you can do nothing" (John 15:5).

We *can* learn to love God with all our strength. We *can* choose to follow Christ and travel the path of spiritual maturity. We *can* resist temptation and grow in virtue. We *can* make a difference in the world, building Christ's kingdom and encouraging others to do the same. If we couldn't, none of the New Testament letters would have been written, since they all contain passionate encouragement to make practical, daily choices worthy of our Christian calling. If knowing the truth were sufficient for our spiritual growth, and if we were not free to choose to live according to that truth, St. Paul, for example, would never have written this:

> Put to death, then, the parts of you that are earthly: immorality, impurity, passion, evil desire, and the greed that is idolatry. . . . Put on then, as God's chosen ones, holy and beloved, heartfelt compassion, kindness, humility, gentleness, and patience, bearing with one another and forgiving one another, if one has a grievance against another; as the Lord has forgiven you, so must you also do. And over all these put on love, that is, the bond of perfection. . . . And whatever you do, in word or in deed, do everything in the name of the Lord Jesus, giving thanks to God the Father through him. (Col. 3:5, 12–14, 17)

When our hearts desire God above all things, and our emotions are joyfully subject to an intellect enlightened by faith and a will strengthened and aligned by grace, we can truly love God with all our heart, soul, mind, and strength, just as Jesus commands.

Questions for Personal Reflection or Group Discussion

1. What idea in this chapter struck you most and why?

2. What is your knee-jerk reaction to the concept of "obedience"? Where does that reaction come from?

3. In what kinds of situations do you feel more acutely the temptation to accept the lie that truth and freedom are enemies instead of co-principles of spiritual maturity?

4. A visitor once asked Blessed Mother Teresa of Calcutta what he could really do to help the poor, since he felt so small and un-influential. She answered, "Pick up a broom." What will you do today to obey Jesus better by putting your freedom at the service of the truth, to be a better "co-worker in the truth"? (3 John 8).

- I will make a good examination of conscience and go to confession.

- I will think about my own persistent unhealthy behavior patterns and try to figure out where their roots are. Then I will think of what kind of behaviors I could develop to correct those unhealthy patterns. I will talk to God about it and ask for his help.

- I will read the explanation of the Ten Commandments in the *Catechism*.

- (Write your own resolution) I will _____

  _____

  _____

  _____

Concluding Prayer

O Lord and Master of my life,
grant not unto me a spirit of idleness, of discouragement,
of lust for power, and of vain speaking.
But bestow upon me, Thy servant, the spirit of chastity,
of meekness, of patience, and of love.
Yea, O Lord and King, grant that I may perceive
my own transgressions, and judge not my brother,
for blessed art Thou unto ages of ages. Amen.

—ST. EPHREM THE SYRIAN[16]

Persevering

At no stage of life can people feel so secure and committed that they do not need to give careful attention to ensuring perseverance in faithfulness; just as there is no age at which a person has completely achieved maturity.
— St. John Paul II, Vita Consecrata, 69

I T'S ONE THING TO MAKE good choices, to use our freedom to grow in love, as we are called to do, rather than forfeiting our freedom to the slavery of attachments and sin. But the power of the human will isn't exhausted by only choosing to follow the right path in isolated moments. Loving God with all our strength also means persevering on that path. Our Lord left no room for doubt on this: "But the one who perseveres to the end will be saved" (Matt. 24:13). And just to make sure we understand, he illustrated this fundamental truth with a visual metaphor: "No one who sets a hand to the plow and looks to what was left behind is fit for the kingdom of God" (Luke 9:62).

LEVELS OF MATURITY

Babies are immature; their will is undeveloped, just as are many other of their natural powers. They have no conscious awareness or control over their emotions, their whims, their passions, and their drives. Their spiritual freedom is in an embryonic state: They are completely dependent on the care and education of others. Just as they need to be potty-trained, they also need to be feelings-trained; they need to learn how to integrate their passions into a harmonious, mature personality under the guidance of their intelligence and their will. In the meantime, they are overly swayed by the pleasure and whim of the moment, by their bio-rhythms and their moods.

Adolescents are usually more mature. They can make independent, creative plans, and they can follow through on them, if they like them and feel the immediate rewards—just think of how much dedication a boy can put into mastering a video game. The will has grown and developed and can be directed toward achievements that take time and perseverance. But adolescents usually remain inordinately attached to immediate gratification, to easy pleasure. Even physiologically, certain areas of the brain that enable more mature judgment are still developing until we reach our twenties. The will, too, is still developing, and still needs training. This is why it is often so hard for adolescents to persevere in tasks where the reward is distant or in jobs that they simply don't enjoy. They need help to discipline themselves in those areas where they feel less immediate gratification and where over-indulgence in pleasure can cause them moral or emotional damage.

The adolescent may or may not show up to fulfill his commitments. He will begin grand projects on a whim, in the wake of an emotional high, and then leave them half-finished. The adolescent can make excellent and numerous resolutions for personal, academic, extracurricular, or spiritual improvement. But those resolutions will quickly fizzle out, and they will be replaced by another set of resolutions, which will also fizzle out, and the pattern continues. This is the activity of a will that is still immature. A person with an immature will would like to do many worthy things, but in actual practice, the "I would like" may never upgrade itself to the full, mature "I will."

Mature adults have developed the capacity for self-governance. They are able to navigate the ebb and flow of emotional energy and maintain a steady, determined pace in pursuit of worthy goals. They are responsible, dependable, and persevering. Without denying their real and legitimate needs for healthy pleasure and gratification, mature adults are able to keep their internal stature ordered and secure, so as to continue worthwhile pursuits over the long haul. They are able to envision how much effort certain commitments or objectives will take, and so they make their decisions with sufficient reflection, knowing what will be required of them. They are committed enough to follow through even though it will be costly, because they have maturely judged (intellect) and maturely decided (will) that the endeavor is worthwhile.

The Cost of Discipleship

Jesus described this steadiness, this healthy realism, this capacity of perseverance, with two of his vivid parables. He emphasized how essential mature willpower—a will liberated from inordinate attachments that inhibit the freedom to love fully (renouncing all possessions)—really is for Christian discipleship:

> "Which of you wishing to construct a tower does not first sit down and calculate the cost to see if there is enough for its completion? Otherwise, after laying the foundation and finding himself unable to finish the work, the onlookers should laugh at him and say, 'This one began to build but did not have the resources to finish.' Or what king marching into battle would not first sit down and decide whether with ten thousand troops he can successfully oppose another king advancing upon him with twenty thousand troops? But if not, while he is still far away, he will send a delegation to ask for peace terms. In the same way, every one of you who does not renounce all his possessions cannot be my disciple." (Luke 14:28-33)

It is possible to have reached adulthood physiologically and to still be an infant or an adolescent as regards the maturity of one's will. In this case, even full-grown, worldly, successful adults may be unable to love God as much as they really want to, because a lot of that strength is simply not yet available to them; in some senses, they are still babies. But growth in this area can happen very quickly, once we plug in to God's grace and make a firm decision to follow him more closely each day. (We will look more into how to do that in the last part of this book.)

It is also possible to be a child or an adolescent physiologically and have already developed a relatively mature will. But maturity doesn't mean that love has reached its limit. As the mind and soul continue to grow in "wisdom and in stature, and in favor before God and man," the "all" of a person's love for God will also continue to grow (Luke 2:52, RSV).

Whatever our current level of spiritual maturity, we do well to remember that love is intrinsically dynamic, and it will always have room to keep on expanding. Obeying the command to love God with all our strength, therefore, is a lifetime project.

Questions for Personal Reflection or Group Discussion

1. What idea in this chapter struck you most and why?

2. In which areas or relationships of your life do you still lack maturity or interior freedom?

3. What life experiences have helped you the most along your path of becoming more mature, responsible, and dependable as a person? How and why did those experiences help you so much?

4. Strengthening your will is much easier to do than you might think. Willpower is like a muscle, and the more we exercise it, the more it grows. The key is to exercise it with faith and prayer, so that we always stay under the light of God's grace and never start thinking we can simply achieve spiritual maturity by trying harder. What will you do today to strengthen your will in loving service of God's plan for your life?

   • I will follow through on a task or commitment that I have been procrastinating.

   • I will start my day by doing the least pleasant item on my to-do list, saving the more pleasing things for later (as a kind of reward).

   • I will make a weekly schedule around my most important priorities and then make a concerted effort to follow that schedule, saying "no" to nonessential, unplanned needs and opportunities that pop up.

- (Write your own resolution) I will _____

_____

_____

_____

Concluding Prayer

I arise today,
through God's strength to pilot me;
God's might to uphold me,
God's wisdom to guide me,
God's eye to look before me,
God's ear to hear me,
God's word to speak for me,
God's hand to guard me,
God's way to lie before me,
God's shield to protect me,
God's hosts to save me
from snares of the devil,
from temptations of vices,
from every one who desires me ill,
afar and anear,
alone and in a crowd . . .
Amen.

—ST. PATRICK OF IRELAND[17]

DAY 23

This Present Darkness

*For in spite of all the witness of creation and of the salvific economy
inherent in it, the spirit of darkness is capable of showing God as
an enemy of his own creature, and in the first place as an enemy of
man, as a source of danger and threat to man. In this way Satan
manages to sow in man's soul the seed of opposition to the one who
"from the beginning" would be considered as man's enemy—and not
as Father. Man is challenged to become the adversary of God!*
—St. John Paul II, Dominum et Vivificantem, 38

SECULAR ATHEISTS CAN DEVELOP STRONG willpower and natural prudence,
and they can put them to work in the service of impressive and
useful achievements. They can develop the natural virtues of responsibility and dependability through persevering effort. But when we
aim at serving God's kingdom instead of the kingdom of this world,
an additional set of obstacles gets involved. The spiritual battle kicks
in, a struggle, as St. Paul explains, that "is not with flesh and blood
but with the principalities, with the powers, with the world rulers of
this present darkness, with the evil spirits in the heavens" (Eph. 6:12).

THE SPIRITUAL STRUGGLE

Developing willpower always demands effort and sacrifice, but align-
ing our will with Christ's and growing in Christian courage and
perseverance—which always require obedience, not just sheer deter-
mination—will demand even more. Both our intellect and our will
are wounded by original sin, as we have seen, and when we launch
out on the path of healing and make loving obedience to God's

plan the desire of our hearts, our spiritual enemies become intensely interested in deterring us. St. John Paul II explained this is in his
encyclical on the moral life, *Veritatis Splendor*:

> This obedience is not always easy. . . . Man is constantly
> tempted to turn his gaze away from the living and true God.
> . . . Man's capacity to know the truth is also darkened, and
> his will to submit to it is weakened. Thus, giving himself over
> to relativism and skepticism (cf. John 18:38), he goes off in
> search of an illusory freedom apart from truth itself.[18]

The Enemy's First Strategy: Corrupt the Heart

Jesus had to fight this battle in his life, too. His nature wasn't
wounded by original sin or personal sins, but he had to do combat
with our ancient enemy, the devil. And in that combat, he revealed
the devil's three basic strategies.

At the beginning of his public life, Jesus went into the desert for
forty days for prayer and preparation. During that period, he was
"tempted by Satan" (Mark 1:13). In these temptations, the devil tried to
divide Jesus's heart, in order to remove or at least corrupt his core
desire of loving and obeying his Father. The devil tried to replace it
with a desire for pleasure and comfort when he tempted our Lord to
turn stones into bread. When that didn't work, the devil tried to
replace it with a desire for earthly power and dominion, showing our
Lord all the kingdoms of the world and promising to put them under
his control for the simple price of worshipping the devil. That didn't
work either. And so the devil tempted Jesus to seek first popularity and
adulation by performing a dramatic miracle of jumping off the top of
the temple without being hurt. That temptation failed as well. The
devil's first strategy, to corrupt the heart, was laid bare.

The Enemy's Second Strategy: Turn Aside the Will

St. Luke finishes his narration of the temptations in the wilderness
by pointing out that "when the devil had finished every temptation, he departed from him for a time" (Luke 4:13). That time came

to an end on the eve of our Lord's passion. After Jesus was betrayed, St. Luke tells us, the Lord explained that "the time for the power of darkness" had returned (Luke 22:53). During Jesus's passion, we learn about our enemy's other two strategies.

In the Garden of Gethsemane, the devil bombarded Jesus with temptations so deep that they inspired fear and confusion and caused him "sorrow and distress" (Matt. 26:37). So profound was the struggle that Jesus sweated blood (see Luke 22:44) and even exclaimed to his companions, "My soul is sorrowful even to death" (Matt. 26:38). For centuries, theologians have debated the exact nature of these temptations, but all agree that whatever their content (and this is where temptations try to corrupt the intellect, sowing false ideas or deceptive half-truths), their goal was clear: The devil was trying to get Jesus to disobey his Father's will, to say no to what his Father was asking of him. And this is the second strategy, to turn aside our will from God's will—to make God's will seem so unreasonable or painful or difficult that our courage fails, and we choose a different path.

The devil can't create reality; he is not God. And so he has to distort it in order to frighten us. To keep us from entering a path that God is inviting us to follow, he has to exaggerate the danger or the difficulty. We already know that it will be difficult, because Jesus revealed this to us:

> "Enter through the narrow gate; for the gate is wide and the road broad that leads to destruction, and those who enter through it are many. How narrow the gate and constricted the road that leads to life. And those who find it are few." (Matt. 7:13–14)

But Jesus would never ask something of us that is absolutely impossible. This is what the devil wants to make us forget. He wants us to see God's invitation only from a human, mundane perspective. That is when our courage will likely fail. But God always reminds us that such a perspective is incomplete (see Matt. 19:26).

THE ENEMY'S THIRD STRATEGY: GETTING US TO GIVE UP

Jesus resisted the devil's onslaught in the Garden of Gethsemane, mainly through fervent prayer (see Luke 22:44). And so the enemy switched to his third basic tactic. He couldn't dislodge the Lord's heart, and he couldn't convince him not to set out on the path of the Father's will, so he made following that path agonizingly difficult. The passion and death of our Lord involved suffering betrayal, injustice, physical and psychological torture, humiliation, calumny, rejection of all types, and even witnessing heartrending sorrow in those whom he loved most, such as his Mother. Every step along the path of his Father's will increased his suffering. Every increase of suffering required a renewal of his loving obedience. The devil was simply trying to wear him out, trying to make him suffer so much that he would eventually rebel against his Father's plan and turn aside from the path he had freely chosen to follow—the right path, the path of loving God with all his heart, soul, mind, and strength. Continuing down that path required perseverance; it required mature human willpower, infused with and elevated by divine grace.

Questions for Personal Reflection or Group Discussion

1. What idea in this chapter struck you most and why?

2. How aware are you of the reality of spiritual warfare in the world and in your own life?

3. Consider the devil's three strategies in relation to the challenges you have faced or are facing now. Which of the strategies seems to be most effective in impeding your spiritual progress?

4. St. Maximilian Kolbe, a Franciscan priest, founder, and martyr of Auschwitz, used to tell his fellow Franciscans that he would be able to help them a lot more once he got to heaven. In heaven, he said, he could use both hands to help them. Here on earth, he could only use one hand, because he had to use

the other hand to keep himself from falling. What will you do today to better unite yourself to Jesus and allow God's grace to strengthen you in the spiritual battle?

- I will think prayerfully about the temptations that most typically trip me up. I will prayerfully come up with a practical way to respond courageously the next time that temptation appears.

- I will memorize the prayer to St. Michael the Archangel (at the end of this chapter), and use it as a spiritual shield the next time I feel tempted.

- I will read about how my patron saint engaged in spiritual battles and draw inspiration from his or her example.

- (Write your own resolution) I will _____

_____

_____

_____

Concluding Prayer

St. Michael the Archangel,
defend us in battle.
Be our defense against the wickedness and snares of the Devil.
May God rebuke him, we humbly pray,
and do thou,
O Prince of the heavenly hosts,
by the power of God,
thrust into hell Satan,
and all the evil spirits,
who prowl about the world
seeking the ruin of souls. Amen.

—Pope Leo XIII

PART VI

GETTING PRACTICAL

"Come to me, all you who labor and are burdened, and I will give you rest. Take my yoke upon you and learn from me, for I am meek and humble of heart; and you will find rest for yourselves. For my yoke is easy, and my burden light."

MATTHEW 11:28–30

DAY 24

The Path of Life

Where can you turn to find answers that satisfy, answers that will
last? The opposite of deception is truth – the person who tells the
truth, the person who is the truth. Yes, the opposite of deception is
Jesus Christ, who tells us: "I am the way, and the truth, and the life"
(John 14:6). Jesus Christ is the Son of God. He reveals the truth of
God. But he is also man. He shares in our humanity and came into
the world to teach us about ourselves, to help us discover ourselves.
– St. John Paul II, Address to Young People, September 12, 1987

WHEN AN APPLE TREE IS mature, when its roots are firmly, deeply grounded in good soil with plenty of water, when its trunk is strong and healthy and protected by sturdy bark, when its branches are smooth and supple and covered with wide green leaves that drink in the sunlight, it blossoms and bears fruit. Its potential is being realized. It has grown in accordance with its nature and is glorifying God, reflecting a small ray of God's own goodness and beauty by being all that it was created to be. The innate powers of the tree are flourishing together harmoniously.

All the innate powers of the human person are enlisted by the Lord in his command to love God with "all your heart, with all your soul, with all your mind, and with all your strength" (Mark 12:30). When each of these powers is harmoniously integrated into the ongoing pursuit of greater union with God, which is the purpose of our existence, our potential is being realized, we are glorifying God, and the fruits of the Spirit are blossoming, ripening, and enriching our lives and the lives of those around us: "The fruit of the Spirit is love, joy, peace, patience, kindness, generosity, faithfulness, gentleness, self-control" (Gal. 5:22–23). Those fruits of the Spirit have no limits. The more we are united to God, the more intense and abundant they become, as Jesus pointed out, and as we have previously noted: "I came so that they might have life and have it more abundantly" (John 10:10).

GROWING IN VIRTUE

Forming these powers so that they are directed in a healthy way, toward the truth and goodness that are in accordance with our nature and our calling, is what the Christian spiritual tradition calls growing in virtue. The virtuous person, from this long-standing perspective, is the one who is most alive, the one whose soul is most mature. Growing in virtue sets the human person free to be all that we were created to be, just as the healthy apple tree, when all its powers reach maturity, is free to fulfill its inherent potential.

Growing in virtue, then, is the same thing as growing in happiness. Just as an apple tree remains frustrated (ontologically, not consciously) if the soil or other conditions inhibit its roots and branches and leaves from growing to maturity, so human beings remain frustrated and unhappy when their hearts haven't discovered and desired to pursue their proper goal, when their intellects aren't being nourished on the eternal truths, when their wills aren't engaged in authentically meaningful and creative activity, and when their passions aren't enjoying docility to the spirit.

Only when we are on the path of learning to love God with all our heart, soul, mind, and strength—only when we are on the path of growing in virtue—do we experience the vitality, the hopefulness, the keen satisfaction that enables mature Christians to say such shocking things as St. Paul did:

> [But] whatever gains I had, these I have come to consider a loss because of Christ. More than that, I even consider everything as a loss because of the supreme good of knowing Christ Jesus my Lord. For his sake I have accepted the loss of all

things and I consider them so much rubbish, that I may gain Christ. (Phil. 3:7-8)

As we move forward along the path of deeper union with God, the path of growing in virtue, our experience of the fulfillment that only God can give increases and intensifies, gradually obliterating all idols.

A Progressive Journey

Here on earth, we never reach the limit of that experience. Rather, God continues to present us with situations in which, if we so desire, our virtue can continue to grow and expand, thereby continuing to intensify our experience of keen inner vitality and clarity. We remain pilgrims, moving along through time and space toward our final destination in heaven, as long as we remain residents of earth. As Christian pilgrims in the world, we are "aliens and sojourners" (1 Pet. 2:11), because " . . . here we have no lasting city, but we seek the one that is to come" (Heb. 13:14). Yet every step of love that leads us closer to the eternal city also increases our union with God, matures our virtue, and enhances our vitality. No one is more alive than a saint.

So even as the circumstances in which we live continue to be marked by the pain, sorrow, and brokenness of this fallen world, our interior experience as we navigate those circumstances takes on more and more the flavor of holiness. We begin to understand, better and better, the peace that Jesus bequeathed to us during the Last Supper—an inner, overflowing peace that differs from any satisfaction available from the goods of this passing world: "Peace I leave with you; my peace I give to you. Not as the world gives do I give it to you. Do not let your hearts be troubled or afraid" (John 14:27). As we grow in virtue, we begin to understand how St. Paul, who was never trite or superficial or overly optimistic, was able to command Christians to rejoice at all times:

Rejoice in the Lord always. I shall say it again: rejoice! Your kindness should be known to all. The Lord is near. Have no anxiety at all, but in everything, by prayer and petition, with thanksgiving, make your requests known to God. Then the peace of God that surpasses all understanding will guard your hearts and minds in Christ Jesus. (Phil. 4:4–7)

THE OPERATIVE QUESTION

This is the path of life that God has called us to. And to follow this path is what we long for. We now know that loving God with our heart, soul, mind, and strength means engaging all the powers of our human nature in the great adventure of seeking first the kingdom of God. But what does it look like to actually do that? How do we go from our immature state of loving to a mature state of loving? We love God already with our heart, soul, mind, and strength — otherwise we wouldn't have read this far. But what activities can we engage in to continue feeding the growth in virtue that will lead us to full maturity, to loving God with *all our all*? That is what the remainder of this book will look into.

Questions for Personal Reflection or Group Discussion

1. What idea in this chapter struck you most and why?

2. When you think of "holiness" and "virtue," what's the first thing that comes to mind? Does that accurately reflect the vitality and abundance that those terms are meant to evoke?

3. How would you define "happiness"? How does that definition compare with the vision of fulfillment we get from God's revelation in Jesus?

4. Today's world — so focused on consumerism — wants us to forget the truth that we can never have perfect happiness until we get to heaven. But when we forget that truth, we will begin to expect perfect happiness on earth. That's a false expectation that fills us with a constant underlying frustration. What will you do today to remind yourself that you are only a pilgrim in this world?

- I will unite some small suffering to Christ's suffering on the cross through a prayer of self-offering.
- I will try to laugh instead of to cry over spilled milk (i.e., the little, frustrating foibles of daily life).
- (Write your own resolution) I will _____

_____

_____

_____

Concluding Prayer

Oh! how I love you, Jesus! My soul aspires to you
And yet for one day only my simple prayer I pray!
Come reign within my heart, smile tenderly on me,
Today, dear Lord, today.

But if I dare take thought of what the morrow brings,
That fills my fickle heart with dreary, dull dismay;
I crave, indeed, my God, trials and sufferings,
But only for today!

O sweetest Star of heaven! O Virgin, spotless, blest,
Shining with Jesus' light, guiding to Him my way!
O Mother! 'neath your veil let my tired spirit rest,
For this brief passing day!

Soon shall I fly afar among the holy choirs,
Then shall be mine the joy that never knows decay;
And then my lips shall sing, to heaven's angelic lyres,
The eternal, glad Today!

—St. Thérèse of Lisieux

A Profile of Virtue

[St. Paul] is concerned with the morally good or bad works, or
better the permanent dispositions – virtues and vices – which are
the fruit of submission to or of resistance to the saving action of
the Holy Spirit. Consequently the Apostle writes: "If we live by
the Spirit, let us also walk by the Spirit" (Galatians 5:25).
— St. John Paul II, Dominum et Vivificantem, 55

A s HUMAN BEINGS IN THE world of time and space, we have to interact constantly with three basic realities: 1) things that cause or promise to cause pleasure; 2) things that cause or threaten to cause pain or harm; and 3) other persons. Our passions tend to react automatically to pleasures and pains, as we have seen. If we form the habit of making our decisions and taking action based only on those automatic, irrational reactions, we will form vices—habits or patterns of acting that contradict what is truly good for our human nature. If we form the habit of taking into account those important emotional reactions as we make our decisions but finally taking action based on the firmer principles of faith and reason, we will form virtues. Virtues can simply be described as our natural powers acting habitually and easily in a proper manner, acting in accordance with the truth of our human nature and vocation. The more virtuous we are, the more doing the right thing and experiencing the internal benefits of doing the right thing—regardless of how difficult or complex that may be—become second nature.

THE CARDINAL VIRTUES

Through the ages, philosophers have identified four basic virtues that are like the hinges of our moral and spiritual life. (The word *cardinal* actually comes from the Latin word that means "hinge.") They correspond to those three realities that we interact with on a regular basis.

If we learn to govern our raw desire for pleasure in accordance with what is truly healthy and in harmony with God's purpose for our lives, we develop the cardinal virtue of *temperance*. Temperance takes different forms in relation to the different types of pleasure that we have to deal with (chastity, sobriety, meekness, humility). If we learn to govern the fear that pain and suffering inspire, so that this never impedes us from doing what is right and necessary according to God's purpose for our lives, we develop the cardinal virtue of *fortitude* or courage, whose sister virtues include patience and perseverance. If we learn to treat all other persons (God as well as our fellow human beings) with the dignity that they deserve, regardless of how we may feel about them or what they may be able to do for or against us, then we grow in the virtue of *justice*, which also has a slew of sister virtues (e.g., honesty, piety, obedience).

Those three cardinal virtues perfect the exercise of our will and emotions in relation to the types of realities that we have to interact with in this world. The fourth cardinal virtue, *prudence* or wisdom, is the development of our intelligence so that it recognizes and discerns what actions are proper (virtuous, healthy, in accordance with our true good) within the myriad and tangled situations of real life.

THE THEOLOGICAL VIRTUES

When we were baptized, we were adopted into God's family, and he infused into our soul capacities to relate to him that did not belong to our pre-baptized nature. This infusion gave the life of grace to our souls. We were enabled to know God, to recognize his voice and his truth, and to accept and believe in him and in those truths that he reveals; this capacity is known as the theological virtue of *faith*. We were also given a deep impulse to expect our fulfillment in life from God himself, not from any of God's creatures, as good and beautiful as they may be. This impulse is known as the virtue, the capacity, of theological *hope*. Finally, were we given the ability, the supernatural capacity, to actually enter into interpersonal communion with the Trinity, to live in friendship with God, as if we were his equals—which by nature we are not; only through grace have we been given this potential. This capacity to engage with the Trinity in a relationship of mutual self-giving is known as the theological virtue, the soul-power, of *love*, also called divine charity.

In a sense, through the infusion of grace at baptism, God "supernaturalized" our human nature. Now faith opens and directs our intellect toward the divine light of God himself, not just to the created lights of finite truths. Now hope spurs our hearts to yearn for completeness in God himself, not only in the good things God has created. Now theological love enables us to converse with and experience an intimate, familial relationship with the infinite God, not only with fellow human beings. It's as if God altered our spiritual DNA on the day of our baptism, so that we are now *truly* members of God's family, not only legally and emotionally, in a way that no merely human adoption can make an adopted child into a member of that adopting family.

New Strength for a New Standard

This may seem abstract and impractical, but it's critical for a clear understanding of what growing in virtue really means for a Christian. Merely natural virtues, which have as their standard and measuring rod human nature unaided by grace, are no longer sufficient for the spiritual maturity we are called to. God's supernatural grace is indeed infused into our human nature, and it works from within that nature. And so the four cardinal virtues that describe the maturation of our natural powers are still valid for the Christian. But they are elevated to a new standard.

For example, self-preservation of the individual and the tribe was the highest value for the pagan world. This led them to see other tribes as inherently less worthy than themselves, as not deserving of the rights (justice) that members of their own tribe enjoyed. In the light of faith, however, and as members of God's family, we now know that every human person has an equal dignity based on having been created in God's image, and so all human persons have equal rights. We no longer reserve our compassion and kindness just for members of our own tribe.

To take another example, we can reflect on how our supernatural faith and hope in God enables Christians to put earthly comfort and success in second place, behind their top priority of friendship with Jesus Christ. This is how so many Christian martyrs have found the strength to refuse to renounce that friendship even in the face of seductive blandishments and agonizing tortures. Only because of this supernatural DNA, this infused grace of God at work within us, does anything in the gospel make sense to us and attract us. Only faith, hope, and love, for example, could motivate a Christian to renounce the goods of this world completely and follow a vocation to the monastery or the cloister: "What profit is there for one to gain the whole world and forfeit his life?" (Mark 8:36).

Questions for Personal Reflection or Group Discussion

1. What idea in this chapter struck you most and why?

2. How would you explain the concept of Christian virtue to someone who asked you about it?

3. Up to this point in your life, what have you consciously and consistently done to exercise the virtues of faith, hope, and charity?

4. When dealing with definitions, as we did in this chapter, virtue can seem dry and abstract. But in fact it's intensely practical, and it's relevant to everything we experience on a daily basis. When we're stuck in traffic and our blood starts to boil, the virtue of patience (a sister virtue of fortitude) keeps us calm and collected instead of getting exhausted by mild (or not so mild) road rage. When the pleasures of video games or TV or social media threaten to sabotage our sense of responsibility to God, family, and ourselves, the virtue of temperance enables us to click the off button. When we are treated unfairly at work or we get laid off and we see no solution on the horizon, the virtue of hope enables us to continue forward without imploding—we know

that resurrections come after crucifixions. What will you do today to exercise intentionally one of the theological virtues?

- I will go out of my way to do something kind for someone I don't really get along with on a natural level, without looking for anything in return (love).
- I will buy a crucifix to hang on my bedroom wall and have a priest bless it (faith).
- I will stop putting something off simply because I am afraid of failing—I will take the next step out of confidence in God (hope).
- (Write your own resolution) I will _____

_____

_____

_____

_____

Concluding Prayer

Lord, holy Father, almighty and ever-living God, I thank you.
For though I am a sinner and your unprofitable servant,
you have fed me with the precious Body and Blood of
your Son, our Lord Jesus Christ. You did this not because
I deserved it, but because you are kind and merciful.
I pray that this holy Communion may not add to my guilt and
punishment, but may lead me to forgiveness and salvation.
May it be for me the armor of faith and a shield of good will.
May it remove my vices and extinguish my evil tendencies.
May it bring me charity and patience, humility and obedience,
and may it strengthen my power to do every kind of good.
May it be a firm defense against the deceit of
all my enemies, visible and invisible.
May it perfectly satisfy all my yearnings, bodily and spiritual.
May it unite me more closely to you, the one true God.
May it bring me to the happy possession of the goal I am seeking.
—Prayer after Communion, St. Thomas Aquinas[19]

Exercising the Virtues

It is not a question of simply knowing what God wants from each of us in the various situations of life. The individual must do what God wants, as we are reminded in the words that Mary, the Mother of Jesus, addressed to the servants at Cana: "Do whatever he tells you" (John 2:5).
— St. John Paul II, Christifideles Laici, *58*

THE PATH OF GROWING IN Christian virtue, of developing all the powers of our nature in harmony with their true purposes, is the path that will lead us to the fulfillment that we are created for and that we long for. But how do we grow in virtue?

Growth in virtue requires exercising virtue. It sounds so simple. And it is. Human nature is made this way. When we nourish and use the powers of our soul properly, they grow, just like muscles. If a young man wants to improve his tennis game, he needs to keep playing tennis; he needs to exercise his skills and abilities so they develop. Just thinking and dreaming about it will get him nowhere. Likewise, if we want to mature in our love for God, if we want to grow in the virtues that unite our heart, mind, emotions, and will to the Lord so we can have deeper communion with him, then we need to nourish and exercise them. And only in that communion will we find lasting happiness.

THE VIRTUES GROW TOGETHER

The history of Christian spirituality has provided various categorizations of the different virtues. It can be helpful to study these and delve, for example, into the distinctions between courage and perseverance, or chastity and purity, or distributive justice and commutative justice. Yet, since the human person is an organic whole, when an individual exercises one virtue, his or her entire spiritual organism is engaged and therefore benefits. In a sense, it is impossible to grow in one of the fundamental virtues without also growing in the others. Just as a baby's five fingers all grow out together—the middle finger doesn't grow to maturity first before the pinky starts to grow—so the Christian who responds docilely and generously to the guidance of the Holy Spirit grows in all the basic virtues simultaneously. The other side of this coin is also true: If we are negligently deficient in any one of the basic virtues, we will only have limited progress in the others. It's important to keep this in mind when we begin discussing what activities you can engage in to exercise your virtue.

THE PRIMARY SPIRITUAL WORKOUT

One activity exercises every Christian virtue simultaneously and intensely. Without it, spiritual maturity is impossible. This activity is prayer.

Prayer is conversation with God, listening to him and speaking to him. It exercises faith, because God's presence, his voice, is almost always mediated by something—the Bible, the beauty of nature, music, other spiritual books. Talking with God simply can't happen without faith: "For we walk by faith, not by sight" (2 Cor. 5:7, RSV).

Prayer exercises hope, because we don't always feel immediate consolation and satisfaction in prayer; our confidence in God's faithfulness motivates us to continue investing in prayer even when results seem long in coming. We know that by praying we are following Christ's command to "store up treasures in heaven, where neither moth nor decay destroys, nor thieves break in and steal" (Matt. 6:20), but often we don't actually enjoy those treasures during our time of prayer.

Christian prayer exercises charity, because we address God as our Father, and we open our hearts to him just as he opens his heart to us; Christian prayer is much more than a mere self-tranquilizing technique or formulaic superstition. The *Catechism* reminds us of this powerfully when it summarizes how we must engage with the mystery of God's revelation in Christ:

> This mystery, then, requires that the faithful believe in it, that they celebrate it, and that they live from it in a vital and personal relationship with the living and true God. This relationship is prayer. (CCC, 2558)

Prayer exercises the cardinal virtues, too, because God deserves our worship and confidence (justice), because prayer takes effort and self-sacrifice since it is not always pleasing (temperance and fortitude), because praying involves overcoming fears and doubts about whether God loves us or what others may say about us (fortitude), and because the true value of prayer is evident only to the wise (prudence). Prayer truly is the one activity that will most help us exercise our heart, mind, soul, and strength in loving God.

How Much Should I Pray?

In our post-modern, secularized culture, growth in prayer requires commitment and discipline—remember, we are to love God with *all* our mind and strength, not only when we happen to feel like it. The basic staples that Christians should include in their spiritual diet include daily, weekly, and seasonal commitments. These will change, vary, and develop as our relationship with God deepens, but here is a sensible starting guideline.

On a daily basis, we need to engage in both vocal and mental prayer. Vocal prayer uses prayers composed by other people—like the prayers that have appeared at the end of each chapter in this book. We can find favorite vocal prayers and use them to offer our day to God in the morning, to put the day in his hands in the evening, or to check in with him at noontime. Mental prayer is more intimate. It involves listening to God through reflecting on a Bible passage or a spiritual commentary on the Bible or on some aspect of our faith. That reflection spurs us to speak to God in the silence of our hearts, using our own words—thanking him, asking for forgiveness, praising him, or simply opening our hearts to him. Without daily mental prayer, without a daily God-time, our other efforts to grow spiritually lose their grip; we end up just spinning our wheels. Ten minutes a day of mental prayer, preferably in the morning, is a reasonable place to start. Many solid and substantial daily devotionals are available to help our mental prayer.

Weekly, God commands us to come alongside the rest of our spiritual family to worship him by attending Sunday Mass (and living the Lord's Day well). We should do everything possible to receive Holy Communion on the Lord's Day. The Eucharist is the grace-filled food for our Christian journey, without which we will surely "collapse on the way" (Matt. 15:32).

Seasonally, we should follow closely the rhythms of the liturgical year, using the sacrament of confession (another guaranteed outpouring of grace) during each period and staying engaged in the parish celebrations (processions, penitential services, special feast days). The Holy Spirit uses this liturgical rhythm to form our hearts according to God's priorities and not the world's. A yearly spiritual retreat or pilgrimage is also as essential as a yearly medical checkup, if we are serious about seeking first Christ's kingdom.

Books and seminars and formation videos that can teach us how to live more and more deeply each of these prayer commitments abound (you can find some recommendations in the Appendix). But none of them can make the commitment for us, and none of them can pray for us. Not even God can do that. We must decide to put our heart, soul, mind, and strength to work in "seeking the face of the Lord" through the great gift of Christian prayer (see Ps. 27:8).

Questions for Personal Reflection or Group Discussion

1. What idea in this chapter struck you most and why?
2. How would you describe the frequency and quality of your prayer life?

3. When have you had a positive experience of prayer? What led to it, and what did you do to follow up with it?

4. Archbishop Fulton Sheen created a television program called *Life Is Worth Living* that became the highest-rated prime-time show in American during the fifties. He reached tens of millions of viewers every single week. When asked what his "secret" was, he said that it all flowed from his unbreakable commitment to spend at least a full hour in personal prayer, in a chapel where the Holy Eucharist was present, every single morning. What will you do today to begin improving your prayer life?

- I will buy a good Catholic prayer book.
- I will talk to someone I know who has a mature prayer life and ask them how they got there.
- I will find a friend and make a daily prayer pact, agreeing to hold each other accountable for this commitment
- (Write your own resolution) I will _____

    _____

    _____

    _____

Concluding Prayer

My Jesus, on this new day I renew my consecration and offer myself to you, for you to make use of my soul, my body, my strength, my mind, and my will as you please. I am totally yours; keep me faithful to your friendship. Enable me to live this day with the eager desire to glorify the Father, fulfilling his will faithfully and constantly. Give me a steadfast heart, that will not forsake you by squandering my love, a generous chaste heart, unstained by any unworthy affection, an unselfish heart, only consumed by your love and the interests of your kingdom, a conquering heart, like your very own. Grant, Lord Jesus, that all of us who are consecrated to you in your holy Catholic Church will be more faithful and courageous apostles of your kingdom. Amen.

—FROM THE PRAYER BOOK OF THE LEGIONARIES OF CHRIST

Spiritual Input

Since man can neither live nor understand himself without love, I want to
appeal to you to grow in humanity, to give absolute priority to the values
of the spirit, and to transform yourselves into "new men" by increasingly
recognizing and accepting the presence of God in your life: the presence of
a God who is Love; of a Father who loves each one of us for the whole of
eternity, who created us by love and who loved us so much that he gave
up his Only Son to forgive us our sins, to reconcile us to Him, and to
enable us to live with Him in a communion of love which will never end.
—St. John Paul II, Message for World Youth Day, 1987

I N OUR POST-CHRISTIAN CULTURE, THE spiritual, moral, and intellectual atmosphere that surrounds our daily activities contains anti-
Christian values. Our cultural environment is polluted by a worldview
that promotes hedonism, secularism, relativism, consumerism, and
a host of other toxic perspectives. These can steadily corrode our
Christ-centered way of seeing ourselves, others, and the world around
us, just as coal dust gradually sickens a miner's respiratory system.

In previous eras, popular culture itself was imbued with the
Christian worldview, so even popular books and dramas reinforced
the Christian value system. But now that is no longer the case.
Instead, our minds are flooded every day by messages (advertisements,
films, TV shows, news, music) that directly contradict the Christian
worldview. That will have its effect on how we think and what we
value. In fact, this is one of the reasons the Church is suffering so
much from so-called cafeteria Catholicism. Cafeteria Catholics get

much of their Catholic formation from secular sources (*The New York Times, Newsweek*), and so they simply can't understand why the Church would ever suggest alternatives to such popular and seemingly reasonable (from a secular point of view) propositions like artificial contraception, artificial reproduction, and gay marriage.

Because of this ongoing flood of secular ideas, we have to consciously nourish our minds with authentic Christian teaching in order to avoid being poisoned. If we don't intentionally and intelligently counteract this cultural pollution, we will fall away from healthy spiritual fervor into spiritual mediocrity, which is only a short distance away from habitual, soul-killing rebellion against and abandonment of the one thing needed for our authentic fulfillment now and forever (see Luke 10:42). We have to breathe fresh spiritual air every day if we want to keep our spiritual organism healthy and growing.

Spiritual Reading

Spiritual reading is one tried and true antidote to cultural pollution. It consists of regularly (daily is best) reading something that explains an aspect of Catholic truth in an attractive, enriching way. Its function is to help reinforce and deepen our Christian view of ourselves and of the world around us. It's ongoing formation for a Christian mind.

Spiritual reading is either instructive or refreshing. It either informs our minds so that we learn to think and understand more and more in harmony with God's revelation, or it refreshes what we already know or have learned by making it shine out more clearly once again. In either case, it counteracts the seductive, secularizing messages that saturate our cultural milieu. This is why it's such an important spiritual discipline. It plants seeds of Christian truth in our mind, and they grow and germinate in our subconscious as we go about our daily business. These seeds often flower during our times of mental prayer. In fact, spiritual reading frequently provides topics, ideas, or insights that are excellent material for Christian meditation.

How to Do Spiritual Reading

Spiritual reading differs from regular reading not only in the content, but also in the method. You don't need to spend a lot of time doing spiritual reading, and you don't need to read fast. The idea is simply to taste, chew on, and swallow some healthy Catholic concepts every single day.

The distinction between spiritual reading and mental prayer (or meditation) is the end result. The goal of your meditation is to converse with the Lord about what matters to him and what matters to you. The reflection and consideration that forms part of your meditation is meant to spur that conversation in your heart. The goal of spiritual reading is to inform your mind; it doesn't advance or finish with a prayerful conversation (though that can sometimes pop up spontaneously, which is fine).

Today's Catholics have at their fingertips an abundance of good material for spiritual reading—old and new books easy to find, old and new articles and websites easy to access. But if you're not a reader, or if you think you don't have time, you can get creative. Listening to recordings of spiritual talks, homilies, or conferences (or books on tape, or even good Catholic podcasts) while you drive or exercise can also do the trick.

An Eye to Entertainment

We all need to rest and relax sometimes, and enjoying a good movie, game, novel, show, or trip downtown can often help that happen. Unfortunately, however, this area of human endeavor has also been affected by post-Christian cultural pollution. Pastimes we engage in for necessary rest and relaxation should be both enjoyable and edifying. They should refresh us, but they should also encourage our Christian values—or at least not discourage them.

This doesn't mean that we should hide away in a Christian bunker somewhere and avoid looking at or listening to anything not explicitly biblical—the Puritan experiment failed in the end, after all, and generations of saints have nourished their minds and hearts on all the great artistic achievements of the human family, including pagan ones. But it does mean that we need to be smart and intentional about the food we give our imagination and the stimulation we give our emotions. We need to avoid input that could be an occasion of sin for us or for others, and we need to find out what truly helps us get the rest and relaxation necessary to maintain a healthy emotional and physiological profile. Proper rest and entertainment are in the service of our life mission; they are not our goal. Christians don't live for the weekend; we live for loving Christ and building up his kingdom.

NEWS AND CURRENT EVENTS

A final area of input that can help us show and grow our love for God has to do with staying informed about current issues and events. With the digital news cycle that never ends, we can be tempted to think that we need to know the backstory behind every headline that pops onto our mental screen, from whatever source. Not true. The digital world of information allows us, for the first time in history, to stay duly informed about the issues and events most relevant to us as Christians. We can choose the sources of our information so that we fill our minds with what we choose to think about, not what a secular producer wants us to think about. And that choice should be made regularly and intentionally with our life's true purpose in mind.

In short, moving forward along the path of Christian virtue requires paying attention to the map the Lord has given us and avoiding seductive sidetracks. As St. Paul put it:

Finally, brothers, whatever is true, whatever is honorable, whatever is just, whatever is pure, whatever is lovely, whatever is gracious, if there is any excellence and if there is anything worthy of praise, think about these things. (Phil. 4:8, RSV)

Questions for Personal Reflection or Group Discussion

1. What idea in this chapter struck you most and why?
2. In your daily life, what are the most common sources of the ideas that go into your mind and imagination?

3. What do you usually do for rest and relaxation? What can you do to make your relaxation activities healthier?

4. One of the most admirable and inspiring aspects of monastic architecture is the balance it achieves between visual silence and visual stimulus. In order to create an atmosphere conducive to prayer, recollection, and interior depth, architects carefully choose and arrange all the external décor, from the plants in the courtyard to the paintings on the walls of the dining room. The result is a physical atmosphere of harmony, beauty, and a sense of peace that you can almost touch. This is one reason monasteries have been able to produce so many saints. What will you do today to fill your mind and soul with what is true, honorable, just, pure, lovely, and gracious?

- I will visit a monastery and spend some time absorbing the atmosphere.
- I will decide at the start of each week what I will use for entertainment and recreation, and I will stick to that decision.
- I will consciously decide how much time each day (or week) I really need to dedicate to staying caught up on current events, and then I will stick to that time allotment.
- (Write your own resolution) I will _____

_____

_____

_____

Concluding Prayer

Lord Jesus, I give you my hands to do your work. I give you my feet to follow your path. I give you my eyes to see as you see. I give you my tongue to speak your words. I give you my mind so you can think in me. I give you my spirit so you can pray in me. Above all I give you my heart so in me you can love your Father and all people. I give you my whole self so you can grow in me, till it is you who live and work and pray in me. Amen.

—FROM THE PRAYER BOOK OF THE REGNUM CHRISTI MOVEMENT

Hungering for God's Will

*Yes, discovering Christ is the finest adventure of your life. But it is
not enough to discover Him just once. Discovering Him becomes
an ongoing invitation to seek Him always more, to come to know
Him still better through prayer, participating in the sacraments,
meditating on his Word, through catechesis and listening to the
teachings of the Church. This is our most important task.*

— St. John Paul II, Message for World Youth Day, August 1989

J ESUS IS THE CENTER OF every authentically Christian life. Loving
God with all our heart, soul, mind, and strength means loving
Jesus more and more and more, because Jesus is God-become-man,
God-with-us. And loving Jesus means following him, learning from
him, obeying him, becoming more like him, and letting him be our
strength and salvation, as he continually invites us to do:

> "Come to me, all you who labor and are burdened, and I
> will give you rest. Take my yoke upon you and learn from
> me, for I am meek and humble of heart; and you will find
> rest for yourselves. For my yoke is easy, and my burden light."
> (Matt. 11:28–30)

WHAT MADE JESUS TICK?

If the spiritual life is, in its most basic elements, nothing less than
following Christ and imitating him—and that is precisely how St. Paul
summed it up: "Be imitators of me, as I am of Christ" (1 Cor.
11:1)—then Christ's deepest desire should be our deepest desire.

During his life on earth, his very food, the thing that he hungered for and the thing that nourished and strengthened him, was "to do the will of the one who sent me" (John 4:34). So central was this idea to his life and teaching that he placed it at the very heart of the one prayer that he taught us, the Our Father: "This is how you are to pray: Our Father in heaven, hallowed be your name, your kingdom come, your will be done, on earth as in heaven . . . " (Matt. 6:9–10).

WHAT IS GOD'S WILL?

The Father's will—finding it, accepting it, and carrying it out with love—was the rule for Christ's life, and so it should be the rule for the life of every Christian. And indeed, if we make this our food, as Jesus did, then our heart, soul, mind, and strength will find themselves fully engaged in our task of loving God, because the essence of love is union, becoming one with the beloved.

God's will is his wise and loving project for the full flourishing of all his creatures, especially those of us created in his own image and likeness. By striving to identify with that project in the here and now of our daily lives, we become co-workers in bringing it to completion. What greater love could we show him than that? And what more direct way could we find to achieve the purpose for which we were created? This is why Jesus, who modeled perfectly the love and purpose we are called to pursue, hungered and yearned "to do the will of the one who sent me" (John 4:34). As he explained to his persecutors: "I cannot do anything on my own. . . . I do not seek my own will but the will of the one who sent me" (John 5:30).

But the phrase God's will can be abused. People have distorted it to justify irresponsible passivity in the face of evil, self-centered and damaging manipulation of others, and exaggerated asceticism. We need to unpack the term so we can better understand what Jesus wants and better unite ourselves to him. Breaking down the concept into two broad sub-categories will help avoid confusion. From our human perspective, God's will can be either indicative or permissive.

God's Indicative Will

God can indicate that he wants us to do certain things. This is his indicative will (as opposed to his permissive will, the things he permits to happen without actually commanding them; this will be discussed in the next chapter). God's indicative will always flows from his wisdom and his love. In other words, whatever he wants us to do is for our greatest good. In this category we find the Ten Commandments, the commandments of the New Testament, the commandments and teachings of the Church, the responsibilities of our state in life, and specific inspirations of the Holy Spirit. If we want to know God's will for our lives, those are the places we need to start.

The field of God's indicative will is vast. It touches all the normal activities and relationships of every day, which are the arenas where, through our choices, we grow in virtue or in vice, thus deepening or dampening our communion with God. It also includes the endless possibilities of the works of mercy (feeding the hungry, instructing the ignorant, comforting the sorrowful, etc.), by which we carry out our Lord's commandment to "love your neighbor as yourself" (Mark 12:31).

Going Even Deeper

Yet God's indicative will not only consists of *what* we do, but also in *how* we do it. This opens up another path of growth in Christian virtue, most especially the theological virtues. We can wash the dishes (responsibilities of our state in life) with resentment and self-pity, or with love, care, and supernatural joy. We can attend Sunday Mass (the third commandment and a commandment of the Church) apathetically and reluctantly, or with conviction, faith, and attention. We can drive to work (responsibilities of our state in life) seething at the traffic jams, or exercising patience. When we ask ourselves, "What is God's will for me?" 88 percent of the time (more or less), God's indicative will is crystal clear: lovingly follow the commandments, lovingly carry out our daily responsibilities, and look for practical ways to love our neighbors as God has loved us. To seek, accept, embrace, and fulfill this will for our lives is the surest way to engaging our heart, soul, mind, and strength fully in loving God.

Much of the Church's tradition of spiritual teaching is dedicated to exploring the implications of and the reasons behind these indicative commandments; the more thoroughly we understand them, the more of our heart, soul, mind, and strength we can put into obeying them. And that obedience is the path to the wisdom, peace, and fulfillment we yearn for—what Jesus referred to as blessedness: "Blessed are those who hear the word of God and observe it" (Luke 11:28).

Questions for Personal Reflection or Group Discussion

1. What idea in this chapter struck you most and why?

2. Make a list of the responsibilities of your state in life and put them in order of importance. How easily and fully do you recognize and embrace God's will in those responsibilities?

3. How deeply do you hunger to discover and fulfill God's will in your life?

4. Although most of the time we know what God's indicative will is for us (through the commandments, Christ's teachings, and our normal life responsibilities), there are times when we aren't sure: *Should I accept this new job offer? Should we move? Should I join the seminary? Should I intervene in a family member's difficult situation?* In these cases, the traditional path of discerning God's will for us consists in asking for light and guidance in prayer, getting good advice from trusted sources, and taking time to reflect on the different options. Usually in the end the path becomes clear. And even if it doesn't, as long as we have done our homework, so to speak, God will work with whatever we decide. What will you do today to become more aware of God's will for your life?

- I will ask myself after each meal, "God, what is your will for me right now?" And I'll listen for whatever answer comes to my mind and my heart.

- I will find and read a good article describing one of my key life areas (a good article on fatherhood or motherhood, for example, or one on ethics in the workplace, etc.).

- I will pay attention to my initial reaction the next time I am not sure what to do. How spontaneously do I involve God in my efforts to find an answer?

- (Write your own resolution) I will _____

  _____

  _____

  _____

Concluding Prayer

Holy Spirit, gentle guest and consoler of my soul,
Enlighten my mind to know the divine will for me;
Inflame my heart to love it passionately;
Strengthen my will to accomplish it as perfectly as you ask of me;
Lastly, Spirit of love, grant me the grace I need to
respond faithfully to your holy inspirations. Amen.

—FROM THE PRAYER BOOK OF THE LEGIONARIES OF CHRIST

Taking Up the Cross

For if, in fact, the Cross was to human eyes Christ's emptying of himself, at the same time it was in the eyes of God his being lifted up. On the Cross, Christ attained and fully accomplished his mission: by fulfilling the will of the Father, he at the same time fully realized himself. . . . Suffering is also an invitation to manifest the moral greatness of man, his spiritual maturity. Proof of this has been given, down through the generations, by the martyrs and confessors of Christ, faithful to the words; "And do not fear those who kill the body, but cannot kill the soul" (Matthew 10:28).
– St. John Paul II, Salvifici Doloris, 22

S EEKING AND FULFILLING GOD'S INDICATIVE will in our lives – his commandments, his inspirations, and the normal responsibilities that we have simply because we are members of a family, a workplace, a community, and a society – is our sure path to spiritual growth. It unites us to Christ, who made his Father's will the overarching rule of his life, and thereby deepens more and more our intimate union and communion with God. And that is the source of our happiness.

God's Permissive Will

But the phrase God's will also touches another category of life-experience: suffering. Suffering, of one type or another, is our constant companion as we journey through this fallen world. God has revealed that suffering was not part of his original plan, but rather the offspring of original sin, which shattered the harmony of God's creation. His indicative will to our first parents in the

Garden of Eden was for them not to eat the fruit of "the tree of the knowledge of good and evil" (Gen. 2:17, RSV). They disobeyed. Human nature fell; creation fell; evil attained a certain predominance in the human condition, giving rise to "the overwhelming misery which oppresses men and their inclination towards evil and death" (CCC, 403).

Here is where the distinction between God's indicative and permissive will comes in. God did not desire or command Adam and Eve to rebel against his plan, but he did *permit* them to do so; he gave them a certain degree of freedom that made disobedience to his indicative will (moral evil) possible. Likewise, throughout human history, God does not will evil to happen, but he does *permit* it. He certainly didn't explicitly will the Holocaust, for example, but, on the other hand, he certainly did permit it. His indicative will doesn't lead to the abuse of innocent children, but his permissive will sometimes allows his free creatures to disobey his indicative will and commit such evils.

The question of why God permits some evil and the suffering that comes from it, even the suffering of innocents, is an extremely hard question to answer. Only the Christian faith as a whole gives a satisfactory response to it, a response that can gradually penetrate our hearts and minds through prayer, study, and the help of God's grace.

St. Augustine's short answer is worth mentioning, however. He wrote that if God permits evil, it is only because he knows he can bring out of that evil a greater good. We may not see that greater good right away; we may not see it at all during our earthly journey, in fact. But Christ's resurrection (Easter Sunday) is the unbreakable and undying promise that God's omnipotence and wisdom are never trumped by the apparent triumphs of evil and suffering (Good Friday).

Thus, only by faith can we begin to understand why obedience to God's will also includes accepting the painful things that he permits, trusting that in our Christ-centered response to them (which often involves resisting and correcting evils) we will be contributing to building up his eternal kingdom in our hearts and in the world.

TAKE UP YOUR CROSS

In this context we can brave a brief comment on the one condition that Jesus lays down for anyone who wants to follow him:

> Then [Jesus] said to all, "If anyone wishes to come after me, he must deny himself and take up his cross daily and follow me. For whoever wishes to save his life will lose it, but whoever loses his life for my sake will save it." (Luke 9:23-24)

Growing in love requires self-denial, self-forgetfulness, self-giving. And in this fallen world, self-giving is often painful (in heaven it won't be). It involves taking up the cross, just as Jesus took up his own cross in order to show the extent of his love for the Father and for us. The cross symbolizes the painful self-sacrifice that growing in love requires in this fallen world. If we truly desire to grow in loving God, to learn to love him with all our all, we will have to carry crosses.

The cross is suffering made fruitful through faith and love. When God's indicative or permissive will in our life contradicts our natural preference (our self-centered, human will), we experience the cross. His will is like the vertical beam, and our natural preference is like the horizontal beam. When they are opposed, we are faced with a grace-filled opportunity. By choosing to accept God's will when we would prefer something else, we exercise our faith, hope, and love more intensely than in any other possible situation. We show that we trust him, not because he fits into our limited, human calculations, but precisely because we believe and hope in his infinite wisdom, power, and goodness. *That's* the supernatural virtue that unites us more fully to God, deepening our trust in him, the trust which is found at the heart of all interpersonal relationships. And when we exercise that virtue more intensely, it grows more quickly and surely, and our communion with God expands and deepens.

THE HIGH ROAD TO HOLINESS

The Lord sends and permits crosses in our lives because he knows they are the high road to holiness when we live them in union with him, saturating them with faith, hope, and love. As Jesus explained to his twelve apostles, almost all of whom ended up dying martyrs' deaths, he prunes the branches of his vine only so that those branches will bear more fruit:

> "I am the true vine, and my Father is the vine grower. He takes away every branch in me that does not bear fruit, and every one that does he prunes so that it bears more fruit." (John 15:1–2)

When we feel the pruning shears purifying our still-imperfect hearts, when we feel the weight of the cross pressing down on our limited minds and souls and strength, we know God is hard at work, and we can abandon ourselves to his care. It is then, above all, when we recognize that growth in love, holiness, and lasting happiness is only 1 percent up to us and 99 percent up to the Lord. And "therefore," as St. Paul explained, "I am content with weaknesses, insults, hardships, persecutions, and constraints, for the sake of Christ; for when I am weak, then I am strong" (2 Cor. 12:10).

It is through bearing our crosses with Christ that we enter into the indescribable experience of joy that comes with the Resurrection. For Jesus, the darkness and suffering of Good Friday blossomed into the brilliant light of Easter Sunday—as a medieval phrase put it: *per crucem ad lucem* (through the cross to the light). If we are in him, the same will be true for us.

Questions for Personal Reflection or Group Discussion

1. What idea in this chapter struck you most and why?

2. How do you usually respond to suffering in your own life, and why? How do you usually respond to suffering in the lives of those around you?

3. What are your most common daily crosses right now, and how are you responding to them? How would the Lord like you to respond to them?

4. When St. Joan of Arc was being burned at the stake as a martyr, she asked for one thing. While the flames began to climb up toward her and burn her, she cried out for "a cross, hold up a cross!" One of the soldiers nearby had compassion on her and made a makeshift cross out of pieces of wood, attaching it to the tip of his pike. He then held it up high, above the flames so St. Joan could see it. As soon as she caught sight of the cross, while the flames were burning into her own flesh, she smiled. She died gazing on Christ's cross and drawing all her strength from it. What will you do today to remind yourself that the cross is really the high road to the lasting happiness that you yearn for?

- I will watch the movie *The Passion of The Christ* from the following perspective: "Jesus suffered all of this in order to prove that absolutely nothing, not even my most horrible sins, can diminish his love for me."
- When I find myself complaining about something, I will turn that complaint into a silent prayer to God, just as Jesus did on the eve of his crucifixion when he was sweating blood in the Garden of Gethsemane.
- When some suffering is happening in my life, either to me or to a loved one, and I can't do anything to alleviate it, I will say a prayer to the Blessed Virgin Mary and use my imagination to picture her standing at the foot of the cross, helplessly watching her innocent son suffer his horrible crucifixion.
- (Write your own resolution) I will _____
  _____
  _____
  _____

Concluding Prayer

*Pierce, most sweet Lord Jesus, my inmost heart with the most
dear and penetrating wound of your love. . . . May my heart
ever draw near to you, seek you, glimpse you, be drawn to
you and find you, think of you, speak of you, and do all that
it does for the glory of your name, humbly and carefully and
delightedly, eagerly and passionately and persevering to the end.
Thus may you alone always be my hope, all my confidence,
my joy, my rest and my peace, all that charms me, my
fragrance, my sweetness, my food, my nourishment, my
refuge, my help, my wisdom, my portion, my possession, my
treasure. In you may my mind and my heart be fixed and
secure and rooted forever without any change. Amen.*

—St. Bonaventure[20]

Loving One Another as Christ Loves Us

To be able to discover the actual will of the Lord in our lives always involves the following: a receptive listening to the Word of God and the Church, fervent and constant prayer, recourse to a wise and loving spiritual guide, and a faithful discernment of the gifts and talents given by God, as well as the diverse social and historic situations in which one lives.
—St. John Paul II, Christifideles Laici, 58

ALTHOUGH EACH ONE OF US has a personal relationship with God, that relationship takes root and grows within a larger network of relationships within the Church. When we are baptized, we are inserted into Christ's mystical body; we are made members of "a chosen race, a royal priesthood, a holy nation, a people of his own," as St. Peter reminds us in 1 Peter 2:9.

THE CHRISTIAN IDENTIFICATION CARD

The fact that we are called to be Christ's companions (in the plural), called to walk with him in loving fellowship with our brothers and sisters in the Church, is so important to Jesus that he made it the main identification badge of all Christians. During the Last Supper, he told his apostles that to be his disciples meant following his commandments, and he condensed those commandments to one: "Love one another as I have loved you" (John 15:12).

He went on to say that the world will recognize us as his followers precisely through our fellowship, through our living in love and faith-filled union with each other: "This is how all will know that you are my disciples, if you have love for one another" (John 13:35). The key theological reason behind the importance Jesus gives to this loving unity among his followers goes back to the very beginning when God created us. He created the human family "in his image . . . in the image of God he created them" (Gen. 1:27). God's core identity is a Trinity: one divine nature and three divine persons. He is a community, a family—a unique one, because he is only one God, not three gods. The Church is God's way of redeeming this damaged aspect of the fallen human race, this divine image in which we were created:

> [God] calls together all men, scattered and divided by sin, into the unity of his family, the Church. To accomplish this, when the fullness of time had come, God sent his Son as the Redeemer and Savior. (CCC, 1)

But there is a practical reason, too. Simply put, we need each other. We can't finish our Christian pilgrimage alone. We need the strength, the light, the guidance, the encouragement, and the help that comes from traveling with other pilgrims.

THE FIRST FORM OF FELLOWSHIP

The first and fundamental manifestation of Christian fellowship comes in the worship of the Christian community, and this is expressed most intensely and fully in the celebration of the sacraments. Christian fellowship is only Christian because its core is Christ himself. This is why Jesus summoned his first apostles "that they might be with him" (Mark 3:14). He is the Savior; he is the Redeemer. It was through the mystery of his passion, death, and resurrection that the Church—the renewed communion of mankind with God and in God with each other—was born.

The celebration of the sacraments links the Church to that mystery. The whole liturgical life of the new people of God is like the heartbeat of that Church: "Through the liturgy, Christ, our redeemer and high priest, continues the work of our redemption in, with, and through his Church" (CCC, 1069). The liturgy also introduces us to the spiritually fruitful, and even necessary, devotion to saints and angels and, in a special way, to the Blessed Virgin Mary—important allies in our spiritual battles.

The Sunday Eucharist is the center of the Church's liturgical life. But the other sacraments are also opportunities to live and grow and benefit from this fellowship. We go to confession to ask for and receive God's forgiveness and also for reconciliation with the community that we damage by our sins. We comfort the sick and dying by bringing them Christ's holy anointing. We gather with our fellow Christian pilgrims for baptisms and confirmations, for marriages and ordinations, supporting and being supported by one another even as we open up the floodgates of God's grace toward every corner of human experience.

And the primary place for this sacramental fellowship is the parish—a kind of local incarnation, through the Church's diocesan structure, of the universal Church. Staying plugged in and contributing to our parishes or our religious communities is the bread and butter of Christian fellowship.

The Second Form of Fellowship

The Christian family, built up around the sacrament of marriage, is another place where this loving fellowship is meant to be lived out. In fact, Christian tradition, spiritualizing a term originally used to refer only to buildings, has come to see the family as a "domestic church." The natural bonds and affection that flow from familial relations are bridges, so to speak, over which God's grace can flow in wonderful abundance if we consciously build our families around their real center: Jesus and his truth, his love, his mission.

It has never been easy to do this, because the effects of original sin are still with us, and our selfishness and woundedness make healthy family life a demanding work in progress. In a post-Christian culture, where family life is under attack legally, economically, educationally, and culturally, building the domestic church is harder than ever; it takes an almost heroic effort. But God's grace will always come to our aid.

THE ROLE OF FAITH-BASED FRIENDSHIPS

Friendship is one of the most beautiful human experiences, and Jesus himself praised and prized it. "I no longer call you slaves," he told his apostles at the Last Supper, "because a slave does not know what his master is doing. I have called you friends, because I have told you everything I have heard from my Father" (John 15:15). Friendship has been valued in every period and place of human history, even long before the time of Christ. It is another manifestation of our being created in the image of God, created to live in communion of life with other persons. It contributes joy, comfort, inspiration, and meaning to our lives.

But with the coming of Christ, even this beautiful human reality has been enhanced. A faith-based, Christ-centered friendship is a deeper, stronger, and longer-lasting friendship than any of the ancient philosophers could have imagined, for one simple reason: Christ himself is part of it. He promised this in one of the most beautiful verses of the New Testament: "For where two or three are gathered together in my name, there am I in the midst of them" (Matt. 18:20, RSV).

Faith-based friendships are an important aspect of Christian fellowship; they help keep us accountable, they help support us in times of temptation, they help heal our emotional wounds, they spur us on to growth in virtue, they delight and comfort us at the deeper levels of our soul, and they help keep Jesus close to us.

Of course, this doesn't mean that we can't have non-Christian friends, but we do need to make a point of investing in some friendships that are built with natural as well as supernatural ties. If our faith is our highest priority, we will feel the need for friends who share that priority. And if we don't look for them and invest in them, we may gradually find our priorities getting confused. St. Paul gave a warning in this regard to the Christians in Corinth: "Do not be led astray," he wrote to them; "bad company corrupts good morals" (1 Cor. 15:33, RSV).

THE BENEFITS OF SPIRITUAL DIRECTION

Finally, growing to spiritual maturity requires the direct assistance of a spiritual coach, which Christian tradition generally calls a spiritual director. We need an ongoing relationship with someone who knows the spiritual ropes, who has traveled the road ahead of us and has a healthy share of the gift of counsel, who can help uncover our blind spots and discern how the Holy Spirit is moving in our lives and how we should respond. We need teachers, mentors, coaches, trainers, and guides in every other area of human life where we want to improve and grow, so it only makes sense that we would need one here as well. As Pope Benedict XVI explained to a group of future spiritual directors:

> The Church continues to recommend the practice of spiritual direction, not only to all those who wish to follow the Lord up close, but to every Christian who wishes to live responsibly his baptism, that is, the new life in Christ.[21]

Questions for Personal Reflection or Group Discussion

1. What idea in this chapter struck you most and why?

2. What characteristics of your daily life make it hard for you to have meaningful fellowship?

3. What have been your most meaningful family experiences? What can you do to contribute more to building up your family as a domestic church?

4. The Book of Proverbs observes: "Iron is sharpened by iron; one person sharpens another" (Prov. 27:17). What will you do today to take better advantage of this part of your Christian life?

   - I will invest meaningfully in one of my faith-based friendships by spending time with someone I haven't spent much time with lately.
   - I will start asking around to see about finding a spiritual director.

- I will take some time to see all of the different programs and activities offered by my parish, and I will sign up for one of them.

- (Write your own resolution) I will _____

  _____

  _____

  _____

Concluding Prayer

It is truly right and just that we should always give you
thanks, Lord holy Father, almighty and eternal God.
For you do not cease to spur us on to possess a more abundant
life and, being rich in mercy, you constantly offer pardon
and call on sinners to trust in your forgiveness alone.
Never did you turn away from us, and, though time and again
we have broken your covenant, you have bound the human
family to yourself through Jesus your Son, our Redeemer, with
a new bond of love so tight that it can never be undone.
Even now you set before your people a time of grace and
reconciliation, and, as they turn back to you in spirit, you grant
them hope in Christ Jesus and a desire to be of service to all,
while they entrust themselves more fully to the Holy Spirit.
And so, filled with wonder, we extol the power of your love, and
proclaiming our joy at the salvation that comes from you, we join in
the heavenly hymn of countless hosts, as without end we acclaim . . .

—ROMAN MISSAL, PREFACE FOR RECONCILIATION I

PART VII

YOU ARE CALLED

"The kingdom of heaven is like a landowner who went out at dawn to hire laborers for his vineyard. After agreeing with them for the usual daily wage, he sent them into his vineyard. Going out about nine o'clock, he saw others standing idle in the marketplace, and he said to them, 'You too go into my vineyard, and I will give you what is just.' So they went off. . . . [And] he went out again around noon, and around three o'clock, and did likewise. Going out about five o'clock, he found others standing around, and said to them, 'Why do you stand here idle all day?' They answered, 'Because no one has hired us.' He said to them, 'You too go into my vineyard.' When it was evening the owner of the vineyard said to his foreman, 'Summon the laborers and give them their pay, beginning with the last and ending with the first. . . .'"

MATTHEW 20:1–3, 5–8

There Is Work to Do

The gospel parable sets before our eyes the Lord's vast vineyard and
the multitude of persons, both women and men, who are called and
sent forth by him to labor in it. The vineyard is the whole world
(cf. Mt 13:38), which is to be transformed according to the plan
of God in view of the final coming of the Kingdom of God.
—St. John Paul II, Christifideles Laici, 1

I N THE EARLY CHURCH, SOME fresh Christian converts had the wrong
idea of how Christ's followers were supposed to behave in this
world. They focused so much on Jesus's promise to come again and
bring human history to its fulfillment that they unplugged themselves from normal life. They idly awaited the Lord's Second Coming,
refraining from any productive activity besides prayer. This caused
problems, as can be imagined, for the Christian communities. St. Paul
actually had to address it explicitly in one of his letters, correcting
those Christians in Thessalonica who were remiss in even the most
basic responsibility to make a living:

> In fact, when we were with you, we instructed you that if
> anyone was unwilling to work, neither should that one eat.
> We hear that some are conducting themselves among you in
> a disorderly way, by not keeping busy but minding the busi-
> ness of others. Such people we instruct and urge in the Lord
> Jesus Christ to work quietly and to eat their own food. But
> you, brothers, do not be remiss in doing good. (2 Thess.
> 3:10–13)

Hearts in Heaven — Feet on the Ground

This problem has cropped up at various times in the history of the Church. Outsiders criticized members of the Church for being so focused on the life to come that they disengaged from life here on earth. Perhaps in certain cases the criticism was valid. Yet the actual doctrine of the Church has always stressed the importance of Christians staying engaged in earthly life in order to redeem human experience and shape it in accordance with God's wise plan. Here is how the Second Vatican Council expressed the critics' point of view in its modern context:

> Not to be overlooked among the forms of modern atheism is that which anticipates the liberation of man especially through his economic and social emancipation. This form argues that by its nature religion thwarts this liberation by arousing man's hope for a deceptive future life, thereby divert-ing him from the constructing of the earthly city.[22]

And here is how that same Council asserted the proper understand-ing of the relationship between hope in heaven and active engage-ment here on earth:

> This council exhorts Christians, as citizens of two cities, to strive to discharge their earthly duties conscientiously and in response to the gospel spirit. They are mistaken who, knowing that we have here no abiding city but seek one which is to come, think that they may therefore shirk their earthly respon-sibilities. For they are forgetting that by the faith itself they are more obliged than ever to measure up to these duties, each according to his proper vocation.[23]

In other words, Christians should be hard workers. A follower of Christ knows that this earthly life is an opportunity to develop one's potential and make a difference in the world. As Christian disciples, that opportunity is the arena we are given to exercise our love, to show and grow our commitment to God and neighbor by putting our lives and talents at the service of others.

A Fruitful Partnership

The landowner in the parable of the vineyard goes out to look for work-ers, and he gives them work: "You too go into my vineyard." The vine-yard image appears throughout the history of salvation as recorded in the Bible. The vineyard is a powerful image for the Christian adventure, even on a merely natural level. The Lord owns the vineyard, and the Lord gives the vines the power to produce grapes. He also provides the sunshine, air, and water the vines need to grow and bear fruit. But those God-given elements will only reach their full potential through cultiva-tion by human beings. The vineyard needs intense labor from many workers in order to produce the fine wine it is capable of producing.

It is no coincidence that Jesus's first miracle consisted of turning water into wine. In a sense, the reproduction of that miracle throughout history is the primary work of the Church. Through the cultivation of the vineyard of the world, the Church infuses God's grace into human affairs, transforming the basic elements of the earthly community into the fine wine of "a chosen race, a royal priesthood, a holy nation, a people of his own" (1 Pet. 2:9).

Our Best Work

There truly is work to do—both normal earthly work that needs to be seasoned with Christian love and grace in order to reach its full potential, as well as the more directly supernatural work of spread-ing faith in Jesus Christ. This is the work Jesus calls us all to engage in by sending us into his vineyard. This is the work his Church was established to accomplish.

And it is this work that will give the deepest meaning to our lives. As Pope Francis explained it:

> When the Church summons Christians to take up the task of evangelization, she is simply pointing to the source of authentic personal fulfillment. For here we discover a pro-found law of reality: that life is attained and matures in the measure that it is offered up in order to give life to others. This is certainly what mission means.[24]

And so St. John Paul II tells us that the Church wisely and lovingly invites each one of us, today and every day, to take our unique place in the vineyard of the Lord:

> The mission of salvation is universal; for every person and for the whole person. It is a task which involves the entire People of God, all the faithful. Mission must therefore be the passion of every Christian; a passion for the salvation of the world and ardent commitment to work for the coming of the Father's kingdom.[25]

Questions for Personal Reflection or Group Discussion

1. What idea in this chapter struck you most and why?

2. How fully do you feel part of this work that God has given us to do? In other words, to what extent do you feel you are working in the Lord's vineyard?

3. When you think about this work the Church is called to be engaged in, how does it make you feel? Excited, eager, intimidated, overwhelmed? Why do you think you feel that way?

4. Various secular sociological studies point out that an important ingredient for a happy life is meaningful work. This coheres with the biblical account of the creation of man and woman. When God created us, he gave us work to do—"to cultivate and care for" the earth (Gen. 2:15). Our very nature requires that we feel in some way useful and productive in order to feel fulfilled. The rest of this book will explore the different ways God gives us for meeting this fundamental need as completely as possible. But for today, how will you raise your awareness of this need and seek to fulfill it more healthily?

- I will take time to think about how even my most mundane activities can be useful and meaningful in God's eyes, and I will try to live them with a greater sense of purpose.

- I will identify one of my talents or gifts that tends to be underutilized and find a way to make it productive today.

- I will reflect on which of my duties and responsibilities seem to be the least fulfilling to me and try to figure out why. Then I will commit to a practical or attitudinal adjustment that may help them become more fulfilling and meaningful.

- (Write your own resolution) I will _____

_____

_____

_____

Concluding Prayer

O God, Creator of all things,
who laid down for the human race the law of work,
graciously grant that
by the example of Saint Joseph and under his patronage
we may complete the works you set us to do
and attain the rewards you promise.

—Roman Missal, Collect for May 1,
Feast of St. Joseph the Worker

The Church's Deepest Identity

Evangelizing is in fact the grace and vocation proper to the Church,
her deepest identity. She exists in order to evangelize, that is to say, in
order to preach and teach, to be the channel of the gift of grace, to
reconcile sinners with God, and to perpetuate Christ's sacrifice in the
Mass, which is the memorial of His death and glorious resurrection.
— St. Paul VI, Evangelii Nuntiandi, *14*

W HEN YOU THINK OF THE Catholic Church, what's the first thing
that comes to mind? For many, the Catholic Church is primarily an organization. It has a hierarchical structure that moves from
a local parish priest up to a local bishop and then all the way up to
the pope, the head of the Church. And all the individuals who call
themselves "Catholics" are members of that organization, similar to
the way soldiers are members of an army, or college students are
members of a fraternity or a sorority.

That is true, as far as it goes. The Catholic Church is an organization, with a structured hierarchy and a wide membership. Yet to think
of the Church primarily in that way is like thinking of a human being
only as a skeleton holding together different muscle groups and biological systems, not as a real *person*. The concept is too reductive.

MORE THAN JUST AN ORGANIZATION

What does this organization do? Where does it come from? Where
is it going? What is its purpose? And what characterizes the Church's
members? These questions point toward a more robust understanding of the Church's identity—and therefore a more robust

understanding of our own identity as Catholics. And at the core of
everything is the Church's mission to spread the gospel: "Evangelizing
is in fact the grace and vocation proper to the Church, her deepest
identity. She exists in order to evangelize. . . . "

The word *evangelization* can be used in many different ways, but
we need to distill it down to an essential meaning in order to
achieve clarity in our search for understanding the commandment
to love our neighbors as ourselves. Here is how the *Catechism's* glos-
sary defines evangelization: "the proclamation of Christ and his
gospel (Greek: *evangelion*) by word and the testimony of life, in fulfillment of Christ's command."[26]

The Greek word *evangelion* literally means "good news." From it
derive the English words *evangelist*, which means one who proclaims
the good news, and *evangelize*, which means to proclaim or spread
the good news, and other cognates like *evangelism* and *evangelization*.
The English word *gospel* is a translation of those terms. Just as *gospel*
in Old English comes from two words meaning "good story," so the
original Greek word comes from two words meaning "good
announcement, or news." Latin adopted the Greek word itself,
Latinizing it into *evangelium* and sometimes translated it literally
into *bona anuntiatio*. The same Greek root gives us our word *angels*,
the spiritual beings who often serve as God's "announcers" or messengers throughout the history of salvation.

In the early years of Christianity, the word *evangelion* referred
primarily to all the Church's activity of spreading and promoting
the Christian faith and message (the content of the "good news").
And since all Christians were involved in that activity, all
Christians were evangelizers. Eventually the four authors of the
written accounts of Jesus's life and ministry were referred to as
Evangelists in a more technical sense, and their individual
accounts were entitled Gospels (the Gospel according to Matthew,
Mark, Luke, or John).

Today these technical senses are the most well known, and
unfortunately that reflects a general diminishment of the everyday
Catholic's understanding of the Church's true mission. After all, if

the four Evangelists have already written down the gospel defini-tively in the Gospels, then what's all this talk about evangelization? It's already happened, hasn't it?

THE DYNAMISM OF EVANGELIZATION

Yes and no. This particular piece of good news is more than simple information, though it includes information. The Word of God—what God speaks to us and announces to us in Jesus—is actu-ally alive. It takes root and grows, like a seed, bearing spiritual fruit and transforming human lives, communities, and cultures. The Book of Hebrews alludes to this:

> Indeed, the word of God is living and effective, sharper than any two-edged sword, penetrating even between soul and spirit, joints and marrow, and able to discern reflections and thoughts of the heart. (Heb. 4:12)

So the gospel, the good news about the salvation of sinners through God's grace and mercy, refers to something that has indeed already happened (the coming of Jesus Christ and the accomplishment of his mission on earth). But it also refers to something that is ongoing: a multi-dimensional process of spreading this grace and mercy that will continue until the very end of history, when Jesus comes again to put an end to all evil and suffering.

THE DIMENSIONS OF EVANGELIZATION

The work of evangelization, then, the spreading of the gospel, involves three basic activities, and engaging in these activities con-stitutes the deepest identity of the Church. The Church's organiza-tion is at the service of these activities, of this mission that announc-es and promotes the good news of Jesus Christ. Here are the three dimensions or "moments" of evangelization:

- *Spreading the knowledge of Jesus Christ and his saving mission to those who have not yet heard about it.* This is traditionally called the "mission *ad gentes*," which is Latin for "to the peoples."

Many times, when we think of missionaries, we think of people who are primarily engaged in this work of spreading the gospel to those corners of the world that haven't yet heard it even for the first time. Though a critical dimension of evangelization, this is not the only sector of missionary activity.

- *Instructing and initiating into the life of the Church those who have heard and accepted the gospel but are not yet mature in their faith.* The traditional term most often associated with this work is *catechesis* (another word with Greek roots—this time the Greek origin refers to "instruction by word of mouth").

- *Cultivation toward full spiritual maturity and fruitfulness of the seed of grace in the lives of those who have received it,* such that it transforms individuals, families, communities, and entire cultures in harmony with God's will for the human family. This is often referred to as the work of *sanctification,* or "making holy."[27]

The Church's mission is to evangelize, and evangelization involves all these dimensions, along with all their logical corollaries and implications: "The Church 'exists in order to evangelize'; that is the carrying forth of the Good News to every sector of the human race so that by its strength it may enter into the hearts of men and renew the human race."[28]

This is what the twelve apostles and the rest of Christ's first followers were sent out to do by the Lord; it is the Church's reason for being.

> He [Jesus] said to them, "Go into the whole world and proclaim the gospel to every creature." (Mark 16:15)

In fact, the word *mission* comes from the Latin word for "sent out" (*missio*), which in Greek is related to *apostello,* the same root that gives us *apostle* and *apostolate.* Mission, evangelization, spreading the gospel, apostolate—this lexicon begins to unveil the richness of the Church's deepest identity—which, as we will see in the next meditation, also gives us a clue about our own deepest identity.

Questions for Personal Reflection or Group Discussion

1. What idea in this chapter struck you most and why?

2. When you think about the Catholic Church, what images or concepts come spontaneously to mind? Why? What do they tell you about your attitude toward the Church?

3. Try to explain in your own words the different nuances of these terms related to the Church's deepest identity: mission, evangelization, apostolate, gospel.

4. The concept of evangelization is so rich that it can't really be defined exhaustively with mathematical precision. The Vatican's *General Directory for Catechesis* points out: "However, no such definition can be accepted for that complex, rich and dynamic reality which is called evangelization. There is the risk of impoverishing it or even of distorting it. . . . Evangelization must be viewed as the process by which the Church, moved by the Spirit, proclaims and spreads the gospel throughout the entire world" (46-48). Considering how rich and multi-dimensional this reality is, what will you do today to engage more intentionally in the Church's work of evangelization?

- I will make a visit to the Eucharist and pray for missionaries who are struggling against taxing and dangerous difficulties.

- I will take five minutes to write a thank you note to God for all the evangelizers whose efforts went into my receiving the Catholic faith (try to list as many of those people as you can think of).

- I will get together with a friend and talk about how the Church in my area is continuing the work of evangelization. Then I will pray for the success of those efforts and brainstorm about how I can join in.

- (Write your own resolution) I will _____
  _____
  _____
  _____

Concluding Prayer

O God, in the covenant of your Christ
you never cease to gather to yourself from all nations
a people growing together in unity through the Spirit;
grant, we pray, that your Church,
faithful to the mission entrusted to her,
may continually go forward with the human family
and always be the leaven and the soul of human society,
to renew it in Christ and transform it into the family of God.

—ROMAN MISSAL, COLLECT FOR MASS FOR THE CHURCH, B

You Too Go into My Vineyard!

"You go too." The call is a concern not only of pastors, clergy, and men and women religious. The call is addressed to everyone: lay people as well are personally called by the Lord, from whom they receive a mission on behalf of the Church and the world.
— St. John Paul II, Christifideles Laici, 2

DEEP WITHIN EVERY HUMAN HEART burns a desire for lasting purpose, for a truly meaningful life. In some hearts, this desire burns quietly, like a small ember waiting under thick layers of cold ash. People in that condition may try to fill their lives with earthly comforts and achievements, thinking that those things will be enough to satisfy them. They try to ignore or quench the deeper yearning.

In other hearts the desire flames out violently, impatiently belittling anything that doesn't directly contribute to whatever particular cause such individuals have dedicated themselves to. In this case, life can lose its balance and harmony, and people can turn even legitimate and necessary human works (i.e., curing cancer, ending world hunger) into a kind of idol. This can even lead to violence and destruction when the adopted cause or chosen means to promote it contradicts human dignity. Killing people in order to save an endangered animal or plant species, for example, is dangerously off-kilter.

THE SOURCE OF MEANING

Neither earthly comforts and achievements nor ideological idols can fulfill the longings of the human heart. Our hearts are made for God and his kingdom, for everlasting life. Nothing on this side of eternity can truly satisfy them. Here we can only begin to experience the fullness of life to which God is leading us, but even that beginning is far superior to anything the secular world can give us.

God wants us to find and follow that path of true meaning. He wants us to experience the growing fullness of life that comes with following that path. In fact, Jesus summed up his life's mission in those terms: "I came that they might have life, and have it more abundantly" (John 10:10).

Being evangelized by the Church gives us access to this path. It actually sets us on "the road that leads to life" (Matt. 7:14) by uniting us to the source of life himself—Jesus.

Through baptism we become members of this Church that is Christ still present in the world, renewing and redeeming the human family from within. Our spiritual DNA is enhanced by baptism, so that in a sense every Christian becomes another Christ. As St. Cyprian put it way back in the third century: "*Christianus alter Christus*"—"Every Christian is another Christ." The other sacraments nourish that divine life of Christ in each baptized person, as does the instruction and guidance that each receives from more mature members of the Church—parents, teachers, priests, and so on.

HEALTHY PLANTS BEAR FRUIT

The healthy growth of this divine life of grace tends irresistibly to produce fruit. Healthy Christians naturally share with others the gifts of grace they have received. As they grow to spiritual maturity, they produce spiritual fruit analogous to how mature plants produce material fruit. Jesus used this image in Mark 4:26-29 to describe the growth of his kingdom.

A healthy seed grows and bears fruit—that's what it does. The seed of grace, according to the Lord, is no different. The urge to help others live life to the fullest, the desire to help them discover the liberating truths of the gospel and experience the revitalizing mercy and love of Jesus Christ, surges up from within every mature Christian. It's part of who we are. It's a spiritual vital sign.

The classic expressions of this yearning to spread the love we have been given are found strewn throughout the New Testament writings of St. Paul, the quintessential missionary. "For the love of Christ impels us," he wrote to the Christians in Corinth (2 Cor. 5:14). In a previous letter, he had explained his own sense of mission with another phrase that has been taken up by every Christian generation since: "If I preach the gospel, this is no reason for me to boast, for an obligation has been imposed on me, and woe to me if I do not preach it!" (1 Cor. 9:16).

PEOPLE VERSUS PLANTS

Of course, human beings are different than plants. Plants grow and bear fruit unconsciously. In the spiritual life, however, growth and fruitfulness are linked to our free cooperation, to our decision to listen and obey as "the voice of Lord clearly resounds in the depths" of our souls, to quote St. John Paul II again. As baptized Christians we are evangelizers in our very nature, but we are capable of denying that nature, of starving it or hiding it or otherwise acting against it. When we do so, we impede the Church's mission, we fail in our call to love, and we deviate from the path of meaning that alone will satisfy the deepest longings of our heart.

Jesus's description of this missionary aspect of our Christian identity illustrates both these dimensions—that we are evangelizers by nature ever since our baptism, but that we can act against that nature. During his Sermon on the Mount, for example, he explained:

> "You are the salt of the earth. But if salt loses its taste, with what can it be seasoned? It is no longer good for anything but to be thrown out and trampled underfoot. You are the light of the world. A city set on a mountain cannot be hidden. Nor do they light a lamp and then put it under a bushel basket; it is set on a lampstand, where it gives light to all in the house. Just so, your light must shine before others, that they may see your good deeds and glorify your heavenly Father." (Matt. 5:13–16)

Christ's followers *are* the salt of the earth and the light of the world.

Our identity involves bringing flavor and illumination to a world deadened and darkened by sin. As St. John Paul II said:

> God calls me and sends me forth as a laborer in his vineyard. He calls me and sends me forth to work for the coming of his Kingdom in history. This personal vocation and mission defines the dignity and the responsibility of each member of the lay faithful.[29]

And yet it is possible for us to become insipid salt or obscured light. As members of the Church, we are sharers in her mission, but we have to decide to live in accordance with that identity, to let our light shine before others and thus fulfill the commandment of love. That's what we are created to do, that's what we are called to do, that's what the world needs us to do, and that's what will satisfy our existential thirst for lasting fulfillment—for making a truly meaningful contribution to history. When the Lord of the vineyard looks at you and says, "You too go into my vineyard" (Matt. 20:4), he says it with a warm, eager, loving smile.

Questions for Personal Reflection or Group Discussion

1. What idea in this chapter struck you most and why?

2. When have you experienced most acutely the thirst for meaning and purpose God has placed in the depths of your soul? What did you do about it?

3. How deeply do you identify with this aspect of being a follower of Christ? How does your condition of being a missionary, being salt and light for the world, make you feel? Why?

4. Becoming aware of this missionary dimension can be overwhelming. We don't always feel up to such a high calling. We don't always feel properly equipped, trained, gifted, or talented. And yet the fact remains that we all share "the common vocation of all Christ's disciples, a vocation to holiness and to the mission of evangelizing the world" (CCC, 1533). In the coming

chapters we will explore the many different ways that mission can be lived out, which can help it be less overwhelming. But for today, how will you consciously express this core aspect of your deepest identity and deepest source of meaning?

- I will visit my parish church and take a few moments to reflect on all the artwork and decoration inside of it, asking myself what those images say to me about my identity as a Christian missionary.

- I will read a description of the life of my favorite saint, paying special attention to how that person lived out the missionary dimension of being a Christian.

- I will bring up my faith in a conversation where it wouldn't usually come up, even if indirectly, and see how God uses that.

- (Write your own resolution) I will _____

  _____

  _____

  _____

Concluding Prayer

O God, you have willed that your Church
be the sacrament of salvation for all nations,
so that Christ's saving work may continue to the end of the ages;
stir up, we pray, the hearts of your faithful
and grant that they may feel a more urgent call
to work for the salvation of every creature, so that
from all the peoples on earth one family and one
people of your own may arise and increase.
Through our Lord Jesus Christ, your Son,
who lives and reigns with you in the unity of the Holy Spirit,
one God, for ever and ever.

— ROMAN MISSAL, COLLECT FOR THE MASS
FOR THE EVANGELIZATION OF PEOPLES

Thy Kingdom Come!

The kingdom is the concern of everyone: individuals, society, and the world. Working for the kingdom means acknowledging and promoting God's activity, which is present in human history and transforms it. Building the kingdom means working for liberation from evil in all its forms. In a word, the kingdom of God is the manifestation and the realization of God's plan of salvation in all its fullness.
— St. John Paul II, Redemptoris Missio, 15

WHEN JESUS BEGAN PREACHING HIS message to the world, he referred to a kingdom, saying: "The kingdom of God is at hand. Repent, and believe in the gospel" (Mark 1:15). When Jesus taught his disciples to pray, he instructed them to aim all their desires at that same kingdom:

> "This is how you are to pray: Our Father in heaven, hallowed be your name, your kingdom come, your will be done, on earth as in heaven . . . " (Matt. 6:9–10)

When Jesus's enemies turned him in to the Roman authorities, they charged him with trying to set up an independent kingdom in opposition to the Roman emperor. Pontius Pilate, the Roman governor at the time, asked Jesus if this accusation was true. The Lord answered, in the most critical moment of his life, by affirming that he was indeed a king, and that his kingdom was utterly unique.

> Jesus answered, "My kingdom does not belong to this world. If my kingdom did belong to this world, my attendants [would]

be fighting to keep me from being handed over to the Jews. But as it is, my kingdom is not here." (John 18:36)

Jesus linked the spreading of his message—the spreading of the gospel, the work of evangelization—to his kingdom. In this sense, the work of evangelization can be described as the work of building up Christ's kingdom—"working for the kingdom" and "building the kingdom" as St. John Paul II put it.

KINGS AND FAIRY TALES

Some people consider this concept out of date. In the postmodern world, they say, kings and queens are obsolete. Even the ones who still survive are mere figureheads, symbols of archaic and irrelevant glory. To think of Christ as a king and the Church on earth as the "seed and beginning of [his] kingdom" (CCC, 541), these critics claim, is to mistakenly relegate Christianity to the realm of fairy tales.

And yet, as we have seen, Jesus used this concept continually. And the Church's official teaching has done the same, even into our own day. In fact, at the beginning of the postmodern era, when the human family was being thrown into historically unparalleled cataclysms of totalitarianism, world wars, global depression, genocides, and massive religious persecution, the Church invoked Christ's kingship as a rallying cry to restore a vestige of sanity.

In 1925 Pope Pius XI instituted throughout the whole Church the Feast of Christ the King. Its official liturgical name is now the Solemnity of Our Lord Jesus Christ, the King of the Universe. We are all familiar with it, since we celebrate it every year on the last Sunday before Advent—the Sunday that brings the liturgical year to its close. But we may be less familiar with the reasons behind its establishment.

CHRIST'S KINGDOM AS THE SOUL OF THE WORLD

Pius XI recognized that the ills of a decadent Western civilization, which were beginning to infect the rest of the world, were linked to a philosophical and cultural rejection of God and Jesus Christ. The modern world began to put its faith more in mankind—and mankind's ability to control its circumstances through science and technology—than in God and the wisdom of the gospel. As a result secularization advanced throughout countries whose popular culture for centuries had been imbued with a Christian worldview and Christian values. Here is how Pope Pius XI explained it in his second encyclical letter, which established the Feast of Christ the King:

> In the first Encyclical Letter which we addressed at the beginning of our pontificate to the bishops of the universal Church, we referred to the chief causes of the difficulties under which mankind was laboring. And we remember saying that these manifold evils in the world were due to the fact that the majority of men had thrust Jesus Christ and his holy law out of their lives; that these had no place either in private affairs or in politics: and we said further, that as long as individuals and states refused to submit to the rule of our Savior, there would be no really hopeful prospect of a lasting peace among nations.[30]

By instituting the liturgical celebration of Christ the King, the Holy Father hoped to set up a counteroffensive to this insidious cultural trend of secularization. He hoped to remind all Catholics of their primary allegiance to a kingdom that is not limited to this passing world, a kingdom that allows the human spirit to flourish instead of flounder, because it leads people to live in obedience to the infinite wisdom and merciful love of Jesus. Only a life in harmony with God's will, in other words, can restore order and sanity to a world gone mad.

> This kingdom is spiritual and concerned with spiritual things. . . . When once men recognize, both in private and in public life, that Christ is King, society will at last receive the great blessings of real liberty, well-ordered discipline, peace and harmony. . . . That these blessings may be abundant and lasting in Christian society, it is necessary that the kingship of our Savior should be as widely as possible recognized and

understood, and to that end nothing would serve better than the institution of a special feast in honor of the Kingship of Christ.[31]

LETTING CHRIST REIGN IN EVERY SECTOR OF THE HUMAN SOUL

This reminder and celebration, enshrined in the liturgy, could both help inoculate Catholics against the virus of secularization and also spur them on to live as faithful subjects and followers of the Lord.

The faithful, moreover, by meditating upon these truths, will gain much strength and courage, enabling them to form their lives after the true Christian ideal.... [I]t must be clear that not one of our faculties is exempt from his empire. He must reign in our minds, which should assent with perfect submission and firm belief to revealed truths and to the doctrines of Christ. He must reign in our wills, which should obey the laws and precepts of God. He must reign in our hearts, which should spurn natural desires and love God above all things, and cleave to him alone. He must reign in our bodies and in our members, which should serve as instruments for the interior sanctification of our souls, or to use the words of the Apostle Paul, as instruments of justice unto God. If all these truths are presented to the faithful for their consideration, they will prove a powerful incentive to perfection.[32]

Christ's kingdom comes whenever a person hears his message of truth and heeds his loving, redeeming will. This is why Jesus linked these two phrases in the Our Father: "Thy Kingdom come; thy will be done . . . "

Using the phrase "to build up the kingdom of Christ" as an expression of what the Church seeks to do through her evangelizing efforts has a profound benefit. It keeps us grounded in a fundamental truth, a truth easy to forget in a post-Christian world—namely, that we are not God, that the power of redemption and renewal that flows from the gospel comes not from us, who are merely messengers, but from the Lord. He is the king of the universe, and it is the grace of his kingdom that frees humble and obedient hearts from the deadening and destructive shackles of meaninglessness, falsehood, and sin. The mission of the Church, and the mission of each Christian, is to extend the breadth and the depth of that kingdom, the only kingdom that will last forever.

Questions for Personal Reflection or Group Discussion

1. What idea in this chapter struck you the most and why?

2. Express in your own words how the specific concept "building the kingdom of Christ" contributes to the general concept of evangelization.

3. When you use your imagination to picture Christ as the perfect king who is, through his Church, building up an eternal kingdom, how does it make you feel? Why? How does it make you feel to picture yourself as a member of this kingdom and a partner of the king in building it?

4. In early twentieth-century Mexico, a rabidly secularized government initiated a violent persecution of the Catholic Church. This led to the confiscation of Church property, the expulsion of clergy, and a general attempt to extinguish the practice of the Catholic faith. Catholics resisted this persecution, both peacefully and violently. The clash led to a decade of deadly unrest that witnessed, in addition to pitched battles between government forces and a Catholic citizen militia dubbed the "Cristeros," public executions and gruesome martyrdoms of clergy and laity throughout the nation. The Church has beatified many of these martyrs, including a young fourteen-year-old boy named José Sanchez del Río. Perhaps the most famous martyr from this era is the Jesuit priest, Blessed Miguel Pro. In many cases, the martyrs would be killed by a firing squad, and right before the final order to shoot was given, they would lift their voices with the Cristero battle cry: "¡Viva Cristo Rey!" ("Long live Christ the King!"). These martyrs refused to abandon their

allegiance to Jesus and his kingdom, even at the cost of their lives. Today, how will you live out your faithfulness to Jesus, your Savior and King?

- I will make time to go to confession, using that sacrament both to confess my sins and to renew my desire to follow Jesus and live under the guidance of his wisdom and love.

- I will reach out to someone I know who is struggling with his or her faith, being for that person a reflection of God's goodness and interest.

- I will take some extra quiet time in prayer to ask the Lord how he wants me to contribute to building up his kingdom. I will say yes to whatever he asks of me.

- (Write your own resolution) I will _____
  _____
  _____
  _____

Concluding Prayer

O God, who in your wonderful providence
decreed that Christ's kingdom
should be extended throughout the earth
and that all should become partakers of his saving redemption,
grant, we pray, that your Church
may be the universal sacrament of salvation
and that Christ may be revealed to all
as the hope of the nations and their Savior.

—ROMAN MISSAL, COLLECT FROM THE MASS FOR THE CHURCH, A

DAY 35

The Motor of the Mission

Mother and Teacher of all nations—such is the Catholic Church in the
mind of her Founder, Jesus Christ; to hold the world in an embrace of
love, that men, in every age, should find in her their own completeness in
a higher order of living, and their ultimate salvation. She is "the pillar and
ground of the truth" (1 Timothy 3:15). To her was entrusted by her holy
Founder the twofold task of giving life to her children and of teaching them
and guiding them—both as individuals and as nations—with maternal care.
  —St. John XXIII, Mater et Magister, 1

S OME PEOPLE WANT TO CONQUER the world because they are megalo-
maniacs. Conquest is all about extending their egos, manifesting
their power through domination of others. These are the would-be
emperors of earthly kingdoms who will stop at nothing to achieve
their goal—Napoleon, Stalin, Hitler. Every age of human history has
figures like these. They echo the devil's own rebellious self-assertion,
recorded in Scripture as a snapshot of the attitude behind sin in
general: "Long ago you broke your yoke, you tore off your bonds. You
said, 'I will not serve'" (Jer. 2:20).

Some critics of Christianity accuse Jesus, as the Church presents
him, of being just one more of these. The leaders of the Catholic
Church, according to them, seek to control and dominate people,
to enslave them with the chains of ignorance and superstition
through a millennia-long exercise in self-aggrandizement.

A DIFFERENCE IN MOTIVATION

But that is not what Jesus's command to "Go, therefore, and make

196

disciples of all nations!" is all about. That is not the goal of evangelization—not at all. Jesus—unlike the dictators whose failed totali-
tarian regimes litter the floor of human history—acted out of love.
He is, in fact, the revelation of God's unlimited, unconditional love:
"For God so loved the world that he gave his only Son, so that everyone who believes in him might not perish but might have eternal
life" (John 3:16).

Evil dictators may not be fully responsible for their atrocities. Their
psychological brokenness may absolve them from much of their culpability—or it may not; that is for God to judge. Yet in every case, they
seek to enlarge themselves—their image, their reputation, their influence, their power—at the expense of others. They use others.

This contradicts true, Christlike love. The example and teaching
of Jesus was the exact opposite. He gave himself, literally, for the sake
of those he loved—all of us. He lowered himself to take on human
nature through the Incarnation. He lived an obscure, working-class
life in Nazareth for thirty years. He exhausted himself preaching, healing, and teaching his followers during his three years of public ministry. And he offered his own life in loving obedience unto death on a
cross to atone for the sins of each and every member of the human
family. He summed up his own earthly mission by saying: " . . . [T]he
Son of Man did not come to be served but to serve and to give his life
as a ransom for many" (Matt. 20:28).

A High Purpose for a Heartfelt Command

When Jesus commanded his apostles to make disciples of all
nations, then, that command didn't flow from megalomania. It
flowed from love, from the sincere, heartfelt desire to rescue every
human soul from the existential frustration that is our natural
inheritance due to original sin. His life and mission fulfilled the
Old Testament prophecy:

> The people who walked in darkness have seen a great light; upon
> those who lived in a land of gloom light has shone. You have
> brought them abundant joy and great rejoicing . . . (Isa. 9:1-2)

Jesus desires people to believe in him, follow him, and obey his teachings because he wants them to live life to the full: "I came that they might have life, and have it more abundantly" (John 10:10). He knows that all of the good things of the earth—wealth, pleasure, popularity, achievements, power—cannot satisfy the human heart. And when we seek to fill our hearts with them, they become twisted, destructive idols that actually thwart our progress toward fulfillment. Following them and putting our hopes in them, we become lost, confused, desperate, even twisted ourselves. Jesus alone, through the gift of divine grace, can save us from that, and he wants to do so; that's why he established a missionary Church.

SEEKING THE TROUBLED AND ABANDONED

This deep connection between love and mission comes across beautifully in a passage from St. Matthew's Gospel. Jesus had finished his Sermon on the Mount, and he had proven the trustworthiness of the words in that sermon by an astonishing series of miracles. At that point, St. Matthew gives us a glimpse into what's going on in our Lord's heart:

> Jesus went around to all the towns and villages, teaching in their synagogues, proclaiming the gospel of the kingdom, and curing every disease and illness. At the sight of the crowds, his heart was moved with pity for them because they were troubled and abandoned, like sheep without a shepherd. Then he said to his disciples, "The harvest is abundant but the laborers are few; so ask the master of the harvest to send out laborers for his harvest." (Matt. 9:35–38)

Jesus encountered people who felt "troubled and abandoned, like sheep without a shepherd." This is the perennial struggle of the human heart, the reason behind the sincere but often desperate forays of philosophers and religious thinkers of every place and time. The human heart yearns for wisdom and completeness but cannot find it in this fallen world; it yearns to make sense out of life but is stymied at every turn by the paradoxes of evil, suffering, and human misery. Jesus was moved by this human condition, by the angst of the human predicament.

FROM WORTHY FEELINGS TO EFFECTIVE ACTION

And what was his reaction? In the very next verses of St. Matthew's Gospel, Jesus called his twelve apostles, gave them a share of his authority and power, and sent them out as his messengers to bring hope, guidance, and healing to all those who are "troubled and abandoned" and otherwise trapped by the forces of evil.

> Then he summoned his twelve disciples and gave them author-
> ity over unclean spirits to drive them out and to cure every
> disease and every illness. . . . Jesus sent out these twelve after
> instructing them thus, " . . . As you go, make this proclamation:
> 'The kingdom of heaven is at hand.' Cure the sick, raise the
> dead, cleanse lepers, drive out demons . . . " (Matt. 10:1, 5-8)

Jesus enabled and commanded his followers to do precisely what he had just been doing—preaching, teaching, healing, serving, bringing light into the darkness of needy human hearts. Clearly, the mission of the Church is the outpouring of God's own love for every person.

The commandment "love your neighbor as yourself" should be understood in this context. It embraces much more than a passive avoidance of harm. To love someone, in Christ's mind, is to affirm the goodness of his or her existence and to help that existence flourish. If every Christian is called to participate in the Church's mission of evangelization, it is only because every Christian—and indeed, every human being—is created for love, to be loved, and to love in return. Only this gives our lives the meaning we crave.

--------*Questions for Personal Reflection*--------
or Group Discussion

1. What idea in this chapter struck you most and why?
2. Why do you think so many people today consider *obedience* to be a bad word—or at least a bad idea? How would you express

in your own words why God wants us to obey his teaching and commandments?

3. What teachings of the Church make you uncomfortable? Which ones do you often feel interior resistance toward? Why? What should you do about that?

4. People can often do the right thing for the wrong reasons. We can do a favor because we want to ask for a favor in return. We can compliment someone because we want to be liked. We can show kindness in order to manipulate. In those cases we are not truly loving the other person — at least, we are not loving that person with a pure heart. This impurity leads to frustration and resentment when we don't get what we want. The path of love that Jesus invites us to follow is different. It seeks to honor the person we are serving, to give of ourselves in a way that will truly help that person, but also respect him or her. This form of love requires more reflection and sensitivity, as well as a denial of our own deep-seated selfish tendencies. But it also creates a climate of interior freedom for us, and an unambiguous experience of goodness on the part of the one we are serving. Today, how will you seek greater purity of heart in your words and gestures of kindness?

- I will do a hidden act of kindness, something that only God and myself will ever know about.

- I will reflect on situations where I typically end up feeling resentful or frustrated and ask God to show me where those feelings are really rooted.

- I will spend ten minutes today in silent adoration of a crucifix, gazing at Jesus dying on the cross and thinking about the revealed truth that he did it in order to show me how much he loves me.

- (Write your own resolution) I will _____
  _____
  _____
  _____

Concluding Prayer

*Jesus, the beginning and fulfillment of the new man, convert
our hearts so that, abandoning the ways of error, we may
walk in your footsteps on the path which leads to life. Make
us live our faith steadfastly, fulfilling our baptismal promises,
testifying with conviction to your word, that the life-giving light
of the gospel may shine in our families and in society. . . .
Jesus, only-begotten Son of the Father, full of grace and truth, the
light which illumines every person, give the abundance of your life
to all who seek you with a sincere heart. To you, man's Redeemer,
the beginning and the end of time and of the universe, to the
Father, unending source of all good, and to the Holy Spirit, seal
of infinite love, be all honor and glory, now and for ever. Amen.*

—Prayer of St. John Paul II
for the Great Jubilee of the Year 2000

A New Evangelization?

Over the years, I have often repeated the summons to the new
evangelization. I do so again now, especially in order to insist that we must
rekindle in ourselves the impetus of the beginnings and allow ourselves to
be filled with the ardor of the apostolic preaching which followed Pentecost.
—St. John Paul II, Novo Millennio Ineunte, 40

I F EVANGELIZATION IS THE DEEPEST identity of the Church, and if the
Church has been engaged in evangelization without interruption
since the beginning of Christian history, why has the Holy Spirit
moved all the postmodern era popes to call so energetically for a "new"
evangelization? What does that mean, and what does it have to do
with our personal mission as members of the Church?

THE NEED FOR SOMETHING NEW

The call for a new evangelization has permeated Church teaching since
the mid-twentieth century. The Second Vatican Council, in a sense, set
the stage for it. Unlike most ecumenical councils through the ages, this
one focused not on clarifying doctrinal issues, but on updating pastoral
ones. It was an invitation to reflect on how to make the gospel message
resound more effectively in postmodern minds and hearts.

St. Paul VI, pope for the conclusion of the Council and for the
years immediately following it, echoed that same desire for a new energy
and effectiveness in evangelization. On the tenth anniversary of the
closing of the Second Vatican Council, he published an apostolic
exhortation dedicated entirely to evangelization. In it, he explained:

The conditions of the society in which we live oblige all of us therefore to revise methods, to seek by every means to study how we can bring the Christian message to modern man.[33]

Then he posed three questions at the heart of this call and impulse toward a new evangelization:

In our day, what has happened to that hidden energy of the Good News, which is able to have a powerful effect on man's conscience? To what extent and in what way is that evangelical force capable of really transforming the people of this century? What methods should be followed in order that the power of the gospel may have its effect?[34]

The concept of a new evangelization, therefore, involves recognizing that the world of the third millennium is fundamentally different than the world of previous epochs. Its culture is different. The obstacles and opportunities it offers to the gospel message are different. And so the Church's ongoing work of evangelization must adjust.

THE CLASSIC VERSION: NEW ARDOR, METHODS, AND EXPRESSION

The way St. John Paul II put it has become the classic expression of what the new evangelization really is. In a speech he gave to the bishops of Latin America on the eve of the fifth centenary of the arrival of Christianity to the American continent, he called for a renewed commitment of the Church, a commitment "not of re-evangelization, but rather, of a new evangelization; new in its ardor, methods and expression . . . "[35] Throughout his quarter-century-long pontificate, St. John Paul II continually reiterated this call to give the ancient thrust of evangelization new forms and new energy.

NAMING THE NEW CHALLENGES

Pope Benedict XVI took up the same baton and identified two of the key challenges the new evangelization faces: the globalization of a technocratic, secularized mentality and the resultant spiritual numbing of cultures that have had long traditions of vibrant Christian living.[36]

This growing awareness of the need for a new evangelization crystalized in Pope Benedict XVI's erection of a new Pontifical Council explicitly dedicated to promoting it. In its letter of establishment, he mentioned all three cultural climates that the new evangelization must find ways to renew with the gospel message: fervent Christian cultures that need to continue maturing; ancient Christian cultures that have lost their fervor or even rejected completely their former Christian identity and so need to be re-evangelized; and cultures that still have not heard or accepted the gospel and require a newly energized generation of missionaries to reach them.

The secularized, digitalized, global culture of third-millennium humanity does indeed pose unprecedented challenges to evangelization. To make the gospel relevant in this new, "post-Christian" environment may be much more difficult than it was to make the gospel relevant to pre-Christian pagans. Post-Christian people assume that Christianity has been tried and has failed. To evangelize them does indeed require the grace of new, truly inspired "ardor, methods, and expression." Are you ready?

Questions for Personal Reflection or Group Discussion

1. What idea in this chapter struck you most and why?

2. How would you explain the term "new evangelization" to a Catholic friend who hasn't read this chapter?

3. What are some of the common objections or criticisms you hear applied to Christianity? How do you usually respond to them? How would you like to be able to respond?

4. C.S. Lewis had a personal policy of reading one old book (from a previous period of history) for every four or five contemporary books. He did this because he felt that we all have a tendency to be blind to the errors and prejudices of our own historical epoch. What will you do today in order to remind

yourself that your primary citizenship is in heaven, and that you are only on a passing journey through life on this earth?

- I will visit the grave of a loved one and pray for the repose of his or her soul, maybe bringing flowers for the tombstone.
- I will spend a few hours entirely "unplugged" from technology.
- I will read one of the older papal encyclicals, like Pope Pius XI's *Quas Primas* (Introducing the Feast of Christ the King), St. Pius X's *E Supremi* (On the Restoration of All Things in Christ), or St. Paul VI's apostolic exhortation *Evangelii Nuntiandi* (On Evangelization in the Modern World).
- (Write your own resolution) I will _____
  _____
  _____
  _____

Concluding Prayer

Heavenly Father, pour forth your Holy Spirit to inspire me with these words from Holy Scripture. Stir in my soul the desire to renew my faith and deepen my relationship with your Son, our Lord Jesus Christ, so that I might truly believe in and live the Good News. Open my heart to hear the Gospel and grant me the confidence to proclaim the Good News to others. Pour out your Spirit, so that I might be strengthened to go forth and witness to the Gospel in my everyday life through my words and actions.

—USCCB, Prayer for the New Evangelization

To Teach the Art of Living

"Life" indicates the sum total of all the goods that people desire, and
at the same time what makes them possible, obtainable and lasting.
. . . Jesus came to provide the ultimate answer to the yearning for life
and for the infinite which his Heavenly Father had poured into our
hearts when he created us. . . . "I came that they might have life" (John
10:10). But what life? Jesus' intention was clear: the very life of God,
which surpasses all the possible aspirations of the human heart.
—St. John Paul II, Message for the VIII World Youth Day[37]

EVANGELIZATION INVOLVES SPREADING THE GOOD news of Jesus Christ
and finding ways for his grace and truth to touch, penetrate,
and transform human hearts, communities, and cultures. The new
evangelization strives to do that with new ardor, methods, and
expressions.

That's a lot of words and a lot of concepts. What does it all
really boil down to? Pope Benedict XVI, before he became pope,
summarized it with a beautiful, powerful phrase:

How does one learn the art of living? Which is the path
toward happiness? To evangelize means: to show this path—to
teach the art of living.[38]

THE LOST ART OF LIVING

The art of living is exactly what was lost by original sin. The human
family was created in a condition where our first parents lived in a
fruitful and dynamic harmony with the rest of creation, harmony

with each other, and harmony with God. That harmony was God's plan for us, and it gave zest and meaning to life.

The great adventure of human existence originally took place in that spiritual arena, when "the Lord God then took the man and settled him in the garden of Eden, to cultivate and care for it" (Gen. 1:28), blessed Adam and Eve, and said to them: "Be fertile and multiply; fill the earth and subdue it" (Gen. 2:15). The happiness we were created to experience was already present from the moment the Lord set the human family on that path. It was a dynamic happiness, meant to grow to fulfillment through loving obedience to God's plan.

Original sin, our first parents' rebellion against God's plan instigated by the deceptions of the devil, shattered that original harmony. Human life became tangled up in confusion and oppressed by misery, as the *Catechism* explains in paragraph 40.

Every aspect and sector of human experience suffered the consequences of original sin—and the expanding stain of sin that even today continues to spread out from that epicenter of evil. The human heart still yearns for its original harmony and purpose, but this fallen world frustrates it at every turn. Because of original sin, the original art of living degenerated into a struggle merely to survive and a desperate search for lost meaning.

Recovering the Lost Art of Living

As dire as this situation is, God refused to abandon us. The coming of Jesus, prepared for through God's patient accompaniment and education of the people of Israel, marked the culmination of his plan to restore and even enhance his original design for the human family. To cite Pope Benedict XVI once again:

At the beginning of his public life Jesus says: I have come to evangelize the poor (cf. Luke 4:18); this means: I have the response to your fundamental question; I will show you the path of life, the path toward happiness—rather: I am that path.[39]

Jesus came to show us how to live and to give us the grace—the divine strength, the forgiveness, the hope, the desire—to live that way. Everything he says and does reveals and enables that fullness of life.

The essence of evangelization, then, is not complicated. It is as simple as introducing someone to a friend—Jesus. As Jesus's followers and messengers, we don't have all the answers and all the solutions. We too are simply learning the art of living, and that apprenticeship ends only when we die and enter the heavenly kingdom. However much or however little of that art we have learned, though, we can still find ways to share it with others. And when they too meet the Lord, he will take over as their Master, and we will take our proper place as his assistants.

THE BENEFITS OF LEARNING THE ART OF LIVING

Simply discovering that the answers to our hearts' deepest questions and longings really do exist begins to spark joy and hope. Simply knowing that there truly is an art of living, a way of living that brings lasting fulfillment, begins to relieve the tense oppression of existential angst and scatter the darkness. Evangelization starts with the announcement that there is an answer, a purpose, and a path, and its name is Jesus. Evangelization moves forward by fostering a deeper and deeper knowledge, love, and following of Jesus. As that increases, the angst and darkness continue to diminish, sin and evil start to lose their grip, and the art of living—along with its resulting experience of joy, hope, and fulfillment—advances.

That's why we say that evangelizing means to teach the art of living, and that's why it is so important.

> The deepest poverty is the inability of joy, the tediousness of a life considered absurd and contradictory. This poverty is widespread today, in very different forms in the materially rich as well as the poor countries. The inability of joy presupposes and produces the inability to love, produces jealousy, avarice—all defects that devastate the life of individuals and of the world. This is why we are in need of a new evangelization—if the art of living remains an unknown, nothing else works. But this art is

not the object of a science—this art can only be communicated by [one] who has life—he who is the Gospel personified.[40]

The remaining chapters of this book will explore the different ways we can evangelize, and address some obstacles and helps along those ways. But we must never forget the heart of it all: simply saying to others, in whatever language they best understand, *I would love for you to get to know a good friend of mine, who also happens to be the Savior of the world and the King of the universe—his name is Jesus . . .*

Questions for Personal Reflection or Group Discussion

1. What idea in this chapter struck you most and why?

2. When did you first "meet Jesus"? What led to that moment and what was it like? Remember, savor, and thank God for that experience.

3. When have you introduced someone to Jesus, knowingly or unknowingly? What led to that moment, and what was it like? What can you learn from that experience?

4. The art of living—the art of being a Christian, knowing, loving, and following Jesus Christ—never really comes to an end. We grow in virtue gradually, with plenty of failures. We overcome our sinful habits and tendencies gradually, and sometimes it's painful. Our emotional and spiritual wounds heal gradually under the gentle care of God's grace, often not so quickly as we would like them to. Our understanding of Church teaching deepens gradually, with the aid of study, discussion, and meditation. . . . If we keep this reality in mind, it helps us avoid the frustration that comes from false expectations. Today, how will you advance and help someone else advance in the art of living?

   - I will ask a qualified person (mentor, priest, teacher) to help me better understand a particular Church teaching I have always struggled with.

   - I will identify a recurring problem in my life and seek some fresh advice about how better to work on it.

- I will reach out to someone who is suffering and try to be a mirror of God's love for that person.

- (Write your own resolution) I will _____
  _____
  _____
  _____

Concluding Prayer

It is truly right and just that we should always give you thanks,
Lord, holy Father, almighty and eternal God.
For you do not cease to spur us on to possess a more abundant life
and, being rich in mercy, you constantly offer pardon
and call on sinners to trust in your forgiveness alone.
Never did you turn away from us, and, though time and again
we have broken your covenant, you have bound the human
family to yourself through Jesus your Son, our Redeemer,
with a new bond of love so tight that it can never be undone. . . .
And so, filled with wonder, we extol the power of your love,
and, proclaiming our joy at the salvation that comes from you,
we join in the heavenly hymn of countless hosts, as without
end we acclaim: Holy, Holy, Holy Lord God of hosts.
Heaven and earth are full of your glory. Hosanna in the highest.
Blessed is he who comes in the name of the
Lord. Hosanna in the highest.

—ROMAN MISSAL, PREFACE FOR THE EUCHARISTIC PRAYER
FOR RECONCILIATION I

You Are Not Just an Extra Add-On

Pius XII once stated: "The faithful, more precisely the lay faithful,
find themselves on the front lines of the Church's life; for them
the Church is the animating principle for human society."
—St. John Paul II, Christifideles Laici, 9

T HE CHURCH HAS A HIERARCHICAL structure, established by Christ
himself and maintained through more than twenty centuries by
the work of the Holy Spirit. Within this hierarchical structure, the
ordained clergy act with a sacred power that non-ordained members
(the laity) of the Church do not exercise. Christ gives that sacred
power, however, for the sake of the whole body of the Church. It is
a service—this is the meaning of the word *ministry*. In fact, *ministry*
comes from the Latin word *minus*, which literally means "less," in the
sense of servants being under those whom they serve.

GOD GAVE US SHEPHERDS

In the case of the ordained clergy, and in accordance with God's
design, their official service is a necessary ingredient in the life of
the Church. Thus the hierarchy of the Church, the pope and the
bishops along with their collaborators, the priests and deacons, provides the sacramental and magisterial (i.e., dependable teaching) fonts
by which the whole Mystical Body of Christ continues to be nourished
and strengthened.

No Second-Class Citizens

And yet the critical nature of that office and the sacred authority that goes with it do not relegate lay members of the Church to a kind of second-class status. Lay members are not meant to be merely passive collaborators with the ordained clergy. When laypersons think in those terms, they handcuff their evangelizing potential.

The essential identity of the Church is found in its evangelizing mission, as we have seen, and in that mission the laity have a dignity and responsibility as real and substantial as the ordained clergy. Here is how the *Catechism* puts it:

> In virtue of their rebirth in Christ there exists among all the Christian faithful a true equality with regard to dignity and the activity whereby all cooperate in the building up of the Body of Christ in accord with each one's own condition and function. (CCC, 872)

In other words, God has designed the Church in such a way that her mission of evangelizing the world and building up his Mystical Body requires a dual fidelity: ordained ministers must be faithful to their official service, and lay members must be faithful to their identity and mission. The hierarchy cannot sanctify the world without the laity, and the laity cannot sanctify the world without the hierarchy. Lay members are not mere extras or hangers-on; they have real responsibility for the life and work of the Church.

A Change in Mentality

Pope Benedict XVI stressed this aspect of dynamic communion between the hierarchy and the laity in a message to Catholic Action, one of the first lay movements in the modern Church. To describe it he focused on the operative term "co-responsibility":

> Co-responsibility requires a change in mentality, particularly with regard to the role of the laity in the Church, who should be considered not as "collaborators" with the clergy, but as

persons truly "co-responsible" for the being and activity of the Church.[41]

The mentality of co-responsibility implies that lay members of the Church should feel the mission of the Church as their own, whether they are consecrated or non-consecrated laypeople. The laity should feel empowered by their baptism to engage fully in the Church's life and mission, being proactive and not only reactive evangelizers. And the ordained ministers should recognize and respect the spirit of initiative that goes along with this co-responsibility.

COMPLEMENTARY SPHERES

The primary sphere of this lay activity of the Church differs from the primary sphere of the activity of the ordained ministers. The clergy are first and foremost ministers of the Word and the sacraments, as well as of the internal governance of the People of God required for those ministries to be effective. Laypersons, on the other hand, are first and foremost messengers of Christ into the secular world, and the Church needs them to evangelize proactively there, to take the initiative in Christianizing (or re-Christianizing) culture:

> By reason of their special vocation it belongs to the laity to seek the kingdom of God by engaging in temporal affairs and directing them according to God's will. . . . The initiative of lay Christians is necessary especially when the matter involves discovering or inventing the means for permeating social, political, and economic realities with the demands of Christian doctrine and life. This initiative is a normal element of the life of the Church. . . . (CCC, 898, 899)

This doesn't mean that laypeople should never be allowed in the sacristy and priests should never be allowed out of the sacristy. That would be a distorted exaggeration, undermining communion rather than fostering it. But it does mean that the co-responsibility envisioned by the Lord for the Church involves a deep and real complementarity of roles between clergy and laity.

A DYNAMIC AND DETERMINED COMMUNION

If clergy view their own ministry as essential to the Church while viewing an active and engaged laity as a nice extra, or add-on, their service to laypersons will be seriously debilitated. Likewise, if the laity ignores or overrides the sacred power granted to clergy, lay members will thwart the advance of Christ's kingdom.

But the contrary is equally true. If clergy belittle and neglect their ecclesial ministry, the people they serve will become spiritually anemic. And if the laity passively sit around in the pews and wait for "the Church" to do something about the social and cultural realities that need to be evangelized, evil will continue to advance.

We all need to recognize that the critical mission of evangelization requires a Church living in dynamic communion, with clergy and laity creatively working together, each ardently and doggedly engaged in their common mission according to their own roles and gifts.

Questions for Personal Reflection or Group Discussion

1. What idea in this chapter struck you most and why?

2. How would you explain in your own words the concept of ecclesial co-responsibility? In order to understand it more deeply, think of specific examples from your own experience in the Church when that co-responsibility has been lived poorly or especially well.

3. How well do your attitudes toward the clergy and laity you know reflect the dynamic communion that we are all called to live?

4. In the message where Pope Benedict XVI utilized the term "co-responsibility," he gave some advice to the lay members of the Church: "May you feel as your own the commitment to working for the Church's mission: with prayers, study and active participation in ecclesial life, with an attentive and positive gaze at the world, in the constant search for the signs of the times. Through a serious and daily commitment to formation never tire of increasingly refining the aspects of your specific vocation as lay faithful called to be courageous and credible witnesses in all

social milieus so that the gospel may be a light that brings hope to the problematic, difficult and dark situations which people today often encounter in their journey through life." What will you do today to follow that sound advice?

- I will jumpstart my prayer life by reviewing and renewing my daily and weekly prayer commitments, making sure they are substantial but also realistic.

- I will take some time to write down what being a "courageous and credible witness" of the gospel could look like in the milieus of my life.

- I will sign up for a spiritual retreat or pilgrimage as a way to deepen my own Christian formation.

- (Write your own resolution) I will _____

_____

_____

_____

Concluding Prayer

Lord, renew your Church by the light of the Gospel. Strengthen the bond of unity between the faithful and the pastors of your people, together with our Pope, our Bishop, and the whole Order of Bishops, that in a world torn by strife your people may shine forth as a prophetic sign of unity and concord.

—ROMAN MISSAL, FROM THE EUCHARISTIC PRAYER FOR USE IN MASSES FOR VARIOUS NEEDS I

PART VIII

THINGS TO KEEP IN MIND

After this the Lord appointed seventy-two others whom he sent ahead of him in pairs to every town and place he intended to visit. He said to them, "The harvest is abundant but the laborers are few; so ask the master of the harvest to send out laborers for his harvest."

LUKE 10:1–2

You Have What It Takes

Christ's gift of the Holy Spirit is going to be poured out upon you in a particular way. You will hear the words of the Church spoken over you, calling upon the Holy Spirit to confirm your faith, to seal you in his love, to strengthen you for his service. You will then take your place among fellow-Christians throughout the world, full citizens now of the People of God. You will witness to the truth of the gospel in the name of Jesus Christ. You will live your lives in such a way as to make holy all human life. Together with all the confirmed you will become living stones in the cathedral of peace. Indeed you are called by God to be instruments of his peace.
—St. John Paul II, Homily for Pentecost, May 30, 1982

THE CHURCH'S DEEPEST IDENTITY IS found in her mission to evangelize, to proclaim and foster the growth of Christ's kingdom. And God calls every Christian, every member of the Church, no matter how apparently small or unqualified, to join in that mission and make a unique, unrepeatable contribution to it that will reverberate throughout eternity. Making that contribution is every Christian's best way to "love your neighbor as yourself."

This mission can make us feel excited. But it can also make us feel scared, intimidated, and inadequate. You might think, *The great saints were capable of something like that, something so transcendental and amazing, but that's not for me. I can barely keep myself together in the hustle and bustle of daily duties and never-ending mini-crises! Who am I to think that I can help build Christ's kingdom and love like that?*

Feelings Bolstered by Faith

It's understandable to feel that way. But sometimes our spontaneous feelings only give us a partial glimpse into reality, especially in the realm of faith. Feelings need to be educated, taught to incorporate the truths of our faith into all the information they process and communicate to us. And on this point, about the capacity of every Christian to become a saint and make a unique, unrepeatable contribution to Christ's kingdom, our faith rescues us from every feeling of fear or inadequacy, for one simple reason: Our efforts are not just *our* efforts.

Naturally, depending only on hard work and our own natural powers and gifts, the call to holiness and evangelization is indeed far beyond our capacities. Christ's kingdom, as we have seen, "does not belong to this world" (John 18:36). It is a supernatural kingdom, built up by the power of grace and the Holy Spirit. If we were to try to take our place in that kingdom by leaning solely on our earthly smarts and strengths, we would be perennially frustrated, fruitlessly aiming again and again and again at a target impossibly beyond our reach.

New Things Have Come

But part of the good news Jesus brings is that, through baptism and confirmation, our natural gifts and talents—however many or few they may be—are healed and enhanced by grace. They are plugged in to the divine life itself. Baptism makes us adopted children of God, not just as some kind of formality, but in truth. Anyone who is baptized has "come to share in the divine nature. . . . So whoever is in Christ is a new creation: the old things have passed away; behold, new things have come" (2 Pet. 1:4; 2 Cor. 5:17).

We are members of Christ's own body, and through the sacrament of confirmation, the same Holy Spirit that animates Christ and the Church has been abundantly poured into our own lives, animating each one of us as well: "Now you are Christ's body, and individually parts of it . . . hope does not disappoint, because the love of God has been poured out into our hearts through the holy Spirit that has been given to us . . . " (1 Cor. 12:27; Rom. 5:5). And so our human and material limitations, our wounds, our struggles and hardships—none of these things have to inhibit us from engaging in this uniquely fulfilling mission of evangelization. God can work through them all, and when we let him do so, he is glorified even more than when we try to serve him from a place of self-satisfaction and self-confidence.

When We Are Weak, We Are Strong

St. Paul learned this lesson the hard way—through a mysterious struggle against what he calls "a thorn in the flesh" that he simply could never get rid of (see 2 Cor. 12:7-10).

The same Holy Spirit that comes to us through the grace of baptism and confirmation, truly uniting us to God and gradually leading us to spiritual maturity, also equips us and spurs us on toward the fulfillment of our mission in Christ's kingdom. Some Christians are called to carry out dramatic and highly visible missions, like St. Bernardine of Siena, who would habitually preach to crowds of ten thousand people. Others are called to carry out hidden but still beautiful and powerful missions, like St. Joseph, who silently cared for Jesus and Mary, without speaking even a single word in the Bible.

You Are Not Lacking

Whatever he may ask of each one of us, "God is faithful," and through Christ he doesn't call and equip us for something beyond our reach—that would be torture. Rather:

> . . . in him you were enriched in every way, with all discourse and all knowledge . . . so that you are not lacking in any spiritual gift as you wait for the revelation of our Lord Jesus Christ. He will keep you firm to the end, irreproachable on the day of our Lord Jesus [Christ]. (1 Cor. 1:9, 5-8)

When Jesus sent his twelve apostles out on their first mission, St. Matthew tells us that he "summoned his twelve disciples and gave them authority" (Matt. 10:1). When he sent the larger group of seventy-two followers, St. Luke tells us that "the Lord appointed" them (Luke 10:1). At his ascension, Jesus prefaces his great commission that the Church "go, therefore, and make disciples of all nations" with an explanation of whose power will truly be at work within the Church's efforts to fulfill that command: "Then Jesus approached and said to them, 'All power in heaven and on earth has been given to me. Go, therefore . . . '" (Matt. 28:18-19).

As Christians, through the mysterious communion with God given by baptism and confirmation, Christ's own life surges through our veins. His own power gives supernatural force to our evangelizing efforts. Insofar as we intentionally and consistently nourish this communion through a growing prayer life, through a humble and determined participation in the Eucharist and in confession, and through a decent effort to obey the Lord's will in all things, it will mature and expand, bringing God's unique dream for each one of us to fulfillment.[42]

Truly, your part in building up Christ's kingdom is beyond anything you could ever do—on your own. But in the Lord, you really do have what it takes.

Questions for Personal Reflection or Group Discussion

1. What idea in this chapter struck you most and why?

2. When you think about the sacrament of baptism, what comes to mind? Why? Why do you think we celebrate our birthdays, but not many of us celebrate the anniversary of our baptism?

3. When you think of the sacrament of confirmation, what comes to mind? Why? Remember your own experience of receiving this sacrament. What sticks in your mind? Why? What would you like to have done differently?

4. The life of grace within us is invisible and most often works in hidden ways. And yet grace is real, and it has produced and inspired all the works of the Church throughout its history: the spiritual maturity, power, and influence of the saints, and the countless acts of mercy, self-sacrifice, fidelity, and kindness performed by thousands of Christians through the centuries.

What will you do today to allow God's grace to flow freely in and through your life?

- I will find out the baptismal anniversaries of every member of my family (including my own) and plan to celebrate them with the same gusto that we celebrate our birthdays.
- I will take some time to read up on the life of the saint whose name I took when I was confirmed in order to derive some fresh inspiration from how grace worked in his or her life.
- I will renew my commitment to spend time in personal prayer with the Lord every single day in order to keep his grace flowing in my mind and heart.
- (Write your own resolution) I will _____

   _____

   _____

   _____

Concluding Prayer

O God, whose ancient wonders
remain undimmed in splendor even in our day,
for what you once bestowed on a single people,
freeing them from Pharaoh's persecution
by the power of your right hand
now you bring about as the salvation of the nations
through the waters of rebirth,
grant, we pray, that the whole world
may become children of Abraham
and inherit the dignity of Israel's birthright.
Through Christ our Lord. Amen.

—ROMAN MISSAL, PRAYER AFTER THE THIRD READING
FOR THE EASTER VIGIL MASS

The Gifts You May Not Even Know You Have

In our own day, too, the Spirit is the principal agent of the new evangelization. Hence it will be important to gain a renewed appreciation of the Spirit as the One who builds the Kingdom of God within the course of history and prepares its full manifestation in Jesus Christ, stirring people's hearts and quickening in our world the seeds of the full salvation which will come at the end of time.

—St. John Paul II, Tertio Millennio Adveniente, 45

THE DIVINE LIFE THAT MAKES us children of God and equips us to make our unique contribution to the Church's mission of evangelization works in many and mysterious ways. Through the centuries, the Church has gradually come to understand partially and even categorize some of them. Dedicating some time to reflect on this knowledge can bolster our confidence in God. It can also prepare us to grasp the many different (and sometimes surprising) forms that our evangelizing mission can take in the midst of our daily lives.

When the life of grace takes root in us, it grafts onto the natural powers of our souls the supernatural gifts of the Holy Spirit. By doing this, God doesn't override our personalities and use us as some kind of robot-slaves to build up his kingdom. But he does equip us with all we need to live our missionary vocation to the fullest. Our potential to develop natural virtues and reach human maturity is enhanced, so we can also truly develop supernatural virtues (sometimes referred to as *infused* virtues) and reach full Christian maturity—the holiness that brings lasting happiness.

WISDOM FROM NARNIA

C.S. Lewis communicated this relationship between natural and supernatural powers beautifully in his delightful classic, *The Lion, the Witch and the Wardrobe.* As the four children from earth make their way through the magical realm of Narnia, which has long been suffering under the curse of an evil witch, they run across Santa Claus. Jolly Father Christmas gives each of the children a special gift—a sword for Peter, a vial of healing potion for Lucy, and so on. As the four children engage in their mission to liberate Narnia from its curse, each of the gifts is used in critical moments. Those gifts didn't take the place of each child's natural strengths and weaknesses, but rather the gifts were customized in order to allow each child's personality to flourish and expand beyond what he or she could have imagined.

ORDINARY AND EXTRAORDINARY GIFTS

It is likewise with God's grace in our lives. It equips our natural human powers with the seven universal gifts of the Holy Spirit (which every Christian receives; that's why we can call them "universal") and an assortment of other, charismatic gifts as well (distributed only to specific individuals in accordance with God's providence).

Four of the seven universal gifts heal and enhance our mental powers. Through the *gift of wisdom*, the Holy Spirit opens our minds to know about God—not only from a distance, so to speak, but to know God himself directly—to taste the divine goodness itself. This is considered the highest gift, because this experience unfailingly deepens and confirms the soul's union with God.

The second gift that renews our mind in Christ is the *gift of understanding*. This enables us to grasp the truths that God has revealed to us about himself and about our salvation; it gives us the ability to penetrate their depths and see more clearly how they relate to one another. The third gift, the *gift of knowledge*, is similar. It enables us to view and interpret normal human events and earthly realities as God does—in light of eternal truths. The fourth gift, the *gift of counsel*, builds on the third. If the gift of knowledge helps us see ordinary human events and earthly realities from God's perspective, the gift of counsel helps us navigate the extraordinary ones, guiding us when the right course of action is hard to fathom.

The remaining three universal gifts heal and strengthen the powers related to our will, our capacity to make free choices. The first of these, the *gift of piety*, gives us a supernatural affection for God as our loving Father and for other people as brothers and sisters in God's family. In other words, piety fuels a desire to live in a faith-based communion of hearts with God and with others.

If the gift of piety gives us supernatural affections, the next gift, the *gift of fortitude*, gives us supernatural strength in the face of spiritual obstacles and enemies. The third gift that the Holy Spirit uses to heal our fallen freedom is the gift of holy fear, what the Bible calls the "fear of the Lord" (Prov. 9:10). This isn't a slavish fear of punishment, but a filial fear of being separated from God, like an interior warning alarm that goes off when we find ourselves in morally and spiritually dangerous situations. It helps us turn around, flee, or change course, so that we avoid the threat altogether. God gives us these seven universal or ordinary gifts in order to help each of us live more and more as Christ lived, so we can continue his mission on earth.

The Bible and our theological tradition also identify other gifts from the Holy Spirit, sometimes called the charismatic gifts. They can also be called extraordinary gifts, because they are not ordinarily given to every Christian. These include prophecy, special discernment of spirits, healing, and miracles. In contrast to the Christological gifts, these can be understood as ecclesiastical gifts, because they are always given for the sake of building up the community of believers, the Church. They do not necessarily help the person who receives them become holy.

BEYOND FEELINGS

You may feel like the gifts of the Holy Spirit aren't present in your soul, but as long as you are living a life of grace, they are. As your relationship with Christ deepens, as you love him more and more with all your heart, soul, mind, and strength, the gifts work more and more freely. In that way, you become more docile to the Holy Spirit, "the One who builds the kingdom of God within the course of history," as St. John Paul II put it. And increased docility to the Holy Spirit means that God's dream for your life and your unique mission in the Church unfold and flourish more fully, regardless of how palpably you feel it. After all, in Christ's parable about the Last Judgment, many of those who were rewarded for their service to Jesus were surprised to discover that their normal behavior had actually contributed to building up Christ's kingdom; the truth of that eternal kingdom often transcends our temporal awareness (see Matt. 25:31–46).

Questions for Personal Reflection or Group Discussion

1. What idea in this chapter struck you most and why?

2. Which of the seven universal gifts of the Holy Spirit do you think would be most helpful for your life right now and why? Ask the Lord to increase that gift in your soul and enable you to make use of it.

3. The charismatic gifts are spoken about much more frequently than the Christological gifts. Why do you think that is? How do you think the devil feels about that discrepancy, and why?

4. The gifts are present in our souls, but in order for them to flourish we have to cooperate with them. This cooperation can take many forms, including feeding holy desires and accepting holy inspirations. Most of us do desire these things deep down. But more mundane desires seem to occupy our attention more regularly: We think about making more money, feeling more relaxed, climbing social or professional ladders, finding more ways to enjoy ourselves. . . . These natural desires aren't evil, but unless we intentionally feed the holier ones, the natural ones will monopolize our attention and make it harder for us to follow where God wants to lead us. Accepting holy inspiration is another way to cooperate with the Holy Spirit's gifts. God is always nudging us toward actions and decisions that will build up his kingdom in our hearts and in the

hearts of those around us. He gives us little inspirations, gentle whispers that we hear in the depth of our hearts: Call that person today; go and visit that person; take some time to pray before you go to work; take some more time to listen. Often these inspirations aren't attractive on the surface, because they require some self-sacrifice. But if we train ourselves to listen to them and heed them, we give God more room to work in our lives, and our spiritual growth accelerates. What will you do today to feed holy desires and accept holy invitations?

- I will make time to read that spiritual book I have been wanting to read for a long time.

- I will reach out to that person I know I should have reached out to already but haven't gotten around to.

- I will take inventory of the kind of media products I watch and listen to and eliminate one or two that consistently have a bad effect on me.

- (Write your own resolution) I will _____
  _____
  _____
  _____

Concluding Prayer

Confirm, O God, what you have brought about in us,
and preserve in the hearts of your faithful the gifts of the Holy Spirit:
may they never be ashamed to confess Christ crucified before the
world and by devoted charity may they ever fulfill his commands.
Instruct, O Lord, in the fullness of the Law those you have endowed
with the gifts of your Spirit and nourished by the Body of your
Only Begotten Son, that they may constantly show to the world
the freedom of your adopted children
and, by the holiness of their lives,
exercise the prophetic mission of your people.
Through Christ our Lord. Amen.

—ROMAN MISSAL, PRAYER OVER THE PEOPLE FROM THE
MASS FOR THE CONFERRAL OF CONFIRMATION, A AND B

Is Self-Love Good or Bad?

Man as "willed" by God, as "chosen" by him from eternity and called,
destined for grace and glory – this is "each" man, "the most concrete" man,
"the most real"; this is man in all the fullness of the mystery in which he
has become a sharer in Jesus Christ, the mystery in which each one of the
four thousand million human beings living on our planet has become a
sharer from the moment he is conceived beneath the heart of his mother.
– St. John Paul II, Redemptor Hominis, 13

IN THE SECOND OF THE two great commandments, Jesus tells us to "love your neighbor as yourself" (Matt. 22:39). Yet later on, in the Gospel of John, Jesus affirms that "Whoever loves his life loses it, and whoever hates his life in this world will preserve it for eternal life" (John 12:25). St. Matthew also records that saying, but with a slight variation: "Whoever finds his life will lose it, and whoever loses his life for my sake will find it" (Matt. 10:39).

TWO BRANDS OF SELF-LOVE

Is Jesus contradicting himself? On the one hand, he assumes that we love ourselves enough to be able to use self-love as a standard for how to treat our neighbor. On the other hand, he warns us against loving our lives, as if doing so will lead to self-destruction. How are we to understand this? Untangling this knot matters, because without doing so we can't really open the door to the realm of loving our neighbor as Jesus wants us to.

Traditional Christian spirituality identifies two brands of self-love, a healthy one and an unhealthy one. Healthy self-love sees and accepts oneself as created good by God, loved by him personally and unconditionally, appreciated and valued and affirmed by a heavenly Father who loved us so much that "he gave his only Son, so that everyone who believes in him might not perish but might have eternal life. . . . See what love the Father has bestowed on us that we may be called the children of God. Yet so we are" (John 3:16; 1 John 3:1).

Gradually coming to recognize this love that God has for us and accept it wholeheartedly constitutes one of the main dynamisms of spiritual growth. Our fallen nature tends to resist this love, mainly because it is unconditional and therefore outside of our control, but also because we have often been wounded and told that we are unlovable. Our tendency toward pride and self-sufficiency, exacerbated by those wounds, fears what is beyond our control. And so that fallen, broken part of us prefers to earn love, to try and make ourselves lovable through actions and accomplishments. It's hard for us to accept the revealed truth that, from God's perspective, nothing we can do will increase of decrease his love for us. He loves us fully already, because of who we are, not because of what we do or don't do.

Why Healthy Self-Love Is Healthy

As we learn to accept God's love for us, we also learn to love ourselves in a healthy way — not because we are better than other people; not because we have made ourselves so excellent; but simply because we are created in God's image and he rejoices in us: "For the Lord takes delight in his people" (Ps. 149:4). We learn to appreciate and even look with awe at the amazing dignity we have been given, not through any merit of our own, but simply through God's overflowing goodness: "I praise you, because I am wonderfully made; wonderful are your works!" (Ps. 139:14).

The awareness of ourselves as beloved by God nourishes humility and opens our souls to his grace. In so doing it fosters all the other virtues as well, giving us deeper reserves of strength and clearer motives to act in accordance with our true dignity — to be just, and temperate, and courageous, and prudent. This is healthy self-love, a self-love that flows from God and carries us toward God.

SIMPLE SELFISHNESS

Unhealthy self-love is what spiritual writers call *disordered* self-love, an exaggerated and distorted view of one's goodness, as if it were existentially independent and the central value of the entire universe. This brand of self-love is nothing more than self-centeredness, egoism, and self-absorption. It is an interior twistedness inherited from original sin and exacerbated by personal sin and the sinful trends present in many of human society's norms and customs. This kind of self-love sees all things as revolving around oneself, and it idolizes self to the point of seeking self-aggrandizement above anything else. Other people become merely obstacles or tools. God does, too. Life in this world is lived in terms of exalting one's self-image at any price. Happiness is pursued not through loving God and neighbor, but through feeding one's ego by acquiring more and more pleasure, popularity, or power—the focal points of the false promises of a fallen world. It distorts our true identity, the way Gollum's obsession with the Ring of Power twisted and distorted him into a shadow of his true self in Tolkien's *Lord of the Rings*. Disordered self-love is the Gollum syndrome.

A CHALLENGE FOR EVERYONE

Selfishness may seem extreme and rare when described so starkly. And yet we all have a built-in tendency to live that way. Every sin is an effervescence of that tendency, a victory of what St. Paul calls the "old self" (see Eph. 4:22-24).

When Jesus warns us that "whoever loves his life loses it, and whoever hates his life in this world will preserve it for eternal life" (John 12:25), he is evoking this Pauline contrast and admonishing us to avoid unhealthy self-love. He wants us to center our desires on God and his will, rather than on the idols of the world.

On the other hand, when Jesus commands us to "love your neighbor as your self," he is evoking healthy self-love as the core criterion for attitudes and behaviors toward others. The same criterion undergirds the earlier Gospel expression of the Golden Rule:

"Do to others whatever you would have them do to you. This is the law and the prophets" (Matt. 7:12).

LOVING YOUR NEIGHBOR AS YOURSELF

Even before we reach spiritual maturity, our deeper self (as opposed to our derivative, fallen nature) instinctually—and rightly—values and prefers things that help us live life well to things that harm and disorient us. When we are in need, we hope to find assistance. When we make mistakes, we hope to be given a second chance. When we are confused, we hope to be enlightened. Those are legitimate hopes, because assistance and second chances and enlightenment are all directed toward the full flourishing of a person created, redeemed, and unconditionally loved by God.

That full flourishing is a good thing; it is the object of a healthy self-love and the reason why sensible self-care glorifies God. And just as we spontaneously desire and pursue those legitimate hopes for ourselves, true love—the generous, Christ-like, Trinitarian love whose image and likeness constitutes our deepest identity and therefore our most authentic happiness—moves us to desire them and also pursue them for our neighbor.

This is why, as we shall see, evangelization includes not just preaching and praying, but also every good deed within our reach.

Questions for Personal Reflection or Group Discussion

1. What idea in this chapter struck you most and why?

2. How would you describe in your own words the difference between healthy and unhealthy self-love?

3. When have you been the recipient of the love-for-neighbor Jesus commands of us? How did it make you feel and why?

4. Because healthy self-love flows from seeing oneself as God does, it educates us about how to see others, too. God loves us and showers us with his gifts even though we are riddled with flaws, wounds, and sinful tendencies. God loves us in a way that never

stops affirming the sinner even while condemning the sin. God never gives up on us, even when there seems to be little hope for improvement: "If we are unfaithful he remains faithful, for he cannot deny himself" (2 Tim. 2:13). What will you do today to learn better how to see yourself and others as God does?

- I will spend some time today looking at a crucifix and reflecting on the fact that Jesus died for me—to pay the price for my sins, to show me the depths of his love, and to open for me the gates of heaven.

- I will pay special attention today to the needs of those around me and make an effort to meet them whenever I can.

- I will speak a little bit less and listen a little bit more in all my conversations today, to help avoid falling into self-centeredness.

- (Write your own resolution) I will _____

_____

_____

_____

Concluding Prayer

*O God, who have taught your Church
to keep all the heavenly commandments
by loving you and loving our neighbor,
grant us a spirit of peace and grace,
so that your entire family
may be devoted to you wholeheartedly
and united in purity of intent.
Through our Lord Jesus Christ, your Son,
who lives and reigns with you in the unity of the Holy Spirit,
one God, for ever and ever. Amen.*

—ROMAN MISSAL, SECOND COLLECT FOR THE MASS
FOR PROMOTING HARMONY

Where to Start?

To all who are listening to my voice I wish to say that the age of the missions is not over; Christ still needs generous men and women to become heralds of the Good News to the ends of the earth. Do not be afraid to follow him. Share freely with others the faith you have received! No believer in Christ, no institution of the Church can avoid this supreme duty: to proclaim Christ to all peoples.
—St. John Paul II, *Homily in Gambia, February 23, 1992; Redemptoris Missio, 3*

W E ALL REMEMBER THE GOSPEL passages where Jesus multiplies the loaves. On one occasion he fed more than five thousand people with only five loaves of bread and two dried fish (see Matt. 14:13-21). On another occasion he fed more than four thousand people with only seven loaves of bread and a few fish (see Matt. 15:32-39).

DOES GOD ASK THE IMPOSSIBLE?

In both cases it seemed to Christ's apostles that he was asking them something impossible. He longed to feed the hungry crowds who were following him:

> "My heart is moved with pity for the crowd, for they have been with me now for three days and have nothing to eat. I do not want to send them away hungry, for fear they may collapse on the way." (Matt. 15:32)

But the little group of chosen apostles was more practical. "The disciples said to him, 'Where could we ever get enough bread in this deserted place to satisfy such a crowd?'" (Matt. 15:33).

On the first occasion of this miracle, the apostles actually advised Jesus to simply send the crowds away to fend for themselves. It's an understandable reaction. But Jesus turned and looked them in the eye and said: "There is no need for them to go away; give them some food yourselves" (Matt. 14:16). He was not stupid. He knew the scanty resources at their disposal. "But they said to him, 'Five loaves and two fish are all we have here'" (Matt. 14:17). They really did have very little. Their merely natural possibilities to achieve what Jesus was asking them to do were ridiculously inadequate.

FEELING OVERWHELMED

Most of us can identify with that, if we are honest. The moral demands of our faith overwhelm us—it seems impossible to live the life of patience, purity, generosity, and courage we know we are called to live. The apostolic demands of being a Christian missionary weigh us down; we find ourselves barely able to fulfill the basic duties of everyday life, let alone branch out into creative ways to evangelize the world—even if we could think of some.

Truly, we find ourselves looking at Jesus with the same pained—and maybe even frustrated or resentful—expression of the disciples in the Gospel: "Five loaves and two fish are all that we have here." Lord, I just don't have the strength, the time, the knowledge to do this. If I give away the little I have, I don't think I will be able to survive. I really need those few loaves and fish. I can't help you—I can barely help myself . . .

JESUS KNOWS OUR LIMITATIONS

Jesus understands that. In fact, he knows our limitations better than we know them ourselves. When St. John told his version of the multiplication of the loaves, he points this out explicitly, even with a bit of humor.

> When Jesus raised his eyes and saw that a large crowd was coming to him, he said to Philip, "Where can we buy enough food for them to eat?" He said this to test him, because he himself knew what he was going to do. (John 6:5-6)

Jesus knows our limitations. He knows that by our own power the Christian life he invites us to live is a mere pipedream. But at the same time, he doesn't share those limitations. He is God. His grace can radically transform and multiply the slightest and most paltry effort to build his kingdom, to love our neighbors, just as his grace transformed the few loaves and fish into an abundant feast. He just needs us to do one thing, one little thing, to make that happen. "Then he said, 'Bring them here to me'" (Matt. 14:18).

Jesus Works Within Our Limitations

When the apostles placed their meager resources into the Lord's hands, they didn't know what would happen. All they knew was that Jesus could be trusted. Jesus would take care of it. Jesus would find a way to make it work out. Jesus would not waste even a crumb of whatever they put into his hands and offered to him for the advance of his kingdom. Not even a crumb. In fact, after the miracle was over and Jesus had fed thousands with the little his disciples had given him, he still wasn't finished.

> [H]e said to his disciples, "Gather the fragments left over, so that nothing will be wasted." So they collected them, and filled twelve wicker baskets with fragments from the five barley loaves that had been more than they could eat. (John 6:12-13)

This is how it works with the Lord. The gifts he gives us, the gifts of grace and the Holy Spirit, miraculously multiply our slightest effort to live as Christ asks us to live. In order to fulfill our Christian mission in the world, we don't have to have a perfect master plan or a fail-safe formula. All we have to do is offer what we have and let Jesus multiply it. We just have to give to others what Jesus has given to us—a few loaves of faith and a couple words of hope—and he will do the rest. That's the way to start. That's how the Lord wants us to start: leaning not on our natural smarts and strengths, but stepping out of our comfort zone and leaning on him.

FROM PLAIN BREAD TO HOLY HOST

This whole dynamism is beautifully present every time we go to Mass. We offer to God the humble gifts of bread and wine—the most normal, earthly products of nature and human labor. We place them on the altar, in all their plainness, simplicity, and fragility. And what happens? They become hosts of Christ's own precious Body and Blood. God "gracifies" them, transforming them into something that no human effort, however magnificent, could ever accomplish: the Eucharistic presence of the Lord himself.

Questions for Personal Reflection or Group Discussion

1. What idea in this chapter struck you most and why?

2. When have you experienced the power of God's grace transforming your limited efforts into a true advance for his kingdom? Remember, savor, and thank him for those experiences.

3. What are the loaves and fish available to you personally, and how is God asking you to put them at the service of his kingdom?

4. Why do you think God sometimes asks us to do more than we are naturally capable of? A famous story about St. Francis of Assisi illustrates this point. St. Francis was the founder of the Franciscan Order, which has been one of the Church's most fruitful spiritual and missionary powerhouses ever since its foundation in the high Middle Ages. But Francis didn't start off with that in mind. He just wanted to serve the Lord. One day early on in his faith journey, he was praying in front of a crucifix in the church of San Damiano, just outside the walls of Assisi, a small city in the Italian region of Umbria. As he prayed, our Lord appeared to him, and the crucifix spoke to him, saying "Francis,

rebuild my church." The Lord was calling him to his great work of founding the Franciscan Order, an army of Christians dedicated to reform and renewal. But Francis didn't understand that yet. It so happened that the little church of San Damiano, where he was praying, was in a state of disrepair. So Francis obeyed our Lord by doing what he could: He started to replace the stones and bricks that had fallen off the church's walls—he started to repair the little church building of San Damiano. That little gesture of loving and generous obedience was transformed into a religious movement that has pumped new spiritual vitality into the Church and the world ever since. Today, what is the Lord asking you to do, and how will you respond?

- I will review my schedule and commitments and determine where I can make more time to engage in some kind of apostolic activity.

- I will review my budget and see where I can cut down on expenditures in order to give material support to some work of charity and evangelization.

- I will say "yes" to the invitation that I have heard God speaking in my heart for a while, but which I have as yet been too afraid to accept.

- (Write your own resolution) I will _____

_____

_____

_____

Closing Prayer

Blessed are you, Lord God of all creation, for through your goodness we have received the bread we offer you: fruit of the earth and work of human hands, it will become for us the bread of life. Blessed are you, Lord God of all creation, for through your goodness we have received the wine we offer you: fruit of the vine and work of human hands, it will become our spiritual drink.

—ROMAN MISSAL, OFFERTORY PRAYERS (AND PRIVATE PRAYER OF THE PRIEST) AT THE START OF THE LITURGY OF THE EUCHARIST

Daily Life Matters

*There cannot be two parallel lives in their existence: on the one
hand, the so-called "spiritual" life, with its values and demands;
and on the other, the so-called "secular" life, that is, life in a
family, at work, in social relationships, in the responsibilities of
public life and in culture. The branch, engrafted to the vine which
is Christ, bears its fruit in every sphere of existence and activity.*
—St. John Paul II, Christifideles Laici, *59*

JESUS LIVED FOR ABOUT THIRTY-THREE years here on earth. He spent the
first thirty of those years in obscurity. He lived most of that period
in a small town off the beaten path, Nazareth. He spent his days learning from his mother, Mary, and his foster father, Joseph, who ran a
carpenter shop and probably served as the village handyman. For thirty
years the Savior of the world, the Son of God, the incarnate second
person of the Blessed Trinity lived the most normal of human lives.
No miracles, no extraordinary manifestations of anything, no special
privileges, no prodigious signs after the amazing night of his birth. Just
normal daily life.

THE VALUE OF THE PRESENT MOMENT

Why? Why did Jesus choose this path? Did he spend those thirty years
twiddling his thumbs and waiting around for the moment when he
would begin to preach and teach and redeem the world? Not at all.
Everything Jesus did and said was part of God's divine revelation. It
all has a lesson for us. It teaches us about how God sees the world,
and about how we are created and called to live our lives. And the

thirty years during which Jesus and the Blessed Virgin Mary lived outside the spotlight teaches us that daily life matters.

The relationships, experiences, and activities of daily life construct the primary arena where we love our neighbors as ourselves, where we fulfill our mission. Too often we overlook this. Too often we fantasize about different circumstances that, or so we think, would give us a chance to live life to the full and be all we can be. Too often we think that "mission" necessarily implies going to far-off places. Too often we forget the wise irony contained in the proverbial phrase "the grass is always greener on the other side of the fence."

Living in a state of perpetual regret and self-pity because of the challenges of our daily circumstances—thinking that "real life" is actually waiting somewhere around the corner and off in the future—distracts the soul. In fact, it can blind us to the real graces and opportunities that the Lord never ceases to present to us: "At every time and in every place, God draws close to man. He calls man to seek him, to know him, to love him with all his strength," the *Catechism* reminds us. "He never ceases to call every man to seek him, so as to find life and happiness . . . God never ceases to draw man to himself" (CCC, 1, 30, 27). Jesus didn't wait until he left Nazareth to redeem the world; the redemption of the world, in fact, necessarily passed through those thirty years in Nazareth. And our contribution to that work of redemption necessarily passes through our Nazareth.

Not All Saints Are Supernovas

We see this truth reflected in the lives of the saints. The most well-known saints are those who were called by God to truly extraordinary lives and missions. St. Francis of Assisi received the stigmata and preached miraculously even to wild animals. St. Faustina Kowalska received mystical visions and had mystical conversations with the Lord on a regular basis throughout her entire consecrated life. St. Patrick exercised such spiritual force—in his preaching, leadership, and miracles—that he converted the entire Irish people to Christianity in his own lifetime. . . . Because of their dramatic character, these extraordinary manifestations of grace capture our attention and can make us think that holiness consists in being like them.

And yet plenty of other saints reached the pinnacle of holiness and fulfilled their mission on earth without ever leaving the confines of their Nazareth. St. Bede entered the monastery as a seven-year-old boy when his parents entrusted his education to the monks. He died there more than sixty years later, having never left the borders of the double monastery in Jarrow, England. St. Thérèse of Lisieux, whose autobiography led to her being named a Doctor of the Church, died at the young age of twenty-four. At the time of her death, the sisters in her convent were at a loss as to what they should put into the death notice that was customary to send to the other convents—that's how normal and unremarkable her brief consecrated life had been, at least from the outside.

St. Gianna Beretta Molla was an Italian wife, mother, and pediatrician. She liked skiing and fashion and lived amid the normal hustle and bustle of family life. Her holiness took root and flourished there, in her Nazareth. And of course St. Joseph himself, patron saint of the Universal Church, lived and died in the dusty obscurity of the literal Nazareth, speaking nary a single word in the Scriptures.

REDEMPTION IS ROOTED IN NAZARETH

The extraordinary manifestations of grace that capture our attention are gifts God gives to the Church in order to boost our faith. But they are not the substance of holiness and happiness. They are not necessary ingredients in the recipe for Christian faithfulness. Rather, they are simply providential works of grace overflowing from daily lives lived in communion with God. To discover and fulfill our mission in life, to love our neighbor as ourselves and thereby build up the kingdom of God, we must not seek first what is extraordinary and dramatic. We must not vainly hanker after spectacular shows of spiritual power. Rather we must strive to be authentic Christians, fully present and engaged in each duty and interaction that meets us in our Nazareth, where redemption is truly rooted. What flows from that, whether dramatic or not, is up to God.

Moses put it well in his last sermon before the Chosen People of Israel crossed into the Promised Land:

> For this command which I am giving you today is not too wondrous or remote for you. It is not in the heavens, that you should say, "Who will go up to the heavens to get it for us and tell us of it, that we may do it?" Nor is it across the sea, that you should say, "Who will cross the sea to get it for us and tell us of it, that we may do it?" No, it is something very near to you, in your mouth and in your heart, to do it. (Deut. 30:11–14)

The principles, virtues, and activities explored in these chapters are all related to how we can help love our neighbors by spreading Christ's kingdom. But they can all be applied—indeed, they *must* be applied—first and foremost in our daily lives. God's providence has placed us there. God's love longs to meet us there. God's grace will flow through us there, leading us step-by-step to the fullness of our calling.

Questions for Personal Reflection or Group Discussion

1. What idea in this chapter struck you most and why?

2. Describe the circumstances of your Nazareth: the duties, relationships, and activities that form the warp and woof of your daily life. Where is God inviting you to love more in them?

3. How easy or hard is it for you to believe that God is at work through you in those daily circumstances? Speak to God right now and express your faith that he is present and active in your Nazareth. Ask for the grace to find and follow him there.

4. Hypocrisy is one of the biggest obstacles to building up the kingdom of Christ. When we profess to be Christians, followers of Christ, we are claiming to have certain standards of behavior. When we habitually fail to live up to those standards, or when we habitually make no effort to do so, we create a disconnect between what we say and what we do. When people

notice that, it makes them doubt the authenticity of the Christian faith. If Jesus were real, they think to themselves, then his followers would be more coherent. What will you do today to root out any remnants of hypocrisy in your life?

- I will go to confession as a concrete expression of my sincere desire to let God's grace root out my self-centered tendencies.

- I will pay special attention to one relationship that is challenging for me, asking God to help me see that person as he does, and to help me "love my neighbor as myself" in that particular case.

- I will ask forgiveness from someone I may have offended, consciously or not.

- (Write your own resolution) I will _____

_____

_____

_____

Concluding Prayer

O God, who cause the minds of the faithful to unite in a single
purpose, grant your people to love what you command
and to desire what you promise, that, amid the uncertainties
of this world, our hearts may be fixed on that place
where true gladness is found.
May your grace, O Lord, we pray, at all times go before
us and follow after and make us always determined
to carry out good works.
Through our Lord Jesus Christ, your Son,
who lives and reigns with you in the unity of the Holy Spirit,
one God, for ever and ever. Amen.

—ROMAN MISSAL, COLLECTS FOR THE TWENTY-FIRST
AND TWENTY-EIGHTH SUNDAYS IN ORDINARY TIME

Who Is Your Neighbor?

The Lord himself renews his invitation to all the lay faithful
to come closer to him every day. And with the recognition that
what is his is also their own, they ought to associate themselves
with him in his saving mission. Once again he sends them
into every town and place where he himself is to come.
— St. John Paul II, Christifideles Laici, 2

JESUS WANTS HIS GRACE TO touch every human heart. He wants to lead every person out of the darkness of sin and frustration and into the spiritual light and fulfillment of his kingdom. God "wills everyone to be saved and to come to knowledge of the truth" (1 Tim. 2:4).

PREPARING HEARTS FOR THE LORD

Only his grace can work that redemption and pour the Holy Spirit into human hearts. Yet Jesus wants us to be the heralds who announce the Good News of his salvation and so open hearts to receive that grace. This is how he arranged things during his own earthly ministry, and that set the pattern for the rest of human history: "After this the Lord appointed seventy-two others whom he sent ahead of him in pairs to every town and place he intended to visit" (Luke 10:1).

Jesus intends to visit "every town and place" himself. He truly is the Savior, and unless he enters a heart, his kingdom cannot come there. Unless his presence in a heart deepens and expands, his kingdom cannot grow there. But he sends his disciples "ahead of him" to prepare the way, to be messengers of his kingdom and channels of his saving and sanctifying grace. When he commands us to "love your neighbor as yourself," he points out which "town and place" he wants us to go and prepare for him: all the hearts that are within our own actual and potential circles of influence.

BONUM EST DIFFUSIVUM SUI

Have you ever noticed that evil is contagious? As the old saying goes, one bad apple spoils the bunch. Sociological studies have explored the influence of "bad apples" in the workplace, finding statistical evidence that even one employee with a habitually sour attitude has a disproportionately negative effect on the entire workplace atmosphere. If you have children, you are keenly aware of the destructive effects that can flow from them hanging out with the wrong kind of peers. Even St. Paul identifies and applies this principle, quoting an ancient proverb: "Do not be led astray: 'Bad company corrupts good morals'" (1 Cor. 15:33).

But the contrary is also true; goodness is also contagious. An old Latin saying puts it concisely: *Bonum est diffusivum sui* ("Goodness always tends to spread"). If you are a teacher or a coach, you always want students or players who work hard and build up the rest of the class or team. If you are a parent, you want your children to spend time with good kids, knowing this will have a good influence on them.

Jesus's famous images of what a Christian is called to be, which we have already reflected on, invoke this principle. He tells his followers they are "the salt of the earth" and "the light of the world" (Matt. 5:13-14). A little bit of salt flavors a whole plate of food and preserves a much larger cut of meat. One small candle or one small lightbulb can illuminate an entire room and be seen through a window from far away. The goodness and grace that we receive from Christ always tends to spread out and touch those around us—*bonum est diffusivum sui*.

The neighbors we are commanded to love, therefore, are first of all every person we come into contact with. Wherever God's providence sends us, whatever lives we touch, we can season them with love, being a blessing to them in small ways or big ways. In this sense, before reflecting on the specific forms of apostolic activity, it is worthwhile to reflect on the circles of influence that every Christian can inject with gospel goodness.

OUR CIRCLES OF INFLUENCE

The circle closest to our own heart is our family, and most especially our immediate family. Then comes the circle of our friends, the people we lean on and the ones who lean on us to make life bearable, enjoyable, and meaningful. The next circle is all of our colleagues and acquaintances, those brought together with us not by our own intention, but through outside circumstances—we go to the same school, we work at the same company, we live in the same neighborhood, we go to the same parish, and so on.

Moving further out, we reach the circle of strangers, those we come into contact with only once and may never meet again, or those we only hear about or know about abstractly—the flight attendant on the plane, the help desk representative we speak to on the phone, the person who reads an article we write, the people affected by a law we help pass, the citizens of a city far away who are suffering from a recent earthquake.

Finally, our circles of influence also include our enemies—those who are actively working against what we are working for, those who are actively obstructing what we are legitimately pursuing.

These circles of influence often overlap, and their borders are porous, so that a stranger can become a friend, for example, or a family member can become an enemy. And any effect we have on any single person in any of those circles of influence will in turn affect that person's interaction with his or her various circles of influence. And as we grow and engage in the activities of life, our circles can also expand and contract.

BEYOND MATH

Identifying these circles is not meant to turn our lives into some kind of mathematical diagram where we try to categorize and control everyone we meet. Rather, the point is simply to pause and reflect on the truly vast field of influence every human being exerts. Our actions and decisions are like stones being thrown into a quiet lake; their repercussions spread like ripples on the water all the way to the shore.

We don't have to go very far to identify our neighbor. To obey the Lord's command, to find our first and finest field of Christian mission, we only have to seek to treat those within our circles of influence as God would have us, spreading his goodness wherever we go and readying hearts to receive him ever more fully.

Questions for Personal Reflection or Group Discussion

1. What idea in this chapter struck you most and why?

2. Make a drawing that illustrates your different circles of influence. Think about all the people whose lives are touched, directly or indirectly, by your life. How does it make you feel?

3. Which of your circles of influence receives its fair share of your attention? Which one, if any, have you been neglecting, and why?

4. The closer circles of influence deserve our greater attention. Just think, for example, of the busy husband and dad who spends so much time at work that he neglects his wife and children. He has lost his center, and eventually even the good he is doing in the outer circles will suffer because of it. This is an especially important principle of discernment to keep in mind in our digital age. It's so easy now to stay connected—at least apparently—with hundreds of people. It can lead to a dispersion of attention and a distracting fascination with merely superficial experiences and interactions. Living only on the surface of things, however, impoverishes the soul. What will you do today to keep superficial things in their proper place?

   - I will fast from my favorite social media interaction for a day.

   - I will refrain from reading the latest headlines for a day.

   - I will enjoy a lovely experience, and instead of taking a photo of it, I will simply let it seep into my soul and enrich me.

- (Write your own resolution) I will _____

  _____

  _____

  _____

Concluding Prayer

I leave you now with this prayer: that the Lord Jesus will reveal himself to each one of you, that he will give you the strength to go out and profess that you are Christian, that he will show you that he alone can fill your hearts. Accept his freedom and embrace his truth, and be messengers of the certainty that you have been truly liberated through the death and resurrection of the Lord Jesus. This will be the new experience, the powerful experience, that will generate, through you, a more just society and a better world. God bless you and may the joy of Jesus be always with you!

—St. John Paul II[43]

PART IX

YOUR MODES OF APOSTOLATE

"Therefore do not be afraid of them. Nothing is concealed that will not be revealed, nor secret that will not be known. What I say to you in the darkness, speak in the light; what you hear whispered, proclaim on the house-tops. And do not be afraid of those who kill the body but cannot kill the soul; rather, be afraid of the one who can destroy both soul and body in Gehenna. Are not two sparrows sold for a small coin? Yet not one of them falls to the ground without your Father's knowledge. Even all the hairs of your head are counted. So do not be afraid; you are worth more than many sparrows. Everyone who acknowledges me before others I will acknowledge before my heavenly Father. But whoever denies me before others, I will deny before my heavenly Father."

MATTHEW 10:26–33

Your Three Ways to Evangelize

We most earnestly beg all our sons the world over, clergy and laity, to
be deeply conscious of the dignity, the nobility, which is theirs through
being grafted on to Christ as shoots on a vine: "I am the vine; you the
branches." They are thus called to a share in His own divine life; and
since they are united in mind and spirit with the divine Redeemer even
when they are engaged in the affairs of the world, their work becomes
a continuation of His work, penetrated with redemptive power.
— St. John XXIII, Mater et Magistra, 259

NO ONE WILL EVANGELIZE IN the exact same way that you do. Your relationship with God is unique, your social network is unique, your circles of influence are unique, and your mission in the Church and the world is unique. And so how you enter into the universal apostolate (see CCC, 863).[44] will also be unique. In a sense there are as many forms of apostolate as there are individual Christians. This is why the first requirement for carrying out our apostolic mission is to be good listeners—to listen to the whispers of the Holy Spirit directing our desires, our hopes, our thoughts, our actions.

A THREEFOLD RICHNESS

But the Church has also identified three general categories of apostolate. In fact the Second Vatican Council published an entire decree describing the apostolate of the Church, especially of the laity, called *Apostolicam Actuositatem*. Understanding these general categories will help us be better listeners and more effective apostles.

These three forms of evangelization correspond to the threefold mission of Christ, who redeems and sanctifies the world as priest, prophet-teacher, and king. Through baptism every Christian shares in this threefold mission, though clergy and laity share in different ways.

A Way to Bridge Heaven and Earth

The priestly aspect of our mission consists in bringing God's grace to bear on our normal activities. Everything Jesus did, from working in the carpenter shop to dying on the cross, expressed and exhibited his love for and obedience to the Father. Everything Jesus did was an offering to the Father, an act of worship, part of his redeeming sacrifice that reached its culmination through his passion, death, and resurrection. In this way Jesus reconnected the human realm to the divine realm—a connection that had been lost with original sin. Such is the primary function of a priest—to be a bridge between heaven and earth.

But even the lay members of the Church exercise this function when they unite their daily activities and sacrifices to the offering of Christ himself by living them with faith and by placing them spiritually on the altar during Mass. In other words, simply the way we live our daily lives—filled with faith, as expressions of love for God and neighbor—can become a powerful witness in the world to the reality and truth of the gospel, as well as an instrument of God's grace.

Words to Change History

The second category of apostolate flows from the prophetic mission of Christ, which also is shared by every Christian. In this context, *prophetic* doesn't simply mean foretelling the future. Rather it refers to "speaking forth" on behalf of God: announcing the gospel, explaining it, and teaching it by words. The clergy do this in an official way, but all Christians are called to do so in their efforts to evangelize the world: "To teach in order to lead others to faith is the task of every preacher and of each believer" (CCC, 904).

Works to Renew the World

Finally, the third way of evangelizing is linked to Christ's kingly mission, which once again is shared by every Christian. For the clergy, this mission applies particularly to governing the ecclesial structures themselves, although laypersons can also participate in that activity to some extent (see CCC, 910). Primarily, however, for the laity this form of apostolate has to do with bringing the institutions and conditions of society under the rule of Christ, what the Second Vatican Council called "the renewal of the temporal order."[45]

In short, the three ways of evangelization have to do with our priestly and Christ-centered *way* of day-to-day living, our prophetic *words* of Christian wisdom, and our creative *works* directed toward Christianizing human society, institutions, and culture from the inside out. In the following chapters we will dig into some more specific aspects of each.

Questions for Personal Reflection or Group Discussion

1. What idea in this chapter struck you most and why?

2. From the point of view of your sharing in Christ's priestly, prophetic, and kingly mission of redemption, what aspects of your life do not have evangelizing potential?

3. How would you describe in your own words the three dimensions of the Church's apostolate?

4. G.K. Chesterton, a famous convert to Catholicism and prolific author and apologist in the early twentieth century, once quipped that when someone becomes a Christian absolutely everything changes, even brushing one's teeth. His point was that once we are members of Christ's mystical body, which happens through baptism, our smallest actions take on grace-filled meaning. What will you do today to activate this meaning more intentionally?

   • I will say a small prayer before each of my day's activities, consciously offering them up to God for the advance of his kingdom.

- I will light a devotional candle somewhere in my house, to remind me that, because God inhabits my soul through grace, my house is in a certain sense a Christian sanctuary, an outpost of Christ's kingdom here on earth.
- I will arrive for Mass a few minutes early next time so I can focus my heart and prayerfully place on the altar all my activities, intentions, and relationships, thus uniting them to Christ's self-offering and living more purposefully my share in the Lord's priestly mission.
- (Write your own resolution) I will _____

_____

_____

_____

Concluding Prayer

In the Church, God has made known to us his hidden purpose: to make all things one in Christ. Let us pray that his will may be done.
— Father, unite all things in Christ.
We give you thanks for the presence and power of your Spirit in the Church: give us the will to search for unity, and inspire us to pray and work together.
— Father, unite all things in Christ.

— LITURGY OF THE HOURS, PRAYERS AND
INTERCESSIONS FOR EVENING PRAYER FOR THE
SIXTEENTH SUNDAY IN ORDINARY TIME[46]

Your Moral Witness

*Above all the gospel must be proclaimed by witness. Take a Christian
or a handful of Christians who, in the midst of their own community,
show their capacity for understanding and acceptance, their sharing of
life and destiny with other people, their solidarity with the efforts of all
for whatever is noble and good. Let us suppose that, in addition, they
radiate in an altogether simple and unaffected way their faith in values
that go beyond current values, and their hope in something that is not
seen and that one would not dare to imagine. . . . Such a witness is
already a silent proclamation of the Good News and a very powerful
and effective one. Here we have an initial act of evangelization.*
—St. Paul VI, Evangelii Nuntiandi, 21

G OD DIDN'T SAVE US FROM a distance. In Jesus he became one of us,
walked along the paths of life with real human beings through
the streets of Palestine, and made his redeeming love and grace tangible. And he did that for thirty years before he preached his first
sermon. Since every Christian is *alter Christus* (another Christ), every
Christian should do the same.

CHRISTIAN BILLBOARDS

This is one of the meanings of "witness" or "testimony." Our outward behavior shows forth the truth, the goodness, and the beauty
of Jesus Christ. We become, as it were, billboards and advertisements for the abundant life Jesus gives when people accept his kingship and become his followers.

Of course, first of all, moral integrity is its own reward. Living in accord with what is morally right means living in accord with what will lead us toward the fulfillment we long for; it's following the manufacturer's instructions—the manufacturer of human nature being God and the moral law being the instructions for how to make human nature flourish. Telling the truth, honoring our elders, obeying legitimate authority, promoting human life, respecting other people's property, treating people with the dignity they deserve as children of God, courageously facing up to evil and corruption, wisely training and governing our raw emotions and passions, putting our gifts and talents at the service of others—these are clearly steps on the road to spiritual maturity and lasting happiness for anyone who takes them.

And yet they have a corollary effect as well. The more faithful we are to the moral law God has built into the universe, the sharper images of God himself we become. We were created in his image and likeness, but that original identity was obscured by sin and evil. As God's grace works in our lives, and as we cooperate with that grace through freely engaging in the battle for moral integrity and spiritual maturity, that original identity is gradually restored and even enhanced. Our personal existence begins to resonate with God's glory. We become mirrors of God's love and wisdom. We begin to "shine like lights in the world"—a world that is darkened with greed and lust and superficial folly (see Phil. 2:15). We become, without even thinking about it, a scent of heaven that captures the attention of other people and makes them curious: "For we are the aroma of Christ for God among those who are being saved and among those who are perishing" (2 Cor. 2:15).

Our own moral and spiritual growth brings us interior peace and strength and overflows into the world around us; God uses it to invite others to step onto the same path of redemption we are following. This is the first and indispensable form of apostolate for every Christian.

WHEN THE LAWS WERE NOT FRIENDLY

In the first centuries of Christianity, this was in many ways the *only* form of apostolate. Christianity was outlawed. Public displays of faith and public evangelizing activities, therefore, were minimal at best and life-threatening at worst. And yet the Church continued to attract new members. It continued to grow and expand at a truly remarkable rate. How?

Because of the moral witness of the Christians: While still living within the Roman Empire, their faith liberated them from Rome's pagan prejudices and vices. And as a result the moral and spiritual quality of their lives increased drastically. People saw how the Christians lived, it resonated in their hearts, and they wanted to find for themselves that same purpose, depth, and joy. Thus Christianity spread through the silent, moral witness of healthy Christian living.

The Beauty and Power of Martyrdom

Sometimes this witness extended beyond the calm interactions of daily life and became dramatic. The English word *martyr*, in fact, comes from the Greek word for "witness." The early Christian martyrs gave definitive and irresistible witness to the truth of the gospel. These Christians modeled moral integrity through their example of honesty, responsibility, and charity; they modeled spiritual maturity through their courageous fidelity to the unseen realities revealed by Christ, like the Real Presence in the Eucharist and the promise of heaven and eternal life. In addition their example and fidelity endured the hardest test of all: physical and emotional torture—and even death.

St. Lawrence the Deacon was one of these early martyrs, or witnesses, to Christ. He resisted the Roman government's efforts to unjustly intrude on the interior life of the Church. For doing so he was condemned to execution by burning—a truly horrible fate. The night before his martyrdom was spent in a dank prison cell, but instead of bemoaning his fate, he dedicated the whole night to prayer and song, joyfully preparing to meet the Lord. Unbeknownst to St. Lawrence, his pagan guard, Romanus, was watching closely, and such strange behavior caught his attention. The soldier's curiosity led him to question the saint, who gladly explained the Christian faith behind his calm confidence in the face of such humiliation and suffering. Soon Lawrence was baptizing Romanus right there in the prison cell.

Our moral and spiritual witness is our first apostolate. Simply through engaging in the struggle to develop the moral integrity and spiritual maturity allows God's grace to fill our souls and shine forth in surprising ways, catching the attention of our neighbors and opening their hearts to hear news of the kingdom. It is a primary way to love your neighbor as yourself.

Questions for Personal Reflection or Group Discussion

1. What idea in this chapter struck you most and why?

2. When have you been positively influenced by someone's moral and spiritual witness? Remember, savor, and thank God for that experience.

3. In which circumstances in your life do you find it hardest to maintain your moral witness to Christ? Why do you think those situations/relationships tend to be so challenging, and what are you going to do about it?

4. Many Christians complain that the moral standards of today's culture are so upside down that it makes it impossible to live with the integrity we are called to live. And yet that point of view fails to take into account at least two important factors. First, God himself is at work in our souls through his grace. If we cultivate that grace through prayer, study, and the sacraments, it will give us all the strength we need to do what is right. Second, throughout history the Church has frequently had to face aggressively corrosive socio-cultural environments. In fact Jesus himself predicted this: "In the world you will have trouble," he promised his disciples during the Last Supper (John 16:33). And yet, the Church has often ended up influencing the culture itself more than allowing the culture to corrupt the Church. What will you do today to strengthen your moral witness in a world gone morally mad?

   • I will do a hidden act of kindness without seeking any reward.

- I will make sure to speak truthfully in every conversation and meeting I have today, refraining from exaggerations and deceptions that only feed my vanity.
- I will do something special for someone close to me—spouse, parent, sibling—just to show them I love them.
- (Write your own resolution) I will _____

  _____

  _____

  _____

Concluding Prayer

*It is truly right and just, our duty and our salvation,
always and everywhere to give you thanks, Lord, holy Father,
almighty and eternal God. For you are glorified when your saints
are praised; their very sufferings are but wonders of your might:
in your mercy you give ardor to their faith, to their endurance
you grant firm resolve, and in their struggle the victory is yours,
through Christ our Lord. Be merciful now to me, and grant me
the grace I need be true to your will in my life today, that my
witness may shine like a light in this darkened world and spread
the sweet aroma of Christ to those around me who need it. Amen.*

—ADAPTED FROM PREFACE II OF HOLY
MARTYRS IN THE *ROMAN MISSAL*

The Apostolate of Kindness

*For the Church, the first means of evangelization is the
witness of an authentically Christian life, given over to God
in a communion that nothing should destroy and at the
same time given to one's neighbor with limitless zeal.*
—St. Paul VI, Evangelii Nuntiandi, 41

A T ONE POINT, THE BIBLE sums up Jesus's life on earth with
the simple phrase, "He went about doing good . . ." (Acts 10:38).
When it comes to the witness of our lives in this world, to becoming
a mirror of God's love for those around us, a better program is hard
to formulate. Doing unto others what we would have them do to
us, loving our neighbors as ourselves, involves at the very least the
habitual disposition to do good and not harm to those around us.

DISTASTEFUL DO-GOODERS

In some circles the term "do-gooder" has taken on derogatory connotations. Maybe that's because so many do-gooders are, in some
way or another, hypocritical. They go about doing good, but with
ulterior motives. They are expecting something in return—praise,
popularity, payback. Their appearance of being concerned for others masks a self-centered approach to life. And so, when whomever
they want to impress or influence isn't around, their mask falls away
and they revert to pettiness and even cruelty in attitude, speech, and
action. If you want to know a person's true colors, so they say, watch
how he or she behaves when nobody is looking.

That kind of hypocritical behavior clouds our soul. It inhibits our own spiritual growth as well as obscuring our capacity to mirror God's goodness. But it doesn't negate the importance of living with an eye for kindness, of following the example of our Lord who "went about doing good." Kindness, the quality of being friendly, generous, and considerate, is certainly not the pinnacle of moral integrity or the sum total of holiness. But unkindness, being inconsiderate and harsh, is just as certainly incompatible with both. To be kind to others, especially those in need, is the entrance level in the edifice of love.

WHY KINDNESS MATTERS

From a theological perspective, kindness flows from the recognition that every person we meet was created in God's image and likeness, redeemed by Christ's atoning sacrifice on the cross, and called to everlasting life in communion with the Lord and all the saints of heaven. That's every human being, every person we see, hear about, run into, interact with—every single one. As Pope Benedict XVI put it in his inaugural homily as pope: "We are not some casual and meaningless product of evolution. Each of us is the result of a thought of God. Each of us is willed, each of us is loved, each of us is necessary."[47]

This may seem obvious to those of us who have grown up in the Church, but it isn't obvious to citizens of this fallen world. It's something that was revealed to us by Jesus. Before the Christian era and beyond the influence of Christian culture, universal human dignity was and is only vaguely perceived—at best. In non-Christian cultures kindness was and is reserved for people of your own group or caste. Outsiders are automatically considered enemies and threats, not brothers and sisters, until proven otherwise. This logic has produced a large portion of the horrendous injustices that litter the path of human history.

This is not to say that all Christians perfectly follow our Lord's example—non-Christians don't have a monopoly on sin. But the truth that, by nature, every human being deserves to be loved as we love ourselves is a truth that Jesus needed to reveal. Our sin-darkened minds needed the divine light to perceive it clearly.

WORDS FROM THE WORD

Jesus illustrated the importance of this kindness—authentic kindness, not conditional and hypocritical kindness—multiple times. In the Sermon on the Mount, for example, he pointed out that our disposition to do good for others should be habitual and universal, just as God's is (see Matt. 5:43-48).

In the same passage, Jesus talked about carrying someone's burden an extra mile when you only really *have* to carry it (by law) for one mile. He talked about handing over both your tunic and your cloak when someone demands only your cloak. He talked about turning the other cheek in response to humiliations—what St. Paul later described in less metaphorical terms:

> Let love be sincere; hate what is evil, hold on to what is good; love one another with mutual affection; anticipate one another in showing honor. . . . Bless those who persecute [you], bless and do not curse them. . . . If possible, on your part, live at peace with all. . . . Do not be conquered by evil but conquer evil with good. (Rom. 12:9-10, 14, 18, 21)

This is how a Christian is supposed to behave in the world, and this is a fundamental element in how we bear witness to the truth of God's revelation in Christ:

> "I give you a new commandment: love one another. As I have loved you, so you also should love one another. This is how all will know that you are my disciples, if you have love for one another." (John 13:34-35)

KINDNESS VERSUS WEAKNESS

Kindness is not weakness. Kindness doesn't require that we turn ourselves into doormats or become enablers of other people's dysfunctions. Kindness is "going about doing good," and what is truly good for another person will never involve condoning their sin or bolstering their unhealthy coping mechanisms. That would be falling into the trap of crippling codependency. Kindness means staying aware of the needs of our fellow pilgrims as we all make our way along life's journey—and helping them out whenever we can. It's that simple.

St. Thomas More, a layman who was chancellor of England and friend and confidante to King Henry VIII in the sixteenth century, showed a memorable act of kindness just moments before he was martyred. He had refused to accept Henry's repudiation of the Catholic faith, a repudiation that the king promulgated as a law for the entire country when he established the independent Church of England. As a result, St. Thomas was imprisoned and eventually beheaded. When he stepped onto the scaffold, the executioner—as was customary—asked for the victim's forgiveness before performing his deed. St. Thomas embraced him warmly and, sensing the man's anxiety, reassured him, saying with a smile, "Pick up thy Spirits, Man, and be not afraid to do thine Office. My Neck is very short, take heed therefore thou strike not awry . . . "[48] It was a word of kindness—even a cheerful jest—spoken in a moment when kind gestures would be least expected: a fitting conclusion for a life whose daily witness to God's goodness was capped with the martyr's crown.

Perhaps St. Thomas More's kindness on the executioner's block flowed from the faith-filled knowledge that he was only moments away from his definitive encounter with the Lord. Indeed, St. Paul linked his exhortation on Christian kindness to an awareness of Christ's closeness, implying that only through faith and grace can we answer our call to the apostolate of kindness by "going about doing good": "Your kindness should be known to all," he wrote to the Christians in Philippi, adding: "The Lord is near" (Phil. 4:5).

Questions for Personal Reflection or Group Discussion

1. What idea in this chapter struck you most and why?

2. How would you describe in your own words the difference between hypocritical or conditional kindness and authentic Christian kindness? When you find it hard to be kind, does that

necessarily mean your kindness is hypocritical? Why or why not?

3. Acts of kindness will flow naturally from an attitude of true respect and esteem for others. In which of your circles of influence do you find it harder to maintain such an attitude and why?

4. What will you do today to engage in the apostolate of kindness?

    - I will express honest interest in knowing how my immediate family members are feeling about what's going on in their lives.

    - I will volunteer to help out with something I normally try to avoid.

    - I will interrupt my own activities when I detect that someone around me needs a kind word or a bit of help.

    - (Write your own resolution) I will _____
    _____
    _____
    _____

Concluding Prayer

*Lord, make me an instrument of your peace. Where there
is hatred, let me sow love; where there is injury, pardon;
where there is doubt, faith; where there is despair, hope;
where there is darkness, light; where there is sadness, joy.
O, Divine Master, grant that I may not so much seek to be
consoled as to console; to be understood as to understand;
to be loved as to love; For it is in giving that we receive;
it is in pardoning that we are pardoned; it is in
dying that we are born again to eternal life.*

—PRAYER OF ST. FRANCIS OF ASSISI

But What If I Don't Feel Like It?

*Through his Church Christ entrusts you with the fundamental
mission of sharing with others the gift of salvation, and he invites
you to participate in building his kingdom. He chooses you, in spite
of the personal limitations everyone has, because he loves you and
believes in you. Being disciples of Christ is not a private matter.
On the contrary, the gift of faith must be shared with others.*
— St. John Paul II[49]

SOMETIMES KINDNESS OVERFLOWS EFFORTLESSLY FROM a warm and affectionate heart. At other times that same heart feels cold and antagonistic, and even the possibility of kindness is crowded back into a hidden corner of the soul. What's going on when we feel that way? What are we supposed to do about it? We have to wrestle a little bit with this question, and we will do so by looking at attitudes and actions.

DISOBEDIENT FEELINGS

Regarding attitudes, we cannot underestimate the importance of distinguishing between unwilled feelings—spontaneous emotional reactions—and willed decisions. Because of our fallen human nature, our feelings are not always obedient to our faith. We can feel an emotional repugnance toward prayer, for example, even though we firmly believe in the importance and value of prayer. Just so, we can feel an emotional disconnect or distaste toward another person, even though we firmly believe that person is created in God's image, loved by God unconditionally, redeemed by Christ's sacrifice on the cross, called to eternal communion with God in heaven, and therefore deserving of our kindness.

SUBJECTIVE EMOTIONS

Those spontaneous, negative feelings can trace their origin to passing subjective factors, such as tiredness or a bad mood induced by the weather or hormonal fluctuations. They can also stem from subconscious factors—an intangible quality of the other person, for example, may trigger in us a reaction linked to hidden emotional patterns that were formed before we were even self-conscious. These same subconscious factors can be at play in our natural affections and likes: We feel more or less affinity toward Person A simply because his personality somehow harmonizes well with the emotional needs that have been more or less seared into the substrata of our own personality. In these cases feelings of repugnance toward someone are completely unwilled. They are not sinful.

And yet they can be valuable for our own growth in self-knowledge. They are giving us information, and we may grow significantly in self-knowledge through reflecting on their origins and what they reveal about our own interior life. Sometimes they are linked to deep wounds that may need some psychological treatment. Often they simply are linked to normal wounds that can become fruitful catalysts for spiritual growth when we identify them and integrate them into our prayer life.

OBJECTIVE EMOTIONS

On the other hand, negative emotions toward other people can also be caused by objective factors. If another person habitually makes self-centered decisions and so becomes a burden for those around them, this will become a source of tension and perhaps even anger. We see Jesus, for instance, becoming angry with the Pharisees when they simply refused to listen to him, consistently closing their hearts and minds to his saving message.

These emotional reactions are objectively linked to damaging actions of other people, and they also are valuable as sources of information. They are telling us something about the relationship—something is wrong, something is unjust, something needs to be dealt with or changed in order to reorient the relationship and make it healthy. These emotional reactions are not willfully chosen; they happen almost automatically, so they, too, cannot be sinful. They just *are*.

Sometimes objective emotional reactions can be exacerbated by subjective factors, forming a potent emotional cocktail that often produces exaggerated reactions.

THE RIGHT ATTITUDE

And so, clearly the right attitude toward these emotional experiences has to start with humble acceptance. The emotions are there. They are linked to who you are. They are giving you information. They are not evil in themselves, and so they are nothing to be ashamed of or frustrated about. Accept them. Understand them. But don't put them in the driver's seat of your soul.

Our moral responsibility always inhabits the realm of our free actions, so we are not morally responsible for these unwilled emotional reactions. Our responsibility surfaces with regard to how we decide to deal with the emotions that spontaneously surge up in our souls. The bottom line here is that we should not make our choices based solely on emotion, which would be the epitome of immaturity. Rather, we need to make our decisions based on truth—moral truth and the truths of our faith.

Thus, for example, when I feel an emotional distaste toward prayer, I don't stop praying. Instead I humbly persevere regardless of the negative feelings, even though I may reflect on why I am feeling that repugnance and try to learn from it.

ACTING "AS IF . . ."

In the case of repugnance toward others, which threatens to manifest itself in unkindness, the same principle applies. I should treat them, to the extent that is possible for me, *as if* I felt the love I know they deserve as God's child. This is virtuous action, a free choice to love, in spite of contrary feelings. And that love means that I treat them with respect and kindness, willing what is good for them. My actions toward them, then, are consistent with my faith and the commandments of the Lord. I don't torture them, abuse them, talk badly about them behind their back, insult and humiliate them, and so on. I try to help them, affirm them, and encourage them.

Sometimes our subjective repugnance toward someone may be so strong—again, not because we will it, which would be sinful, but just because that's the way it is—that we actually need to avoid that person in order not to treat him or her poorly. This can be painful for us—we wish we didn't have such strong negative emotions toward this person. It hurts our pride to experience our brokenness and woundedness so palpably. But the right action is to avoid, as much as it is possible, situations where we know that our emotions have a chance to get the better of us. Pray for that person. Don't harm that person. Be civil and kind to that person when you have to interact with him or her. But until God's grace heals you a little bit more, until you develop more virtue, you may need to minimize your contact with that person.

Actions as Reactions

In the second case—the case of the objective negative emotions that flow from identifiably problematic behaviors and behavior patterns—the kind and loving thing to do is to communicate about it. Talk with the other person about the behavior patterns, try to understand what's behind them, and try to calmly express why they are so bothersome or destructive. Try to help each other adjust the patterns. This is especially the case if your relationship with the person in question is habitual—if you have to continue to interact with him or her on a regular basis.

In some cases you may run into a person who is not willing to change. He or she won't acknowledge destructive behaviors or take responsibility for them. In that circumstance you may need to sever the relationship, at least temporarily. It is not an expression of love to continue enabling someone's dysfunctional behavior by exhibiting the kind of toleration that tacitly approves of it.

In summary, our spontaneous emotional reactions give us information, and until we are mature enough in Christ that those emotions are in perfect sync with the truths of our faith, they will sometimes clash with those truths. That's OK. Accept that and seek to understand it. But don't let it drive your actions and decisions. Pray for grace and strength to always act in accordance with your faith, with God's will, even if your feelings disagree. Live the apostolate of kindness even when it's tough. Gradually, with God's help, your feelings will catch up to your faith and line up more fully with God's will, increasing the energy at your disposal for loving God and loving your neighbor.

Questions for Personal Reflection or Group Discussion

1. What idea in this chapter struck you most and why?

2. How often do you tend to let your feelings alone drive your decisions and actions? In what specific circumstances does this happen most frequently, and why?

3. How do you feel when you sincerely pray for people even though you do not feel a natural affection for them?

4. Christian maturity recognizes that emotional experience is a gift from God, but we also recognize that our feelings need to be educated and integrated into the deeper levels of faith and freedom. What will you do today to pursue that integration and emotional maturity?

   - If I tend toward the extreme of repression, I will take some time to write in a journal about the emotions I most frequently experience, trying to name, claim, tame, and aim them.

   - If I tend toward the extreme of emotionalism, I will take some time to come up with a strategy regarding how to respond proactively to situations where I know I tend to give too much rein to my feelings.

   - I will think about a person in my life whom I feel an

emotional repugnance toward, and I will try to understand, accept, and maturely deal with those feelings.

• (Write your own resolution) I will _____

_____

_____

_____

Concluding Prayer

With all my heart I seek You; let me not stray from Your commands . . . . Open my eyes, that I may consider the wonders of Your law. I am a wayfarer of earth; hide not Your commands from me . . . . Make me understand the way of Your precepts, and I will meditate on Your wondrous deeds . . . . Your compassion is great, O Lord. . . . To you, Almighty Father, Creator of the universe and of mankind, through Christ, the Living One, Lord of time and history, in the Spirit who makes all things holy, be praise and honor and glory now and for ever. Amen!

—PSALM 119:10, 18–19, 27, 156; PRAYER FOR
THE GREAT JUBILEE BY ST. JOHN PAUL II

Talking Like a Christian

The invitation I offer you to responsibility, to engagement, is
. . . an invitation to place the truth of Christ at the center of
your life to give witness to this truth in the story of your daily
life, in the decisive choices you have to make, in order to help
humanity set its feet firmly on the path of peace and of justice.
— St. John Paul II[50]

St. Philip Neri, the tireless apostle of Renaissance Rome, had a gift for helping people understand Christian teaching. One time he explained the repercussions of careless and uncharitable speech by giving an unusual penance to someone who admitted to those sins in his confession. St. Philip advised the penitent to fill a pillowcase with goose feathers, walk up to the top of a tall hill outside the city walls, and throw all the feathers into the wind. Then, admonished the saint, try to gather up all the feathers that were blown hither and thither.

An impossible task, surely. But a vivid illustration of the power of words—once we have spoken them (or tweeted them, or messaged them, or Facebooked them, or YouTubed them), we cannot retract them. Hence the importance of learning to talk like a Christian—to use words as Christ would have us, thus witnessing on *behalf* of his kingdom and not *against* it.

Seasoned with Salt

So much good can be done with our words! Words can warm cold hearts, enlighten confused minds, and motivate discouraged souls. Words can establish and bolster trust, confidence, community, and human solidarity. The more we understand and master virtue and skill in this arena, the more good we can do—for ourselves and for others—with everything we say.

St. Paul expresses this multiple times in his New Testament writings. He almost always refers to virtuous speech—speech that builds up the community and spreads truth and goodness—in his lists of essentially Christian behaviors, behaviors that image Christ to the world. For example, he writes: "Let your speech always be gracious, seasoned with salt, so that you know how you should respond to each one" (Col. 4:6). Words really do matter. Our words can impart grace, becoming vehicles of salvation. But they can just as easily be vehicles of destruction: "Death and life are in the power of the tongue" (Prov. 18:21).

The Tongue Is a Fire

In his New Testament letter, St. James picks up on this same theme (see James 3:1-6). He not only shows the apparently disproportionate impact of such a small organ as the tongue, but he also explicitly links virtue in speech with spiritual maturity. Evil or foolish words cause damage—sometimes horrible damage. These biblical passages make that clear. Yet the Bible's descriptions tell us only what we have all experienced: the blow that comes from being slandered or wickedly criticized takes a long time—sometimes a lifetime—to lose its sting.

Evil words only work such great mischief, however, because the power of words has such great potential for good. Yes, evil men "sharpen their tongues like swords" (Ps. 64:3), but a sharp sword can be useful for good as well as for evil. A sharp knife is necessary for proper surgery and good cooking; a sharp axe is more effective at chopping wood than a dull one. Words can be used to sin, but as St. James points out, "This need not be so" (James 3:10).

Words without Truth

To use words for good, we need first and foremost to avoid the sinful abuse of words. The most common temptations in this area include violations of the truth through lying, rash judgment, calumny, flattery, and adulation. A lie is an intentional deception of someone who has a reasonable claim on the truth. Rash judgment claims to know the interior motive of someone's action and jumps to a judgmental (and, more often than not, false) conclusion about it, whether that conclusion is voiced only interiorly or also out loud. Calumny is deliberately spreading false or exaggerated affirmations about another person to the detriment of his or her good honor, which always has truly noxious repercussions. Flattery and adulation have to do with exaggerated praise, whether motivated by a desire to manipulate (flattery) or an overblown, unreasonable, and blinding sense of reverence (adulation).

Other temptations to abuse the power of language adhere to the truth, but they use it as a weapon of unjust attack instead of an instrument promoting justice and charity. These include detraction, destructive criticism, disparaging irony, and boasting.

WORDS THAT WOUND

Detraction is often confused with calumny, but it involves an important distinction. Detraction holds to the truth. Detraction is not lying. Yet it yields some of the same hideous by-products of calumny. According to the *Catechism*, someone falls into the temptation of detraction "who, without objectively valid reason, discloses another's faults and failings to persons who did not know them" (CCC, 2477). Calumny invents untrue faults and failings about people and spreads them around. Detraction takes people's true faults and failings and turns them into casual conversation topics, often leading to tale-bearing and toxic gossip.

Like detraction, degrading irony and destructive criticism adhere to the truth, but they still qualify as abusive uses of communication. Unlike detraction, however, these forms of speech address directly the person being cut down. Insults like these sometimes burst out during angry arguments, like verbal blows meant to punish, humiliate, or intimidate someone we feel has wronged us. At other times we wield them with calculated purpose in order to manipulate others and get what we want. In certain contexts and relationships, these forms of verbal abuse become barely perceptible habits, ingrained patterns of behavior that need to be rooted out through repentance and the renewing power of grace.

Good-humored irony brings enjoyment, laughter, and stimulation to conversation. When irony wounds other people, however, it crosses the line from spice to poison. Sincere concern for others requires us to pay attention to the effect our comments have on those around us. What one person may take in stride and enjoy may feel like a slap in the face or a personal attack to someone else. When laughter is bought at the expense of someone's tears, the price is simply too high.

The *Catechism* warns against boasting or bragging in the same paragraph where it warns against degrading irony. A boast may include a dose of the truth, but more often than not it also includes an exaggeration. Even more than faulting against the truth, however, boasting mimics degrading irony in its attempt to belittle other people. When I brag, I am attempting to elevate myself over others—the tone and often the content of a boast show a certain disdain for people who have achieved less than I have. Instead of drawing people together and encouraging them, this kind of speech demeans and discourages.

THE TALKING APOSTLE

These corrosive forms of communication often have roots in our own insecurities and fears. Sometimes they erupt from undisciplined passions. Whatever their cause and wherever they appear—in conversation, print, or digital platforms—they counteract the true purpose of speech, which is to communicate truth and build interpersonal communion.

As our spiritual lives mature, these negative behavior patterns gradually fall away and give room to a manner of communicating that better witnesses to the Lord's desire to redeem and save every person—words that express what we really feel and think in ways that also enlighten, encourage, and edify, even when they have to communicate truths that are hard to hear. In that way talking like a Christian becomes an ongoing answer to the call of evangelization.

Questions for Personal Reflection or Group Discussion

1. What idea in this chapter struck you most and why?

2. Which of the temptations mentioned in this chapter do you struggle with most often? Why? How can you begin to intentionally improve in that area?

3. How would you describe the difference between destructive and constructive criticism? How is that distinction relevant in your life?

4. What will you do today to become a better listener so you can also talk more like a Christian?

   - I will make some space for silence in my day, giving myself a chance to slow down and drink in the sights and sounds of God's creation.

   - I will ask someone what he or she thinks or feels about something before trying to express how I think or feel about it.

   - (Write your own resolution) I will _____

     _____

     _____

     _____

Concluding Prayer

May Mary, Mother of the Church, Star of Evangelization, accompany us on our journey, as she remained with the disciples on the day of Pentecost. To her we turn with confidence. Through her intercession may the Lord grant us the gift of perseverance in our missionary duty, which is a matter for the entire Church community.

—St. John Paul II, Message for
World Mission Sunday 2001

Your Pursuit of Excellence

*Every activity, every situation, every precise responsibility – as, for
example, skill and solidarity in work, love and dedication in the family
and the education of children, service to society and public life and the
promotion of truth in the area of culture – are the occasions ordained
by Providence for a continuous exercise of faith, hope and charity.*
– St. John Paul II, Christifideles Laici, 59

SEEKING EXCELLENCE IN THE NORMAL activities and responsibilities of life
is part of our Christian witness. When we give our best to do our
best in all our works, we are imaging God's love and concern for his
own "work" of creation. We are also showing our gratitude toward God
for giving us the grace to join our own efforts to his as we "cultivate
and care for" the world that has been "given to the children of Adam"
(Gen. 2:15; Ps. 115:16).

Whether it's baking cookies, building a house, drafting a law, or
entering data into a spreadsheet, human work always shares in
human dignity, precisely because it is human, and as such it, too,
can be part of the apostolate of witness, part of our way of living the
gospel. St. Paul expressed this with his usual brevity and vividness:
"So whether you eat or drink, or whatever you do, do everything for
the glory of God" (1 Cor. 10:31).

THE MONKS GOT IT RIGHT (AT LEAST IN THEORY)

The monastic movement that emerged in the early Middle Ages
included this often-overlooked dimension of human life in the motto
that summed up its core values: *ora et labora* ("pray and work").

Monastic communities sought to worship God directly through prayer (especially community, liturgical prayer) and indirectly through excellence in work. Monasteries became real schools that taught and cultivated the art of living in a period when the civilized world was descending into social and political chaos. Monks followed (and still follow) a disciplined daily schedule, combining work, prayer, and study in a balanced rhythm that allowed for the calm pursuit of excellence in each of those arenas. The results were spectacular. Not only did the monasteries become engines of holiness, they also became motors of human advancement, oases of culture that preserved and became the seeds of a new, Christian civilization.

Even today when you visit one of the ancient monasteries, you feel a certain peace and reverence almost emanating from the walls themselves. The physical elements of the monastery, fruit of the monks' labor over the centuries, have taken on an air of beauty and meaning that turns them into songs of praise preserved in stone. The faithfully pursued ideal of *ora et labora*, working hard and praying hard, created a unity of life that resonates with God's original plan for the human person.

ELEVATED FROM WITHIN

The monks lived this unity of life in the cloister, infusing their mundane work with spiritual meaning and thereby pursuing excellence in even the smallest labors. All Christians, however, are called to seek the same ideal in the context of their particular circumstances. St. John Paul II expressed this beautifully in an encyclical letter dedicated entirely to the theme of human work:

> The faithful, therefore . . . must learn the deepest meaning and the value of all creation, and its orientation to the praise of God. Even by their secular activity they must assist one another to live holier lives. In this way the world will be permeated by the spirit of Christ and more effectively achieve its purpose in justice, charity and peace. . . . Therefore, by their competence in secular fields and by their personal activity, elevated from within by the grace of Christ, let them work

vigorously so that by human labor, technical skill, and civil culture created goods may be perfected according to the design of the Creator and the light of his Word.[51]

When you are writing up a report, or fixing a drain, or washing dishes, or designing a skyscraper, or researching new energy sources—whatever form of human work you are engaged in—it is an opportunity for evangelizing the world, that it may be "permeated by the spirit of Christ and more effectively achieve its purpose." To elevate earthly activities, even the most mundane, to this level requires nothing more than infusing it with the "profound motive" our faith offers us, and thus orienting it to the praise of God. Such is the noble vision God offers us for even the least glamorous forms of human work. And that vision is what moves authentic Christians to fight against the petty, lazy tendencies of their fallen nature and pursue excellence in all they do.

THE PATRON SAINT OF EVERYBODY

It is interesting to note that the patron saint of the Universal Church, St. Joseph, is also the patron saint of workers. In Scripture St. Joseph never speaks; he only works, obeying God's call to protect and provide for his family. This aspect of the human condition, the Church seems to be telling us, should never be belittled or overlooked. We truly can witness to God's love and Christ's truth by seeking faith-inspired excellence in our daily duties, which so often seem little more than trifles, and bothersome ones at that. If Jesus, Joseph, and Mary spent their lives among such trifles—and worked the world's redemption by doing so—then it's certainly okay for us to do so, too.

Questions for Personal Reflection
or Group Discussion

1. What idea in this chapter struck you most and why?

2. How deeply do you feel the redemptive value of your normal work activities? How can you intensify your awareness of that value?

3. In which of your normal pursuits have you stopped seeking excellence? Why? In light of the ideas in this chapter, how do you think the Lord is inviting you to proceed in that area from now on?

4. Blessed Mother Teresa of Calcutta used to say, "Not all of us can do great things. But we can do small things with great love." Often we overlook the intrinsic value that our small actions have simply because we are God's children and therefore channels of grace in the world. What will you do today to better connect your daily work with your faith?

    - When I feel frustrated or weighed down, I will invoke and try to enact this attitude: "Whatever you do, do from the heart, as for the Lord and not for others" (Col. 3:23).

    - I will begin and end today's least enjoyable task with a prayer.

    - I will pause in the midst of today's chores and ask myself how I can do what I am doing better than I have done it in the past.

    - (Write your own resolution) I will _____
    _____
    _____
    _____

Concluding Prayer

*O God, Creator of all things, who laid down for the
human race the law of work, graciously grant
that by the example of Saint Joseph and under his patronage
we may complete the works you set us to do
and attain the rewards you promise.
Through our Lord Jesus Christ, your Son,
who lives and reigns with you in the unity of the Holy Spirit,
one God, for ever and ever. Amen.*

—ROMAN MISSAL, COLLECT FOR THE MASS FOR MAY 1,
FEAST OF ST. JOSEPH THE WORKER

DAY 51

Your Way of Loving the Church

*There is thus a profound link between Christ, the Church
and evangelization. During the period of the Church that we
are living in, it is she who has the task of evangelizing. This
mandate is not accomplished without her, and still less against
her. . . . And how can one wish to love Christ without loving
the Church, if the finest witness to Christ is that of St. Paul:
"Christ loved the Church and sacrificed himself for her"?*
—St. Paul VI, Evangelii Nuntiandi, 16

YOU, PERSONALLY, CANNOT SAVE A single soul. Only God saves souls.
Only God's grace redeems and renews the human heart, so
wounded by original sin and all its consequences. Jesus is the source
of that grace, and he has chosen to distribute it through his Church.
The Church, guided and powered by the Holy Spirit, continues to
proclaim the message of Jesus, translating that message into terms
that can be grasped by each new generation and each new culture.
The Church also imparts the sacraments, the objective signs and
instruments of God's saving grace, in each individual life. Without
the Church, who would guarantee the integrity of Christ's message
through the vicissitudes of history? Who would keep the sacramental
economy clicking?

SEED AND BEGINNING OF THE KINGDOM

The Church truly is the mother of Christians, both the origin and
the goal of evangelization:

Henceforward the Church, endowed with the gifts of her founder and faithfully observing his precepts of charity, humility and self-denial, receives the mission of proclaiming and establishing among all peoples the Kingdom of Christ and of God, and she is on earth the seed and the beginning of that kingdom. (CCC, 768)

For this reason, our apostolic witness necessarily includes showing a warm affection and supernatural reverence for the Church. The apostolate consists in bringing people closer and closer to Christ, for which the Church remains an irreplaceable mediator. We cannot pretend to be disciples and messengers of the Lord if at the same time we are indifferent or antagonistic to the Church.

SAVORING THE SACRAMENTS

We bear witness to the Church's essential role in God's plan for the human family in many ways. Our own living of the sacraments and the liturgical year—which implies a conscientious and warm engagement in our local parish—is perhaps the most impactful.

If the celebration of the Eucharist through the Holy Mass and devotion to the Eucharist through adoration of the Blessed Sacrament become pillars of our own personal and familial spirituality, that in itself will be a testimony to others (in addition to nourishing our own growth in spiritual maturity). If the confessional becomes a regular stop on our hectic journey through this fallen world, that too will overflow in surprising ways as a sign of God's presence and power to those who know and interact with us (in addition to flooding our hearts with fresh outpouring of God's redeeming mercy). Even the other sacraments, which we receive only once or, in the case of marriage and anointing of the sick, possibly more than once, can become beacons of Christian witness when we surround them with meaningful family traditions, joyfully celebrate their anniversaries, and intentionally seek to understand and activate their power in our lives.

LIVING THE LITURGICAL YEAR

It is similar with the rhythms of the liturgical year. When a Catholic family makes the liturgical year, as opposed to the civil year, the primary matrix of their weekly, monthly, and annual activities, they become living signs of the spiritual realm and the eternal truths. Sundays and other liturgical solemnities, saints' days, liturgical seasons (Advent, Christmas, Lent, Holy Week, Easter)—the Church offers us these tangible touch points in order to help us keep a truly spiritual, Christ-centered, heavenly trajectory to our lives. We ignore or belittle them (treating Sunday as a normal day, for example) at our own risk, and at the risk of blending in to the secularized culture so much that our Christian witness is watered down, if not completely compromised.

Studying and therefore understanding and knowing how to explain the teachings of the Church (instead of arrogantly setting up our own opinions as a kind of parallel magisterium) is another form of the apostolate of witness. Just as we would expect a medical doctor to be able to speak intelligently, interestingly, and definitively about his or her area of medical expertise, so too unbelievers rightly expect that a self-proclaimed Catholic Christian should be able to do the same regarding the Church's doctrine in relation to faith and morals. Not that every Catholic is called to become a professional theologian, but every Catholic should seek to be well-versed enough in the faith to represent it fairly and warmly when the need or opportunity arises.

POISONING THE WELL

Perhaps the most common way this area of witness breaks down has to do with useless criticism. We all know that the Church, though divine in its origin and in the means by which it carries out its mission, is also human. It is made up of sinners. As a result, members of the Church always have plenty of things to complain about. And yet those complaints, as legitimate as they may be, can easily undermine our testimony to the deeper reality of the Church.

God doesn't need the human side of the Church to be perfect in order to continue his flow of grace into the world. Endless complaining and destructive criticism seem to suppose that he does. Instead of falling into those sterile behaviors, we should follow God's own example of mercy and invest our energies in positive action—taking the initiative to help fix what needs to be fixed, disciplining our own attitudes and words so that any criticism we might have is constructive, and recognizing and speaking freely about the amazing good God works through the Church. In short, by loving the Church, wrinkles and all, we will naturally stimulate interest and curiosity on behalf of those who are outside the Church, giving God's providence plenty of opportunities to open hearts and minds that have long been closed to the love of the Lord. This too is part of the apostolate we can pursue simply by the way we live our daily lives.

Questions for Personal Reflection or Group Discussion

1. What idea in this chapter struck you most and why?

2. How would you describe your engagement with your local parish? How could you improve it?

3. What aspects of the Church do you complain about most often? How would you describe the difference between useless whining, patient acceptance, and constructive action?

4. Every Catholic family is in a sense a domestic church—a mini Catholic community called to reflect and embody the life and mission of the universal Church in its own milieu. The activities of the universal Church, therefore, should in some form be present in this domestic church: prayer, study, fellowship, mutual service, mission, and so on. What will you do today to help develop your domestic church?

   • I will place an inspiring Catholic image (crucifix, picture of the Blessed Virgin Mary, picture of a saint, etc.) in my own room, so as to foster a more prayerful attitude when I am alone and engaged in my personal activities.

   • I will put an image of the Sacred Heart of Jesus and a candle in a visible area of our home as a way of giving testimony to our faith and tangibly consecrating our family to God's service. (If you like this idea, you might want to read about the tradition of Enthroning the Sacred Heart in the home; see sacredheartapostolate.com.)

- I will renew our family's commitment to pray together, at the very least by praying grace before meals.

- (Write your own resolution) I will _____

_____

_____

_____

Concluding Prayer

Increase, O Lord, our faith and our love for you, present in every tabernacle. Grant us to be faithful witnesses to your resurrection to all people, especially the youth, so that, in knowing you, they may follow you and find in you their peace and joy. Only then will they know that they are brothers and sisters of all God's children scattered throughout the world. You who, in becoming man, chose to belong to a human family, teach families the virtues which filled with light the family home of Nazareth. May families always be united, as you and the Father are one, and may they be living witnesses to love, justice and solidarity; make them schools of respect, forgiveness and mutual help, so that the world may believe; help them to be the source of vocations to the priesthood and the consecrated life, and all the other forms of firm Christian commitment. Protect your Church and the successor of Peter, to whom you, Good Shepherd, have entrusted the task of feeding your flock. Teach us to love your Mother, Mary, as you love her. Give us strength to proclaim your Word with courage in the work of the new evangelization, so that the world may know new hope. Mary, Mother of the Church, pray for us!

—ADAPTED FROM ST. JOHN PAUL II'S PRAYER AT THE
END OF ECCLESIA IN AMERICA, JANUARY, 22, 1999

Speaking the Words of Life

Nevertheless this [witness] always remains insufficient, because even the
finest witness will prove ineffective in the long run if it is not explained,
justified—what Peter called always having "your answer ready for people
who ask you the reason for the hope that you all have" (1 Peter 3:15)—and
made explicit by a clear and unequivocal proclamation of the Lord
Jesus. The Good News proclaimed by the witness of life sooner or later
has to be proclaimed by the word of life. There is no true evangelization
if the name, the teaching, the life, the promises, the kingdom and the
mystery of Jesus of Nazareth, the Son of God are not proclaimed.
—St. Paul VI, Evangelii Nuntiandi, 22

I F YOU HAD DISCOVERED THE cure for cancer, the truly loving thing to
do would be to share that discovery with those who suffer from the
disease. Even if the cure were bitter and painful, keeping it to yourself
for fear of offending a cancer victim who may resent the bitterness of
the pill would be a lack of love, a self-centered and vain pretension.

JESUS IS THE CURE

This seems so obvious. And yet, when it comes to spiritual diseases
and spiritual cures, the obvious sometimes gets obscured. Jesus
Christ truly is the cure for life's moral and spiritual ills. As we have
seen, his teaching, preserved and communicated in every generation
by the Church, points the way to healthy and happy living: "I am
the light of the world. Whoever follows me will not walk in darkness, but will have the light of life" (John 8:12). To know him,
accept him, and follow him opens the door to the interior freedom

and fulfillment we all yearn for: "If you remain in my word, you will truly be my disciples, and you will know the truth, and the truth will set you free" (John 8:31–32).

He is not only one worthy figure among the world's great philosophers; he is not only one respectable founder among history's great founders of religion; he is not only one wise teacher among humanity's top gurus: He is the incarnate Son of God, the second Person of the Holy Trinity become man; the sole Savior of the world.

> "I am the way and the truth and the life. No one comes to the Father except through me. . . . " There is no salvation through anyone else, nor is there any other name under heaven given to the human race by which we are to be saved.
> (John 14:6; Acts 4:12)

People searching for happiness, inner peace, and meaning are searching for Jesus, whether they realize it or not. He is the cure—the only cure—for their spiritual diseases, which can be immensely painful and debilitating even for people who seem to be doing pretty well by all external appearances.

YOU HAVE THE CURE

Only Jesus can forgive sins and heal the wounds caused by sin. Only Jesus can give the answers to the deepest questions of the human heart. Only his teaching provides sure guidance through the confused, maddening moral labyrinths of the post-modern world. And you know him. You believe in him. You are familiar with those teachings. You have the cure for your neighbor's spiritual ills—will you keep it to yourself?

We cannot force people to accept Jesus and his teachings, but we are called to tell people about him. If we don't, some of those people in our circles of influence may never even be given the chance to put their faith in the Lord:

> For "everyone who calls on the name of the Lord will be saved." But how can they call on him in whom they have not

believed? And how can they believe in him of whom they have not heard? And how can they hear without someone to preach? (Rom. 13:14)

Telling people about Jesus, sharing the gospel with them, explaining the reasons behind the moral and theological tenets of Christianity—this is a fundamental dimension of every Christian's mission, a central way to "love your neighbor as yourself" and exercise the prophetic facet of our Christian vocation.

DELIVERING THE MESSAGE

The first dimension of mission (which we have been reflecting on in the previous chapters) has to do with our way of daily living, the witness of our own moral integrity, love for the Church, and pursuit of excellence. And that is, in many cases, a necessary precursor to effectively speaking the words of life; people will tend to listen to what we say with a more open mind if they have seen us behave admirably beforehand.

But at times God also nudges us to speak about him regardless of the relationship we have with a person. Sometimes, in other words, he wants us to take the initiative and bring up the topic of religion. We need to be ready and willing to do that. More often, perhaps, we need to be ready to respond to questions that are asked of us directly or that come up indirectly in conversations. We need to know how to express and explain what we believe, and we need to cultivate the courage—based on true love for our neighbor—to do so when the need or opportunity arises.

That requires doing our homework. We can never have all the answers to every question or objection, but we can gradually increase our knowledge and understanding of the faith so as to be better and better at explaining it. A good rule of thumb is to try to avoid having to say, "I am not sure how to answer that" more than once. When someone brings up a question you can't answer, make a commitment to investigate and study until you *can* answer it, so that the next time it comes up, you will able to shed God's light on it.

Our Manner Affects Our Message

Of course, the manner in which we speak about Jesus and his teachings is almost as important as the content of what we say. If our manner lacks respect and humility, our words will simply go unheard. Timing matters. Tone matters. Attitude matters. It is not primarily about winning arguments and making converts in order to feed our vanity—it is about loving our neighbors as ourselves, sharing with them the good news we have received from others. We are simply heralds of Christ's message, ambassadors of his kingdom, and so our egos don't have to get involved. "Whoever listens to you listens to me," Jesus pointed out. "Whoever rejects you rejects me. And whoever rejects me rejects the one who sent me" (Luke 10:16).

True love seeks ways to communicate the truth that truly saves; it doesn't cop out by throwing up its hands and saying, "Whatever you want to do and believe is perfectly fine with me." That's not how Jesus fulfilled his redeeming mission of love, and it's not how we should live our mission, either.

Questions for Personal Reflection or Group Discussion

1. What idea in this chapter struck you most and why?

2. How well do you know your faith? Could you explain the gospel to someone who asked you to? What are you doing to continue deepening your knowledge and your ability to share that knowledge with others?

3. How well do you understand the reasons behind the Church's moral teachings, which are so maligned in today's world? Which ones are you most comfortable talking about? Which ones are you least comfortable talking about? Why?

4. Fear often inhibits us from speaking about what we believe and why. We are afraid of being labeled a fanatic; we are afraid of being rejected; we are afraid of being made fun of or persecuted in some way; we are afraid of being humiliated if we can't hold

up our side of an argument. And yet Jesus himself experienced all of those things in response to his saving mission—he was rejected, humiliated, and persecuted even though his knowledge and love were perfect. What will you do today to overcome your fear of sharing the faith?

- I will publicly display some sign that I am a Christian (a necklace with a cross on it, a rosary bracelet, etc.).
- I will begin researching one of the questions about my faith I don't feel comfortable answering.
- I will find a good Catholic radio station or podcast to start listening to on a regular basis in order to better equip myself for my mission of speaking about the gospel.
- (Write your own resolution) I will _____

_____

_____

_____

Concluding Prayer

Mary, Virgin and Mother, you who, moved by the Holy Spirit, welcomed the word of life in the depths of your humble faith: as you gave yourself completely to the Eternal One, help us to say our own "yes" to the urgent call, as pressing as ever, to proclaim the good news of Jesus. Obtain for us now a new ardor born of the resurrection, that we may bring to all the gospel of life which triumphs over death. Give us a holy courage to seek new paths, that the gift of unfading beauty may reach every man and woman. . . . Star of the new evangelization, help us to bear radiant witness to communion, service, ardent and generous faith, justice and love of the poor, that the joy of the Gospel may reach to the ends of the earth, illuminating even the fringes of our world. Mother of the living gospel, wellspring of happiness for God's little ones, pray for us. Amen. Alleluia!

—POPE FRANCIS, *EVANGELII GAUDIUM*, 288

Your Works of Mercy

*Christians must learn to make their act of faith in Christ by
discerning his voice in the cry for help that rises from this world
of poverty. This means carrying on the tradition of charity which
has expressed itself in so many different ways in the past two
millennia, but which today calls for even greater resourcefulness.*
— St. John Paul II, Novo Millennio Ineunte, 50

BY OUR WAY OF LIVING—our example of striving for moral integrity, acting with kindness, talking like a Christian, loving the Church, and humbly pursuing excellence in everything we do—we give witness to God's goodness and love. That is our apostolate of testimony, by which our lives take on a priestly meaning and bring this fallen world back into communion with God. By proclaiming and explaining the person and message of Jesus with our words, we exercise the prophetic dimension of our Christian vocation and engage in apostolate through a verbal witness to God's truth and love (we explored that in the last chapter). The third mode of apostolate, an expression of the kingly dimension of our vocation as Christ's followers, has to do with our Christian works: specific actions and ongoing projects that "impregnate culture and human works with a moral value."[52]

THE POWER OF MERCY

The first arena of these works is the most basic, and it has to do with actively helping people who are in need. In a certain sense, this is the most obvious expression of obedience to Our Lord's command: "Love your neighbor as yourself. . . . Do to others whatever you would have them do to you" (Matt. 22:39, 7:12).

The Church's long and fruitful tradition of spirituality helps make this basic criteria more concrete by identifying two categories of actions that embody this Christlike, self-giving love: the corporal works of mercy and the spiritual works of mercy.

In biblical language, the term *mercy* refers to the generous love God has never ceased showing to the human family ever since sin entered the world. Mercy is love that reaches out to serve those who are suffering and in need regardless of whether they deserve, strictly speaking, to receive such service. St. John Paul II described it vividly when he wrote about Jesus himself as the incarnation of God's mercy:

> Especially through his lifestyle and through his actions, Jesus revealed that love is present in the world in which we live—an effective love, a love that addresses itself to man and embraces everything that makes up his humanity. This love makes itself particularly noticed in contact with suffering, injustice and poverty—in contact with the whole historical "human condition," which in various ways manifests man's limitation and frailty, both physical and moral. It is precisely the mode and sphere in which love manifests itself that in biblical language is called "mercy."[53]

CHRIST'S STANDARD FOR CHRISTIAN BEHAVIOR

The corporal and spiritual works of mercy, then, are ways of continuing Christ's own loving mission by making love "present in the world . . . particularly noticed in contact with suffering, injustice, and poverty. . . . " In fact, toward the end of his public life, Jesus revealed that the quality of our Christian life is inextricably intertwined with the extent to which we engage in works of mercy. Through his incarnation Jesus has mysteriously but truly identified himself with every human person, and so the way we treat neighbors in need directly manifests the depth of our love for the Lord (see Matt. 25:34–40).

Our example of Christian living and our willingness to speak of Christ to those who don't know him or who resist him must overflow into a practical generosity and spirit of service. Otherwise our love remains immature. St. James emphasized that faith—true belief in Jesus and his message—by its very nature overflows into works (see James 2:14-17). St. John put it even more succinctly, linking the Christian behavior of practical service to the example of Jesus that inspires it:

> The way we came to know love was that he laid down his life for us; so we ought to lay down our lives for our brothers. If someone who has worldly means sees a brother in need and refuses him compassion, how can the love of God remain in him? Children, let us love not in word or speech but in deed and truth. (1 John 3:16-18)

All these passages point in the same direction: Claiming to love God while refusing to reach out and help a neighbor in need when we can is a form of hypocrisy. It constitutes the sin of omission, the sin of omitting to do the worthy (and sometimes necessary) good within our reach.

WHAT ARE THE "WORKS OF MERCY"?

The *Catechism* lists the traditional works of mercy in order to make the commandment of neighborly love practical, to help us keep in mind and stay sensitive to the most common needs that our neighbors experience. It points out that the list is only indicative, not exhaustive.

> The works of mercy are charitable actions by which we come to the aid of our neighbor in his spiritual and bodily necessities. Instructing, advising, consoling, comforting are spiritual works of mercy, as are forgiving and bearing wrongs patiently. The corporal works of mercy consist especially in feeding the hungry, sheltering the homeless, clothing the naked, visiting the sick and imprisoned, and burying the dead. Among all these, giving alms to the poor is one of the chief witnesses to fraternal charity: it is also a work of justice pleasing to God. (CCC, 2447).

We don't have to travel far to find ways to engage in these works—our own living rooms, backyards, and neighborhoods are the right place to start. The important thing is to cultivate the attitude of care, concern, and attentiveness that keeps us aware of the needs those around us may have so we form a habit of living on the wavelength of mercy: "Blessed are the merciful, for they will be shown mercy" (Matt. 5:7).

As that habit forms, we will also become more docile to the inspirations of the Holy Spirit, which often invite individual Christians to create projects and institutions that can serve these needs on a large scale. Such initiatives—from orphanages to hospitals, from schools to treatment centers, from international humanitarian networks to entire religious orders dedicated to serving persecuted Christians—have always blossomed wherever the Church is alive and well.

Whether in day-to-day interactions or vast institutional efforts, the works of mercy remain the most fundamental form of the apostolate linked to the third W (after *way* and *words*): our *works*.

Questions for Personal Reflection or Group Discussion

1. What idea in this chapter struck you most and why?

2. How would you explain the Christian concept of "mercy" in your own words? What are some of the most common misunderstandings or misuses of this term, in your experience?

3. What is the deeper connection between our own personal salvation and our efforts to help those around us? How does that apply to your own life?

4. What arena of basic human need moves your heart most? Have you ever thought that this special sensitivity may be a hidden call from the Lord to become more actively engaged in a specific type of merciful work? Think about it, prayerfully, right now.

Concluding Prayer

Father, by the power of the Spirit,
strengthen the Church's commitment
to the new evangelization
and guide our steps along the pathways of the world,
to proclaim Christ by our lives,
and to direct our earthly pilgrimage
toward the City of heavenly light.
May Christ's followers show forth their love
for the poor and the oppressed;
may they be one with those in need
and abound in works of mercy;
may they be compassionate toward all,
that they themselves may obtain indulgence
and forgiveness from you.
Praise and glory to You, Most Holy Trinity, you alone are
God most high!

—St. John Paul II, Prayer for the Celebration of the
Great Jubilee of the Year 2000[54]

Renewing the Fabric of Society

[Lay people's] own field of evangelizing activity is the vast and complicated world of politics, society and economics, but also the world of culture, of the sciences and the arts, of international life, of the mass media. It also includes other realities which are open to evangelization, such as human love, the family, the education of children and adolescents, professional work, suffering.
— St. Paul VI, Evangelii Nuntiandi, 70

T HE GOAL OF THE APOSTOLATE, the goal of the Church's evangelization efforts, is to bring and constantly deepen the reign of Christ *everywhere* — into every human heart, family, community, and culture. We seek nothing less than to infuse every human reality with the redeeming truth of Christ's message and the redeeming power of Christ's grace. In Jesus's commissioning of his Church to fulfill that mission, notice the universal scope, the unlimited boundaries of his vision:

> "Go, therefore, and make disciples of all nations, baptizing them in the name of the Father, and of the Son, and of the holy Spirit, teaching them to observe all that I have commanded you." (Matt. 28:19–20)

All nations are to become disciples; *all* that Jesus taught and commanded is to be known, loved, and followed by *everyone*. That's the work of evangelization. That's our mission.

TRANSFORMING HUMANITY FROM WITHIN

Jesus used a simple image to describe this process of cultural transformation when he explained the nature of his kingdom: "He spoke to them another parable. 'The kingdom of heaven is like yeast that a woman took and mixed with three measures of wheat flour until the whole batch was leavened'" (Matt. 13:33).

NOT JUST A PIPE DREAM

The development of western civilization in the Christian era demonstrates that this mission is more than a fairy tale. Greco-Roman civilization and Anglo-Germanic culture were both penetrated and transformed by the Christian ethos, creating a new culture. Over the course of a thousand years, the previously pagan scale of values was overturned by the influence of the gospel and its message of human dignity, divine mercy, and everlasting life. The institutions of European society developed under this spiritual tutorship, spreading wherever the Christians went to explore and to build. Many of the ideas found in the gospel were foreign and even contradictory to much of what the Greco-Roman and Germanic peoples adhered to. Concepts like humility and celibacy, care for the poor and inter-communitary justice (equality of human rights), and natural moral law were only vaguely present in pre-Christian worldviews, if they were present at all. Through the work and lives of Christians, they came to become common presuppositions in Western mentalities and legal systems. This led to flourishing achievements in every field of human endeavor, including science and technology, education, literature and the arts, and even politics and economics.

Certainly it wasn't heaven on earth, as some Western civilization apologists like to claim. In fact Jesus had promised it would never be so until his second coming. In the parable of the wheat and the weeds, he promised that good and bad would grow up side by side throughout the history of his Church, and the full purification from evil would only occur at the end of the earthly story (see Matt. 13:37–43).

GOD'S AMBASSADORS TO EVERY SECTOR OF SOCIETY

God calls all of us to share in this aspect, too. The first Christians didn't hunker down and go into hiding in the face of ancient Rome's aggressive, anti-Christian paganism. Yes, they prudently guarded their worship services and formation activities from prying eyes in order to avoid unnecessary trouble, but at the same time they brought their faith to bear on the world in which they lived. They believed in the power of Christ's message to transform the milieus in which they lived and worked.

Christian philosophers challenged and dialogued with pagan philosophers. Christian soldiers courageously imbued their military service with honor and moral integrity. Christian families rescued infants legally abandoned in forest clearings outside the city limits. Christian merchants and politicians battled corruption and worked to transform legal structures and economic customs in harmony with the true common good. Christian doctors and teachers defended moral truth and created new institutions dedicated to serving the underprivileged as well as those who could pay. In short, every sphere of society was penetrated not by "the Church" in the abstract, but by individual Christians whom God endowed and called to be missionaries within particular branches of human endeavor.

The new evangelization must include this same dimension; it must follow this same pattern. Imagine how different our culture would be if every Catholic—or even one in every ten Catholics—was fully aware and fully engaged in this kind of effort. We have no cause to wait for "the Church" to Christianize culture; we *are* the Church wherever we work and live. And we are present in every nook and cranny of society. God is eager to give us the courage and wisdom to proclaim and build up Christ's kingdom right there. We just need to seize the opportunities, to believe, and to launch ourselves into the fray. If we don't, who will?

Questions for Personal Reflection or Group Discussion

1. What idea in this chapter struck you most and why?
2. How firmly do you believe that Jesus really wants to convert the

entire world, every single person? How firmly do you believe that he wants to work through you to help achieve that goal?

3. How can you better infuse gospel values in your workplace or other circles of influence with cultural implications?

4. God calls all of us to bring the gospel into the circles of society where we live and work, through our way of being, our words, and our works. What will you do today to use your personal gifts for God's glory and to further the Church's work of evangelization?

- I will sit down with a friend and ask him or her to help me identify my top three or four personal gifts.

- I will spend some time prayerfully reflecting on the strong desires in my heart to take on a particular project or get involved in a certain apostolic activity, desires that have been resonating in my heart and may be indicating an invitation from the Lord, but which I haven't yet responded to. I will write these down and ask God to show me how to take the next step.

- I will remember the idealistic dreams of doing something great for God that motivated me in the past, and I will prayerfully reflect on what role those dreams should play in my life now.

- (Write your own resolution) I will _____

_____

_____

_____

Concluding Prayer

*I am created to do something or to be something for which no
one else is created; I have a place in God's counsels, in God's
world, which no one else has; whether I be rich or poor, despised
or esteemed by man, God knows me and calls me by my name.
God has created me to do Him some definite service; He has
committed some work to me which He has not committed to another.*

—St. John Henry Newman[55]

Relationships or Activities?

It is not therefore a matter of inventing a "new program." The program already exists: it is the plan found in the gospel and in the living Tradition, it is the same as ever. Ultimately, it has its center in Christ himself, who is to be known, loved and imitated, so that in him we may live the life of the Trinity, and with him transform history until its fulfillment in the heavenly Jerusalem.
—St. John Paul II, Novo Millennio Ineunte, 29

THE INSTRUCTIONS JESUS GAVE WHEN he sent out the first Christian missionaries included a curious directive: "Whatever town or village you enter, look for a worthy person in it, and stay there until you leave" (Matt. 10:11).

CHRISTIAN MISSION IS ABOUT PEOPLE

The implication is clear: Mission, for a Christian, is primarily about people. The whole history of salvation follows this same pattern. God begins to unfold his plan of redemption by establishing a relationship with the chosen people of Israel, and this relationship becomes the central characteristic of Israel's very identity. "Ever present in your midst, I will be your God, and you will be my people" (Lev. 26:12).

Through the Incarnation, God elevates his relationship with us to a shocking new level. By taking on human nature, he enables us to interact with him just as we interact with any human friend: "I no longer call you slaves, because a slave does not know what his master is doing. I have called you friends, because I have told you everything I have heard from my Father" (John 15:15).

Original sin shattered a relationship of trust between God and the human family: "Man, tempted by the devil, let his trust in his Creator die in his heart" (CCC, 397). God originally established that relationship to be the source of meaning and joy for human beings: "Man was made to live in communion with God, in whom he finds happiness" (CCC, 45). And so it makes perfect sense that God's plan for redeeming us from sin involves reestablishing a real, interpersonal relationship with the human family and each member of it, not simply tweaking a damaged social system or repairing a technical malfunction.

THE REAL MEANING OF RELIGION

Whenever we forget the centrality of relationship in the Christian worldview, we play into the hands of critics and cynics who consider religion to be nothing more than empty rituals and soulless formalities. We all know people who have left the Church because of this. They learned how to make the Sign of the Cross; they learned a few answers to questions in *Catechism* classes; they learned when to stand and sit and kneel during Mass; but they never experienced a personal encounter with God. Jesus remained for them a shadowy historical figure, not a real person passionately interested in their lives.

Developing a personal relationship with God in the context of a community of believers who make up the family of God—this is the real core of true religion. Making this possible was a central part of the radical, revolutionary message of Jesus Christ.

And so, as we strive to find creative ways to spread that message, we have to give priority to relationships. Otherwise we will end up betraying the very idea we are trying to communicate. Jesus commanded us to "love your neighbor as yourself" (Matt. 22:39). Love means relationship, personal investment, interpersonal knowledge, and mutual esteem. To be Christ's messengers to the world, his apostles and missionaries, requires us to care enough about the people whom Jesus came to save that we are willing to become vulnerable and enter into relationship with them: "Whatever town or village you enter, look for a worthy person in it, and stay there until you leave" (Matt. 10:11).

BEYOND TECHNIQUES

Any apostolic activity we engage in should include, or at least be open to, this dimension. Christianity is not a technique that people can learn and apply with clinical precision. Christianity is a network of faith-based relationships that flows outward from a personal encounter with the one, true, Triune God—Father, Son, and Holy Spirit—who is relationship and requires relationship: "Whoever is without love does not know God, for God is love" (1 John 4:8). Our apostolic endeavors have to be conceived and executed from that perspective.

Apostolates like camps, schools, Bible studies, service projects, publishing houses, websites, hospitals, professional associations, conferences, radio shows, formation programs, and even whole parishes are never ends in themselves. Rather, every apostolate is an effort to create an environment or situation in which personal encounters with Christ and among actual or potential members of the Body of Christ have a better chance of happening and flourishing. Apostolic activities are meant to be catalysts that initiate or deepen Christian experience, which is always in some way an experience of God and God's family.

AVOIDING A TRICKY IDOLATRY

And so we must resist the temptation to idolize our apostolates, as if the perfect apostolate will be able to conquer evil and usher in a new Golden Age of Christianity. There is no Golden Age, and there never has been. Every period in the history of the Church has had its crises as well as its saints. The age in which we live is no exception. Our Christian mission spurs us on to find creative ways to evangelize, to come up with new apostolates that can expand the reach—both in breadth and in depth—of Christ's message in our world, but in the end they are merely tools. The real heart of evangelization is found not in perfect pastoral programs or killer apps, which are merely useful instruments, but in relationships of love—love for Christ and love for neighbor.

Pope Benedict XVI put this beautifully in his very first encyclical letter, *God Is Love*:

Love of neighbor is thus shown to be possible in the way proclaimed by the Bible, by Jesus. It consists in the very fact that, in God and with God, I love even the person whom I do not like or even know. . . . Then I learn to look on this other person not simply with my eyes and my feelings, but from the perspective of Jesus Christ. His friend is my friend.[56]

"His friend is my friend"—this is the heart of apostolic activity. I want to give to others what Jesus has given to me, and I want to do so because Jesus wants me to. Evangelization is never mechanical; it is never technocratic. It is about people, and relationships, and the living God who is present in all of them.

Questions for Personal Reflection or Group Discussion

1. What idea in this chapter struck you most and why?

2. Considering the reflections in this chapter, what do you think is the best way to evaluate the effectiveness of our apostolic activities?

3. What would you say to someone who wanted to come up with creative means of evangelization to reach as many people as possible? Could an inspiration like that—so focused on visible results and measurable numbers—come from the Holy Spirit? Why or why not?

4. Throughout this book, we have explained that apostolic action can take three forms: the priestly form of living our daily activities as an offering to God and thereby as a witness to his goodness; the prophetic form of telling people about Jesus and his message; and the kingly form of working to transform society in accordance with God's plan. In your own life, which of those three is in the best condition and why? What will you do today to make an improvement in the one that needs it most?

   - I will seek advice from someone I trust about an aspect of my life I have been uncomfortable with for a while.

- I will bring up religion in a normal conversation and see where it goes.
- I will visit my parish or diocesan website and look for opportunities to volunteer my time in some apostolic activity during the coming weeks.
- (Write your own resolution) I will _____

    _____

    _____

    _____

Concluding Prayer

Dear Jesus, help me to spread thy fragrance everywhere I go.
Flood my soul with thy spirit and love.
Penetrate and possess my whole being so utterly that
all my life may only be a radiance of thine.
Shine through me and be so in me that every soul I come
in contact with may feel thy presence in my soul.
Let them look up and see no longer me but only Jesus.
Stay with me and then I shall begin to shine as you
shine, so to shine as to be a light to others.

—PRAYER OF ST. TERESA OF CALCUTTA

DAY 56

Working with Others and Working Smart

A spirituality of communion means, finally, to know how to "make room" for our brothers and sisters, bearing "each other's burdens" (Galatians 6:2) and resisting the selfish temptations which constantly beset us and provoke competition, careerism, distrust and jealousy. Let us have no illusions: unless we follow this spiritual path, external structures of communion will serve very little purpose. They would become mechanisms without a soul, "masks" of communion rather than its means of expression and growth.
– St. John Paul II, Novo Millennio Ineunte, 43

HOWEVER GOD INSPIRES YOU TO engage in the apostolate of works, it will sooner or later involve partnering with others. You may be moved to make rosaries and send them to persecuted Christians; you may be inspired to join your parish's efforts to alleviate poverty in a nearby city; you may feel a call to work full-time as a youth minister or part-time as a Catholic summer camp director; you may be nudged by the Holy Spirit to dedicate all your professional expertise to solving a major humanitarian crisis, like the lack of clean water in some third-world region; you may discover in your heart a burning desire to found a new Catholic research institute dedicated to figuring out how to evangelize the digital continent. Whatever form your apostolate of works takes, you will have to partner with other people in order to fulfill the dream that God planted in your soul. That's just how it is. As Christians, we are never Lone Rangers.

THE GOSPEL ISN'T INDIVIDUALISTIC

Some modern cultures tend to be exceedingly individualistic. Christians in those contexts often prefer an individualistic apostolate—something they can control and keep within the bounds of their comfort zone. But the work of the Church is always the work of the Church. From his encounter with the very first disciples, Jesus called his followers to work in teams. He formed a team of twelve apostles to be his immediate successors in building the Church. And even when he sent out the seventy-two disciples, he sent them out into the villages "two by two" (Luke 10:1).

This was intentional. It reflects the truth of our human nature, as created in God's own image. God, to put it in overly simplistic terms, is a team: Father, Son, and Holy Spirit. And so we, who are called to image God here on earth, live and work and do apostolate not just as individuals, but as members of a community, a team.

THE CALL TO COMMUNION

The theological term most often used to refer to this essential mark of Christian life is *communion*. God has not created us self-sufficient, but interdependent. Each individual and each community has something unique to contribute to the mosaic of the Church as a whole; no one person or single group can fulfill the mission of evangelization all alone.

Working with others always brings challenges. Sometimes it seems so much easier just to launch out on our own and make things happen. Sometimes it seems that the community structure of the Church, with its parishes and dioceses and the proper authorities that go with those entities, is more of an obstacle than a support. And yet this is how God wants us to live and work. Evangelization isn't just a technological challenge whose solution can be engineered through raw creativity and hard work. Evangelization is a journey, a pilgrimage of faith undertaken by the entire people of God. By facing the challenges of working in teams and staying plugged into the broader ecclesial realities, we help avoid fruitless deviations that on the surface may appear to be shortcuts.

Don't Be Afraid of Renewal!

This doesn't mean that we are meant to put up with archaic or dysfunctional patterns of behavior. If a team is unhealthy, we shouldn't just grin and bear it. Seeking constructive ways to renew and reform whatever needs to be renewed and reformed is an important expression of love. Permanent indifference or avoidance in the face of dysfunction is the opposite of love. It breeds cynicism, contempt, and resentment, in addition to inhibiting—or even poisoning—apostolic efforts. "Don't be afraid of the renewal of structures!" Pope Francis exhorted in one of his daily homilies.[57]

Learning from the Children of This World

Whether your apostolate takes place within an official Church structure or not, you can benefit from the best practices applicable to every human group and endeavor. The virtue of prudence involves taking time to build and maintain a healthy team—a healthy communion of persons. It involves taking the time and effort to reflect, plan, evaluate, organize, coordinate with other groups and apostolates, communicate, set goals, and invest time and resources wisely. No human enterprise can flourish without such prudence, and although the apostolate is not *merely* a human enterprise, the human factor is real.

When the Holy Spirit moves us to engage in apostolic activity, he doesn't want us to shelve our intelligence and common sense; instead he wants us to baptize and contribute them to the mission. Jesus actually complained to his followers about the tendency we all have to over-spiritualize our apostolic activity, as if by a sheer act of faith we will be able to bypass the normal requirements for effective action. "For the children of this world are more prudent in dealing with their own generation than are the children of light" (Luke 16:8).

Thinking that God will make everything work out even if we are careless and irresponsible in doing our part is a naïve form of fideism (i.e., an exaggerated reliance on faith to the imprudent exclusion of reason). Human efficiency alone can bear no fruit for Christ's kingdom—"Without me you can do nothing," Jesus reminds us (John

15:5)—but human efficiency is a beautiful offering, a concrete expression of love we can place upon the altar and entrust to the Lord's care—just as we use beautiful vessels and vestments for the celebration of Mass, not just paper cups and rags. Love moves us to give our best to the beloved. By calling us to share in his redeeming mission, Jesus generously gives us the chance to love him in that way, too.

Questions for Personal Reflection or Group Discussion

1. What idea in this chapter struck you most and why?

2. When you face the challenges of living your mission together with others, how do you tend to react? Why?

3. What challenges are you facing right now in your efforts to engage in apostolic works? How would Jesus want you to deal with those challenges?

4. In every period of Church history, God sparks spiritual and apostolic renewal by raising up new spiritual families within the larger family of the Church. In our period of Church history, God continues to raise up new movements and call people to join them and thereby put their lives more concretely at the service of the Church's mission. What will you do today to contribute to these efforts?

    - I will renew my own commitment to an apostolate I know God is inspiring me to be a part of.

    - I will begin looking around to find an apostolate or a Catholic faith-community that resonates with me.

    - I will renew my commitment to being an active member of my parish community.

    - (Write your own resolution) I will _____
      _____
      _____
      _____

Concluding Prayer

O God, You are our Creator. You are good and Your mercy
knows no bounds. To You arises the praise of every creature. O
God, You have given us an inner law by which we must live. To
do Your will is our task. To follow Your ways is to know peace of
heart. To You we offer our homage. Guide us on all the paths we
travel upon this earth. Free us from all the evil tendencies which
lead our hearts away from Your will. Never allow us to stray
from You. O God, judge of all humankind, help us to be included
among Your chosen ones on the last day. O God, Author of peace
and justice, give us true joy and authentic love, and a lasting
solidarity among peoples. Give us Your everlasting gifts. Amen!

—St. John Paul II[58]

PART X

WHAT TO EXPECT

"Go on your way; behold, I am sending you like lambs among wolves. Carry no money bag, no sack, no sandals; and greet no one along the way. Into whatever house you enter, first say, 'Peace to this household.' If a peaceful person lives there, your peace will rest on him; but if not, it will return to you. Stay in the same house and eat and drink what is offered to you, for the laborer deserves his payment. Do not move about from one house to another. Whatever town you enter and they welcome you, eat what is set before you, cure the sick in it and say to them, 'The kingdom of God is at hand for you.' Whatever town you enter and they do not receive you, go out into the streets and say, 'The dust of your town that clings to our feet, even that we shake off against you.' Yet know this: the kingdom of God is at hand. I tell you, it will be more tolerable for Sodom on that day than for that town."

LUKE 10:3–12

Facing Your Challenges

We have every reason to have confidence in Christian youth: youth will not fail the Church if within the Church there are enough older people able to understand it, to love it, to guide it and to open up to it a future by passing on to it with complete fidelity the Truth which endures. Then new workers, resolute and fervent, will in their turn enter upon spiritual and apostolic work in the fields which are white and ready for the harvest.
—St. Paul VI, Gaudete in Domino

SOMETIMES WE MAY WONDER WHY God decided to burden us with this work of evangelization. Why doesn't he just do it all himself, miraculously, as he did at the wedding feast in Cana?

It's because God made us with a purpose, an existential need to have an impact in the world, to make a difference. And we long for that. To make a lasting difference helps give meaning to our lives, and we yearn for meaning. This mission, this call, this cooperation with the Lord in evangelizing the world is an incomparable path of meaning.

LEAVING A LASTING MARK

Pope Benedict XVI beautifully described this yearning and its proper place of fulfillment just a few days before he was elected pope in a passage we have already encountered:

All people desire to leave a lasting mark. But what endures? Money does not. Even buildings do not, nor books. After a certain time, longer or shorter, all these things disappear. The only thing that lasts for ever is the human soul, the human person created by God for eternity. The fruit that endures is therefore all that we have sown in human souls: love, knowledge, a gesture capable of touching hearts, words that open the soul to joy in the Lord.[59]

No greater fulfillment exists than the fulfillment that comes from loving God with all our heart, soul, mind, and strength and loving our neighbors as ourselves, and nothing achieves that more than evangelization through our way of life, our words, and our works.

Why Blessings Sometimes Feel Like Burdens

But even so, heeding this call to "go, therefore, and make disciples of all nations" (Matt. 28:19) can feel more like a burden than a blessing. It feels that way because part of our fallen human nature resists our true calling, and that fallen nature is egged on by some of the standards and behavior patterns present in this fallen world, as well as by the influence of our ancient enemy, the devil, and his minions. Loving as Christ loves brings us fulfillment, but it also encounters resistance.

We need to be prepared for that. It shouldn't surprise us. When internal problems and dysfunctions keep cropping up among our fellow apostles, when external obstacles ceaselessly batter our most sincere apostolic efforts, when opposition arises and difficulties present themselves from the most surprisingly and even seemingly contradictory sources—this is nothing to be disoriented by; it is par for the course, the Lord knows all about it, and he can handle it.

St. Paul's Troubles

St. Paul is known throughout the history of Christian literature as the apostle par excellence. His tireless journeying to spread the message of Christ yielded amazing results and indeed planted the seeds of Christian civilization. When you visit the city of Rome today, you see towering statues and gorgeous monuments dedicated to his pioneering work of evangelization. From the perspective offered by twenty centuries of Christian living, we can clearly see the amazing magnitude of his achievement. We should be inspired by that and give glory to God for it, as Christians have done since the first centuries of our era.

And yet, during the period when he was actually engaged in his evangelizing labors, such glorious success often eluded him. His life unfolded amid constant opposition, persecution, difficulties, challenges, misunderstandings, and, yes, even failures. God was working in him and through him, but the process was not some meteoric rise to glory. Rather, it followed the rhythms of Christ's own life: normal Nazareth, dramatic public life, painful passion, glorious resurrection. All these elements were present throughout his missionary life, and they will all be present throughout our missionary lives, too. We must be ready for that.

In 2 Corinthians 11, St. Paul paints a portrait of what it was like for him to faithfully answer the Lord's call in his life. He issues this enumeration as a self-defense (which he was reluctant to give, but it was necessary) against unjust critics who were maligning him and trying to undermine his apostolic toils.

The Christian mission, the Christian life with its priestly, prophetic, and kingly dimensions, always bears the sign of its Lord and Savior: the Sign of the Cross. Let's decide ahead of time—right now in fact—that we won't let it confuse us.

Questions for Personal Reflection or Group Discussion

1. What idea in this chapter struck you most and why?

2. If we are created to evangelize, to love God and neighbor, why does it often feel so difficult to do? Explain that apparent contradiction in your own words.

3. When have you experienced the blessings that come from evangelizing? Remember, savor, and thank God for that. When have you experienced the burden of evangelizing? Remember, accept, and thank God for that as well.

4. Our crosses are somehow mysteriously part of God's plan for us, just as the passion and crucifixion of Jesus was part of the

Father's plan for redeeming the world. What will you do today to embrace your crosses with faith and love?

- I will make the Sign of the Cross slowly, intentionally, and prayerfully before I pray.

- I will thank Jesus for loving me so much that he was willing to suffer the attacks of evil in order to atone for my sins and those of the whole world.

- I will reach out to someone whose cross is heavier than mine right now and try to help that person carry it.

- (Write your own resolution) I will _____

  _____

  _____

  _____

Concluding Prayer

The Lord is my light and my salvation;
whom should I fear?
The Lord is my life's refuge;
of whom should I be afraid?
When evildoers come at me
to devour my flesh,
these my enemies and foes
themselves stumble and fall.
Though an army encamp against me,
my heart does not fear;
Though war be waged against me,
even then do I trust.
For God will hide me in his shelter
in time of trouble,
he will conceal me in the cover of his tent;
and set me high upon a rock.

—PSALM 27:1–3, 5

Exorcising the Specter of Discouragement

The gospel is certainly demanding. We know that Christ never permitted his disciples and those who listened to him to entertain any illusions about this. At the same time, however, he revealed that his demands never exceed man's abilities. If man accepts these demands with an attitude of faith, he will also find in the grace that God never fails to give him the necessary strength to meet those demands.
— St. John Paul II[60]

DISCOURAGEMENT IS ONE OF AN apostle's greatest enemies. It can sneak up on us. We need to understand it in order to be ready to resist it. A good place to do so is in chapter 24 of St. Luke's Gospel, where we read the familiar story of the disciples on the road to Emmaus.

It was Easter Sunday. The gruesome events of Good Friday were over, and while the eleven apostles were still together, the wider circle of disciples was starting to disperse. Two of these were walking from Jerusalem back to their hometown of Emmaus.

Along the way they were discussing everything that had happened—the life and teaching of Jesus, his trial and crucifixion, and even the first vague reports of the empty tomb. But it was not a happy, enthusiastic discussion. On the contrary, St. Luke tells us they were "looking downcast." They were disheartened—the Greek word has connotations of gloomy and morose. They were experiencing what all of us experience sooner or later in our faith journey: the suffocating weight of discouragement.

THE ROLE OF SADNESS

Simple sadness is different than discouragement. Feeling sad is part of being human, and nothing is wrong with that emotion. But when we let the feeling of sadness seep into our hearts and minds and extinguish our hope, when we let it convince us to relinquish our evangelizing efforts, then it becomes a danger, a temptation, a threat to the health of our souls—that's discouragement.

An old saying among spiritual writers claims that discouragement never comes from the Holy Spirit. The emotion of sadness can be in harmony with the Holy Spirit's work in our souls, because this fallen world has legitimate causes for sadness—death, loss, sin, and the destruction that sin wreaks, for example. To be insensitive to those things would be inhuman and spiritually blind.

In his Sermon on the Mount, Jesus proclaimed that experiencing sadness over these kinds of things, a sadness in harmony with truth, helps us move forward on the path of a meaningful life. "Blessed are those who mourn," he taught, "for they will be comforted" (Matt. 5:4).

Jesus himself sometimes experienced profound sadness: He wept over the city of Jerusalem, which refused to receive his message of salvation; he wept over the death of his friend Lazarus; his soul became "sorrowful even to death" in the Garden of Gethsemane (Mark 14:34).

DEFINING DISCOURAGEMENT

But that kind of sadness is different than discouragement. Since sadness comes simply from recognizing the brokenness of a fallen world, it doesn't paralyze us and extinguish our hope. Rather, it expresses our love for all that is good and true, for all that sin and evil destroy. This kind of sadness, then, strengthens our hearts against evil and actually feeds our courage.

Discouragement, on the other hand, is sadness gone crazy. Like a wound that has become infected, discouragement is sadness that starts to fester, and it produces spiritual poison. The English word *discouragement* expresses this well. It literally means "without courage." To become discouraged is to lose the energy necessary to continue fighting. To become discouraged is to play with the temptation to give up and give in, to stop trying.

Someone who is discouraged no longer strives after the worthy goal he or she used to believe in, because that person no longer has any hope that goal is attainable. And that is precisely why discouragement can never come from the Holy Spirit—in Christ, with the help of God's grace, every worthy goal is always attainable. As the angel said to the Blessed Virgin Mary during the Annunciation: "For nothing will be impossible with God" (Luke 1:37). And Jesus himself said the same thing: "For human beings this is impossible, but for God all things are possible" (Matt. 19:26). That's why discouragement always hides some kind of lie.

THE EXPECTATION TRAP

These two disciples, then, were dragging their feet toward Emmaus, with long faces and downcast hearts. They were in a dangerous situation, spiritually speaking: They were discouraged.

At that point Jesus came up and started walking beside them, although they didn't recognize him. Jesus asked them what they were talking about, and in their explanation of the recent events, they revealed why they were discouraged. After recounting all the wonderful things Jesus had done and the horrible tragedy of his betrayal, crucifixion, and death, they said, "But we were hoping that he would be the one to redeem Israel" (Luke 24:21).

"We were hoping," the two disciples admit. They had hoped in Jesus, but now their hope had died. They had expected so much from him, even changing their lives to follow him, but now their expectations had been shattered, and they were returning to the way things had been.

We have all had that experience. We have expected God to act in a certain way in our life or give us a certain kind of apostolic success, and then had the wind knocked out of us when those expectations were not met. We have all felt the disappointment, the confusion, the frustration—the *discouragement*—that can come with shattered expectations.

The Real Cause of Discouragement

Up to that point in the conversation, Jesus had simply been listening. But once they finished their story, he chimed in with some words that didn't appear to be very comforting, at least not at first: "O how foolish you are!" (Luke 24:25). He called them fools! Most likely he said it with a smile and not a frown, but even so, we can only imagine the shocked look on the faces of these two disciples when this apparent stranger, instead of commiserating with them, upbraided them.

And then Jesus went on to explain *why* they were being foolish, and in so doing, he revealed the real cause of every discouragement, of every festering sadness that threatens to extinguish our hope, paralyze our souls, and halt the advance of evangelization. "How slow of heart to believe in all that the prophets spoke! Was it not necessary that the Messiah should suffer these things and enter into his glory?" (Luke 24:25).

There it is, the source of all spiritual discouragement: a faltering faith, an unwillingness to believe in God's way of doing things, a reluctance to accept the revealed truth that all salvation, all growth in holiness, all progress in spiritual maturity, and all apostolic fruitfulness must pass along the way of the cross. When things go wrong, it doesn't mean God has abandoned us—the Crucifixion isn't the end of the story; the Resurrection is.

Adjusting Expectations

When we expect life to be without the cross, our expectations are false, and they will always end up being shattered. The cross was necessary, Jesus emphasized; it was somehow part of God's plan that the new and eternal life shining out on Easter Sunday should rise from the hideous and painful darkness of Good Friday.

This is true for our own spiritual lives, and it is also true for our evangelizing efforts. Jesus summarized it with one of his favorite images, that of a seed: "Amen, amen, I say to you, unless a grain of wheat falls to the ground and dies, it remains just a grain of wheat; but if it dies, it produces much fruit" (John 12:24).

And throughout the history of the Church, that saying has been verified, over and over again. As the early Christian theologian Tertullian put it, "The blood of the martyrs is the seed of the Church."[61] And since our evangelization efforts are all about spreading and growing the Church, we need not be discouraged when those efforts require our blood—on the contrary, we should rejoice: "Now I rejoice in my sufferings for your sake, and in my flesh I am filling up what is lacking in the afflictions of Christ on behalf of his body, which is the church" (Col. 1:24).

Questions for Personal Reflection or Group Discussion

1. What idea in this chapter struck you most and why?

2. What do you usually do when you experience healthy sadness? How can you better integrate those experiences into your prayer life?

3. When do you tend to get discouraged and why? How do you usually react? How can you infuse more faith into those reactions?

4. In order to integrate our emotions into our spiritual life in a healthy way, we first have to learn to identify and own up to what we feel. Taking some time each day to pray an "examination of conscience" is a good way to do this. We quiet our souls and then reflect on how we have been living the events of daily life. We ask God to enlighten us about how he has been present and how we have been responding to the opportunities and challenges his providence has been dishing up. In that atmosphere of reflective prayer, we can often begin to see and understand our own emotional reaction patterns. What will you do today to increase your self-knowledge?

   • I will start—or jump-start—a daily examination of conscience, looking for a guide to help me if necessary.[62]

   • I will take some time during the following four Sundays to write in a spiritual journal, trying to describe what is happening in my soul and how I am dealing with that.

   • I will find a good book on my vocation (marriage,

315

priesthood, consecrated life), and I will read it with an eye to better understanding God's point of view regarding my state in life and how I can better live in harmony with that.

- (Write your own resolution) I will _____

  _____

  _____

  _____

Concluding Prayer

The Lord is my shepherd; there is nothing I lack.
Even though I walk through the valley of the shadow of
death, I will fear no evil, for you are with me. Indeed,
goodness and mercy will pursue me all the days of my life;
I will dwell in the house of the Lord for endless days.

—FROM PSALM 23

DAY 59

The Perennial Pitfall

*It is important however that what we propose, with the help of God,
should be profoundly rooted in contemplation and prayer. Ours is a
time of continual movement which often leads to restlessness, with the
risk of "doing for the sake of doing." We must resist this temptation
by trying "to be" before trying "to do." In this regard we should
recall how Jesus reproved Martha: "You are anxious and troubled
about many things; one thing is needful" (Luke 10:41–42).*
—St. John Paul II, Novo Millennio Ineunte, 15

O NE OF THE PERENNIAL PITFALLS for Christian apostles is activism. Activism is idolizing our evangelizing activities, behaving and thinking
as if we ourselves were the redeemers of the world and not Jesus.

GETTING THINGS DONE

Some personalities have a built-in propensity for this—they just
want to get things done and have no patience for delays of any kind.
For others the temptation flows more from the depth of their love:
They see how much need the world has for God's grace and thus
keep overcommitting themselves, taking on way more responsibilities and projects than they can effectively handle. That is a formula
for burnout and can serve as a back door for the devil—he can no
longer make any progress by tempting someone with mortal sin and
outright rebellion against God, so he sneaks in under the radar,
stimulating thoughts that appear to be holy (*You need to do more for
the Lord! Don't you love him? Isn't there more you can do?*) only to use
them as a disguise for spiritual pride (*I really have to do this, that, and*

317

the other thing, even though my health and my family life and my prayer life are collapsing—if I don't do all these projects, I will be letting God down, and there is no one else who can possibly do them).

Activism can have truly horrendous consequences. Those who were formerly full of sincere zeal for Christ and his kingdom can become bitter and resentful toward God. They can blame the very people they used to work with in their evangelizing efforts for their own ennui and exhaustion, feeding sentiments of anger as well as violent and destructive criticism. They can even begin to direct their previously apostolic energies toward quixotic causes they believe are necessary to fix all the Church's problems—the problems that, they claim, led to the painful burnout they experienced.

Staying Close to the Vine

One giveaway for creeping activism is usually linked to our prayer life. Prayer always must be our first priority. Without a healthy life of prayer—including vocal prayer, mental prayer, and the sacraments of the Eucharist and confession—our relationship with God will surely languish, and then what do we have to give to others? Unless we keep filling our own souls with God's grace and strength, we quickly run out of the necessary supplies for effective evangelization. As Jesus said: "You are the salt of the earth. But if salt loses its taste, with what can it be seasoned? It is no longer good for anything but to be thrown out and trampled underfoot" (Matt. 5:13).

The apostolic fruit our Christian lives are called to bear is a supernatural fruit. When we cut ourselves off from its source by skimping on our prayer life, we invite barrenness (see John 15:4–8). The evangelizing power of our way of living, the effectiveness of our words of witness, and the success of our apostolic works (the "fruit" Jesus speaks of) all depend primarily on God's grace, because they are all directed toward helping people hear his voice in their lives and respond generously to it. Only a healthy life of prayer can keep that grace flowing through our spiritual veins. Pope Benedict XVI made this point explicitly:

Prayer, as a means of drawing ever new strength from Christ, is concretely and urgently needed. . . . It is time to reaffirm the importance of prayer in the face of the activism and the growing secularism of many Christians engaged in charitable work.[63]

WATCHING THE STRESS METER

Another indicator that activism may be on the rise has to do with the experience of anxiety or stress. When we begin depending excessively on our own efforts in order to build up Christ's kingdom, the pressure becomes unbearable. Our efforts will never be sufficient to save the world. Our efforts will never be sufficient to earn God's unconditional love (we already *have* that as a pure gift from God). If we put those kinds of burdens on ourselves, they constrict our soul and drain it of joy. God is the author of salvation and the real protagonist in every apostolic endeavor. His invitation to join him in the work of redemption flows from the love he already has for us.

In all our evangelizing efforts, a continual purification of our intention is a strong help against falling into the perennial pitfall of activism. What are we truly seeking: to glorify God and help our neighbors and thereby fulfill the true meaning of our lives, or to win popularity contests and achievement competitions? Continually and purposely purifying our intention helps us maintain a healthy balance in our lives, giving proper attention to our circles of influence and keeping us docile to God's direction. Each of us simply needs to listen closely to what he is asking of us and make a decent effort to do that. We are not responsible for saving the world; we are only responsible for doing our part.

Questions for Personal Reflection or Group Discussion

1. What idea in this chapter struck you most and why?
2. In your own life, what are the signs that usually indicate you are falling into your own perennial pitfall?

3. What can you do to keep God first and to increase your trust in him so that you don't put undue pressure on yourself?

4. What will you do today to regain some balance in your life so God's grace can flow more freely in you and through you?

    *   I will take a look at what I do for entertainment and cut out any excesses that don't reflect the purpose of my life here on earth.

    *   I will reflect on the five most important relationships in my life and see which one is the most neglected. I will make a concrete effort to invest in that relationship this week.

    *   I will look at my commitments. I will divide them into categories—essential, useful, and superfluous. I will then drop the superfluous commitments and resolve to take sufficient time to reflect before making new commitments.

    *   (Write your own resolution) I will _____
        _____
        _____
        _____

Concluding Prayer

Holy Mary, Mother of God, you have given the world its true light, Jesus, your Son—the Son of God. You abandoned yourself completely to God's call and thus became a wellspring of the goodness which flows forth from him. Show us Jesus. Lead us to him. Teach us to know and love him, so that we too can become capable of true love and be fountains of living water in the midst of a thirsting world.

—POPE BENEDICT XVI[64]

Avoiding the Rush

*This passion will not fail to stir in the Church a new sense of
mission, which cannot be left to a group of "specialists" but
must involve the responsibility of all the members of the People
of God. Those who have come into genuine contact with Christ
cannot keep him for themselves, they must proclaim him.*
—St. John Paul II, Novo Millennio Ineunte, 40

O UR LORD'S FAVORITE IMAGES FOR his kingdom always had to do
with plants. The sower who went out to sow, the mustard seed,
the grain of wheat, the farmer's field . . . his kingdom is like that. It
grows organically, taking time to put down roots and put up shoots,
going through different seasons as its fruit matures. And just as farmers cannot rush their crops but have to respect the natural rhythms
of growth, so too Christian apostles need patience and perseverance
as they respect the seasons of evangelical growth.

SHARING IN THE LABOR

Sometimes, in fact, we may never see the harvest of the seeds we
planted—at least, not this side of heaven. Sometimes we are called
to plant, other times to water, and still other times to bring in the
harvest (see John 4:37-38). St. Paul picks up on this same image
in order to remind the Christians in Corinth that the spiritual
fruitfulness they have experienced through believing in the gospel
is not the result of merely human activity, and so the men who
preached the gospel (in this case Apollos and Paul himself)
deserve only relative credit (see 1 Cor. 3:5-9).

SEASONS OF SALVATION

Perhaps patience and perseverance are harder for us than they were for Christians in past ages. The pace of life in the digital world is so accelerated and the rate of technological progress so dizzying that we expect quick results, quick fixes, quick progress, and quick resolution. We are products and citizens of an on-demand culture, but spiritual and apostolic growth are not on-demand items—they are seasonal.

Throughout the history of salvation, every major event had its seasons. Moses didn't even begin his mission to free Israel from Egyptian slavery until he was an old man. David had to wait nineteen years—enduring persecution for most of them—between his anointing as the new king of Israel and his actual crowning. Even Jesus, as we have seen, spent thirty years in obscurity before launching out on his public mission, and then he prefaced his first sermon with a forty-day retreat in the desert wilderness. The nascent Church had to wait for seven weeks after the Resurrection before receiving the Holy Spirit at Pentecost. The Church is "God's field," and the fruits of her evangelizing effort take time to mature.

YOU CANNOT RUSH THE EFFECTS OF GRACE

Our apostolic activities deserve our best efforts and our smartest strategies, but unlike mere worldly work, their fruits are not completely in our control. To evangelize is to work with God and for God and allow him to arrange the calendar. The effects of grace go beyond our merely human efforts, and we need to learn to be okay with that.

Evangelization seeks to establish and nurture a living relationship between God and every person, and relationships always take time to develop. This apostolate poses many practical challenges, which we should meet with all the creativity and energy we would apply to any practical challenge. But the central challenge is actually deeper; it involves healing broken hearts and sickened souls, and those things cannot be rushed.

Yearning of Love versus Worldly Rush

Jesus felt the urgent yearning of love; it burned in his heart like a fire: "I have come to set the earth on fire, and how I wish it were already blazing!" (Luke 12:49). But when he commissioned his followers to make disciples of all nations, he let them know how long it would take to finish: "And behold, I am with you always, until the end of the age" (Matt. 28:20). The evangelizing mission of the Church will continue until the end of history. Let's work hard, planting and watering and weeding however the Lord asks us to, but let's do so calmly and wisely, trusting first and foremost in him and his love, not in our human smarts and strengths. Let's avoid the worldly rush and make room for the flow of grace.

Questions for Personal Reflection or Group Discussion

1. What idea in this chapter struck you most and why?

2. When do you tend to get impatient and why? How do you usually respond to that? How would you like to respond?

3. When have you been surprised by how God's grace works? Remember, savor, and speak to God about that experience. What do you think he wants you to learn from it?

4. We are responsible for our input into the work of evangelization God invites us to undertake. But God is responsible for the output. What will you do today to cultivate a humble sense of detachment from visible results and a joyful trust in the fruitfulness of every effort offered to God with love?

   - When things don't go my way, I will say a prayer of trust in God.

   - When things go my way and I experience a success, no matter how small, I will enjoy the feeling and thank God for it.

   - After I do my part, I will say a small prayer commending my efforts to God's care and releasing any self-centered or fear-based expectations I may have regarding the results.

- (Write your own resolution) I will _____
  _____
  _____
  _____

Concluding Prayer

Lord, my heart is not haughty,
I do not set my sights too high.
I have taken no part in great affairs,
in wonders beyond my scope.
No, I hold myself in quiet and silence,
like a little child in its mother's arms,
like a little child, so I keep myself.
Let Israel hope in the Lord
henceforth and for ever.

—Psalm 131[65]

Conclusion

R ESPONDING TO CHRIST'S INVITATION TO love God with all our heart, soul, mind, and strength, and to love our neighbor as ourselves, is a lifetime adventure. It is a journey that will never end. Every time we think we have reached the limit, we suddenly turn a corner and discover new horizons, new depths in our own being as well as new wonders in the inexhaustible mystery of God. God is infinite, and infinitely lovable. Even after our earthly pilgrimage concludes and we find ourselves—please God—face-to-face with the Lord, loving him will continue to surprise and delight us in new, fresh ways for all eternity. This is the only adventure that is worth living and dying for. It is the adventure that we were each created to experience. And each one of us will experience it in a unique way; no one else can love God, or discover God's love, the way you can.

Likewise, God gives each of us a unique call, a unique way in which to share his love. While we are here on earth, there is work to do for Christ and his kingdom, and the Lord has invited each one of us to join in it. No other work can ever be as meaningful. Yet we do not build the kingdom alone, but in cooperation with God and each other.

This is why it's especially important to recall that our love for God never comes first; it is always a response to God's love for us. He is the vine, we are just the branches; as we have seen various times during this book, without him we can do nothing (see John 15:5).

Keeping that in mind is the secret to being a deeply joy-filled Christian, in spite of our many faults and failings, in spite of the twists and turns of the Christian road, and in spite of the reality of evil in this fallen world. By remembering day in and day out that

God is the one most interested in our growth in love, and that he does 99 percent of what needs to be done, we can learn to welcome St. Paul's otherwise puzzling exhortation to "rejoice always. Pray without ceasing. In all circumstances give thanks, for this is the will of God for you in Christ Jesus" (1 Thess. 5:16–18).

This introductory explanation of how to begin living the greatest commandments was not meant to be exhaustive. And it was not meant to provide a connect-the-dots kind of formula for Christian living. Love is too personal and surprising and vital for that kind of thing. But if it has helped you understand a little bit better the common characteristics of the path that every disciple of Christ must somehow follow, and if it has stirred up or reinforced your desire to keep following that path, and if it has provided one or two (or maybe even three) new insights or suggestions that will help you turn that desire into day-to-day decisions that give glory to the Lord and overflow in love, then we can both be grateful to God, the giver of every good gift.

Acknowledgments

This book would not have been possible without the collaboration of a vast team of fellow pilgrims, especially the following, whom I want to thank sincerely: Cecilia Azcunaga, Lisa Brenninkmeyer, Daniel Burke, Luly Fernandez, Debra Graspointner, Lucy Honner, Fr. Owen Kearns, Fr. John Connor, Fr. Steven Liscinsky, Fr. Dermot Ryan, Paul McCusker, Jennifer Meyer, Alli Shoemaker, Michele Sylvestro, Doug Venne, DJ Venne, Claudia Volkman, Mike Williams, the Atlanta, Georgia, community of Consecrated Women of Regnum Christi, the Cupertino, California, community of Legionaries of Christ, and the fledgling "Writers' Team" who took joyful advantage of their hospitality.

Notes

[1]Benedict XVI, Angelus, June 18, 2012.

[2]St. Augustine, *Sermo* 169,11,13:PL 38, 923.

[3]Second Vatican Council, *Gaudium et Spes*, 13, 27.

[4]Prayer of St. Teresa of Avila, quoted in CCC, 227

[5]St. Thomas Aquinas, *Exposition of the Apostle's Creed*, XII.

[6]Pope Benedict XVI, Wednesday Audience, October 17, 2012.

[7]http://www.newmanreader.org/works/meditations/meditations8.html#return1.

[8]C.S. Lewis, *The Great Divorce: Collected Letters of C.S. Lewis* (New York: HarperCollins, Kindle edition 2009) location 731–734.

[9]St. Thomas Aquinas, *De Perfectione Vitae Spiritualis*, VI.

[10]*Confessions*, Book X

[11]Benedict XVI, Homily, April 24, 2005.

[12]http://www.catholicity.com/prayer/prayers-and-hymns-by-john-henry-cardinal-newman.html.

[13]http://www.catholicdoors.com/prayers/english/p00404.htm.

[14]http://www.ourcatholicprayers.com/prayers-before-studying.html.

[15]*Veritatis Splendor*, 120.

[16]http://www.stjohnchrysostom.org/OurTraditions/Prayers/CommonPrayers.aspx.

[17]http://www.worldprayers.org/archive/prayers/invocations/i_arise_today_through_a_mighty.html.

[18]St. John Paul II, *Veritatis Splendor*, 1.

[19]*Roman Missal*, Appendix of Prayers after Communion.

[20]Paraphrase of Prayer from St. Bonaventure, Air Maria, http://airmaria.com/category/subjects/franciscan-things/page/2/.

[21]Benedict XVI, Address, May 19, 2011.

[22]Second Vatican Council, *Gaudium et Spes*, 21.

[23]Ibid., 43.

[24]Pope Francis, *Evangelii Gaudium*, 10.

[25]St. John Paul II, Message for World Mission Sunday, 9; October 24, 1999.

[26]Libreria Editrice Vaticana (2011-11-02). *Catechism of the Catholic Church* (Kindle Locations 27410–27411). United States Conference of Catholic Bishops. Kindle edition.

[27]For this tripartite description of the Church's evangelizing mission, see the Vatican Congregation for the Clergy, General Directory for Catechesis, 49.

[28]Vatican Congregation for the Clergy, General Directory for Catechesis, 46; vatican.va.

[29]St. John Paul II, *Christifideles Laici*, 58.

[30]Pius XI, *Quas Primas*, 1.

[31]Ibid., 15, 19, 21.

[32]Ibid., 33.

[33]Blessed Paul VI, *Evangelii Nuntiandi*, 3.

[34]Ibid., 4.

[35]St. John Paul II, Address at the Opening of the 19th Ordinary Plenary Assembly of the Latin American Episcopal Council, 9 March 1983; *L'Osservatore Romano* English edition, 18 April 1983, p. 9.

[36]Pope Benedict XVI, Homily at Vespers, June 28, 2010.

[37]http://w2.vatican.va/content/john-paul-ii/en/messages/youth/documents/hf_jp-ii_mes_15081992_viii-world-youth-day.html.

[38]Joseph Cardinal Ratzinger, Address to Catechists and Religion Teachers,

Jubilee of Catechists, December 12, 2000. (https://www.ewtn.com/new_evangelization/Ratzinger.htm).

[39]Ibid.

[40]Ibid.

[41]Benedict XVI, Message for the International Forum of Catholic Action, August 10, 2012; http://w2.vatican.va/content/benedict-xvi/en/messages/pont-messages/2012/documents/hf_ben-xvi_mes_20120810_fiac.html.

[42]Those are essential aspects of our Christian discipleship, and they were treated in greater detail earlier in this book and in the author's previous work: *The Better Part: A Christ-Centered Resource for Personal Prayer.*

[43]Address of His Holiness John Paul II to the Students of the Catholic University; Washington, D.C., October 7, 1979; http://w2.vatican.va/content/john-paul-ii/en/speeches/1979/october/documents/hf_jp-ii_spe_19791007_usa_washington_studenti-univ-catt.html.

[44]Following the explanations earlier in this book, I am using the terms evangelization and apostolate interchangeably.

[45]The Second Vatican Council, *Apostolicam Actuositatem*, 7; CCC, 909.

[46]http://www.universalis.com/index.htm.

[47]Benedict XVI, homily, April, 24, 2005; http://w2.vatican.va/content/benedict-xvi/en/homilies/2005/documents/hf_ben-xvi_hom_20050424_inizio-pontificato.html.

[48]The Trial of Sir Thomas More; http://law2.umkc.edu/faculty/projects/ftrials/more/moretrialreport.html.

[49]St. John Paul II, Message for the VII World Youth Day, November 24, 1991; http://w2.vatican.va/content/john-paul-ii/en/messages/youth/documents/hf_jp-ii_mes_24111991_vii-world-youth-day.html.

[50]St. John Paul II, Message for XIX World Communications Day, April, 15 1985; http://www.catholicradioassociation.org/World%20Communications%20Day%20Messages.pdf.

[51]St. John Paul II, *Laborem Exercens*, 25.

[52]The Second Vatican Council, *Apostolicam Actuositatem*, 7; CCC, 909.

[53]St. John Paul II, *Dives in Misericordia*, 3.

[54]http://w2.vatican.va/content/john-paul-ii/en/prayers/documents/hf_jp-ii_1999_jub-prayer-padre.html.

[55]http://www.newmanreader.org/works/meditations/meditations9.html

[56]Pope Benedict XVI, *Deus Caritas Est*, 18.

[57]http://www.news.va/en/news pope-francis-the-holy-spirit-renews-our-lives.

[58]The Pope Speaks 37/4, 1992, 213; https://www.ewtn.com/JohnPaul2/writings/prayers/guidance.htm).

[59]Joseph Cardinal Ratzinger, homily, April 18, 2005; (http://www.vatican.va/gpII/documents/homily-pro-eligendo-pontifice_20050418_en.html).

[60]John Paul II, *Crossing the Threshold of Hope* (New York: Alfred A. Knopf, 1994), p. 222.

[61]Tertullian, *Apologeticum*, chapter 50; http://www.tertullian.org/works/apologeticum.htm.

[62]The conference video from the retreat guide, Sitting in the Side Pew, gives some pointers about how to do this kind of prayer: http://rcspirituality.org/sitting-in-the-side-pew-conference-video/.

[63]Pope Benedict XVI, *Deus Caritas Est*, 36, 37.

[64]Pope Benedict XVI, *Deus Caritas Est*, 42.

[65]Adapted from the *New Jerusalem Bible* translation.

Sophia Institute

Sophia Institute is a nonprofit institution that seeks to nurture the spiritual, moral, and cultural life of souls and to spread the Gospel of Christ in conformity with the authentic teachings of the Roman Catholic Church.

Sophia Institute Press fulfills this mission by offering translations, reprints, and new publications that afford readers a rich source of the enduring wisdom of mankind.

Sophia Institute also operates the popular online resource CatholicExchange.com. *Catholic Exchange* provides world news from a Catholic perspective as well as daily devotionals and articles that will help readers to grow in holiness and live a life consistent with the teachings of the Church.

In 2013, Sophia Institute launched Sophia Institute for Teachers to renew and rebuild Catholic culture through service to Catholic education. With the goal of nurturing the spiritual, moral, and cultural life of souls, and an abiding respect for the role and work of teachers, we strive to provide materials and programs that are at once enlightening to the mind and ennobling to the heart; faithful and complete, as well as useful and practical.

Sophia Institute gratefully recognizes the Solidarity Association for preserving and encouraging the growth of our apostolate over the course of many years. Without their generous and timely support, this book would not be in your hands.

www.SophiaInstitute.com
www.CatholicExchange.com
www.SophiaInstituteforTeachers.org

Sophia Institute Press® is a registered trademark of Sophia Institute. Sophia Institute is a tax-exempt institution as defined by the Internal Revenue Code, Section 501(c)(3). Tax ID 22-2548708.